RURAL WOMEN IN CAMEROON: LEGAL DEVELOPMENT, STAKES AND PROSPECTS

Roland Djieufack
Yvonne Shumbe Nehmamfor

Publisher: Upway Books

Authors: Roland Djieufack, Yvonne Shumbe Nehmamfor

Title: Rural women in Cameroon: Legal development, stakes and prospects

ISBN: 978-1-917916-21-9

Couverture réalisée sur: www.canva.com

This book is a work of non-fiction. The information it contains is based on the authors' research, experience, and knowledge at the time of publication. The publisher and authors have made every effort to ensure the accuracy and reliability of the information provided, but assume no responsibility for any errors, omissions, or differing interpretations of the subject matter. This publication is not intended to replace professional advice or consultation. Readers are encouraged to seek professional guidance where appropriate.

PREFACE

The primary concern of this book is to critically highlight the state of progress of the economic empowerment of rural women in Cameroon as guaranteed by the existing regulations. Rural women in Cameroon are a group of persons that are vulnerable because their daily economic activities come with so many challenges such as discrimination, limited finances, cultural malpractices, ignorance, illiteracy and violence within the society, family and institutional settings. As this this study acknowledges the efforts put in place through existing regulations, it aims at pointing out the hurdles that beset the enforcement of the economic rights of rural women in Cameroon from a purely legal-based approach. Nevertheless, despite these regulatory measures, the pace of economic empowerment of rural women in Cameroon remains alarmingly slow. The study posits that the current regulatory mechanisms are insufficient in empowering rural women economically. Adopting both qualitative and quantitative research methodology, involving in-depth content analysis of primary and secondary data that explicitly address the economic empowerment of rural women in Cameroon, this study notes that the existing standards and regulations are fragmented and inconsistent, creating normative, informational, and implementation gaps that significantly hinder the protection and enhancement of the economic empowerment of rural women. To bridge these gaps, this study recommends the establishment of a comprehensive legislative and institutional frameworks, including the creation of a Gender Equality Observatory, and the enactment of specific legislation focused on the economic empowerment of rural women. Such measures are essential to ensure that rural women in Cameroon are adequately protected and empowered to achieve economic self-sufficiency.

In this book, the authors have carefully discussed their viewpoints from a legal perspective drawn purely from a legal view-point. This current study is a clear reflection of the efforts put in by the authors during years of Doctorate research as we have drawn from the few existing literature superficially on this subject in Cameroon as well as from other jurisdictions, analyzed the relevant statutes and elucidated on material drawn from extensive field research work conducted in some remote areas of Cameroon. The scope of the research coveres the year 2011-2024.

This book is divided into eight chapters numbered sequentially from one to eight. Chapter one is the general introduction in which some background consideration focusing on the historical evolution of the economic empowerment of rural women both at the international and national levels are studied.

Chapter two discusses the rational for the economic empowerment of rural women This chapter examines the importance for the economic empowerment of rural women with particular focus on human rights and economic perspectives.

Chapter three examines the Guiding Principles of economic development of rural women in Cameroon. In this chapter, several principles for development are examined. These include guiding principles postulated for at the international, regional and national levels.

Chapter four highlights the policy standards put in place for the economic empowerment of the rural women. The chapter addresses the policy standard established by national legal instrument, the contribution of regional legal instruments and the role of international legal instruments.

Chapter five considers the institutional framework in place for the economic empowerment of the rural women in Cameroon. The chapter elucidates on the role of national, regional and international institutions in promoting the economic empowerment of rural women. The chapter ends with the study of the contribution of national and international NGOs in promoting the economic empowerment of rural women.

Chapter six critically assesses the measures put in place for the economic empowerment of the rural women. These measures include amongst others, access to communication, education, non-discrimination, customary practices, access to land, finances, right to work as well as measures for the promotion and protection of the rights to social benefits.

Chapter seven articulates on the various limitations to the economic development of the rural women in Cameroon. The chapter brings out limitations within the institutional setting, weak implementation of mechanisms, lack of education, lack of commercial network, gender-based violence, multiple responsibilities and non-enforcement of legal instruments. The chapter ends with the general challenges faced by rural women.

Chapter eight concludes by highlighting major findings and advancing possible suggestions geared at strengthening the enhancement of the economic rights of rural women in Cameroon.

The book is a useful source of reference for students of Business Law, Economic Law, Women Law. Law and Development, Human Rights Law, legal practitioners, magistrates judges, government and non-governmental structures

4

concerned with women's concerns. This study will definitely go a long way to enhance understanding to existing regulations on women's rights in general and particularly rural women in Cameroon.

Roland Djieufack, Ph.D

Yvonne Shumbe Nehmamfor., Ph.D

Cameroon

ACKNOWLEDGEMENTS

This study indeed would not have been conducted without the assistance of many persons who in various ways aided to shape our thoughts. We immensely benefited from the assistance of some staff working in the decentralized services of the Ministry of Agriculture and Rural Development, Ministry of Small and Medium-Sized Enterprises, Social Economy and Handicrafts, Ministry of Social Affairs, Ministry of Women's Empowerment and the Family, Ministry of Vocational Training and Employment, Ministry of Posts and Telecommunications, Ministry of Housing and Urban Development during our different field trips in the major cities of Bamenda, Buea, Douala and Yaoundé in Cameroon.

We also register our gratitude to some rural economic groupings and women associations concerned with women's preoccupations, especially the Bafut Women Ginger Association in Bamenda, and the *Rural Women Development Centre* (RuWCED), Cameroon for responding positively to our questions and provided useful information.

We are thus confident that our findings will be a great importance to the stakeholders involved in the welfare of vulnerable groups in Cameroon particularly rural women.

We humbly accept and take responsibility for all errors and omissions in this book.

Roland Djieufack, Ph.D

Yvonne Shumbe Nehmamfor., Ph.D

Cameroon

TABLES DES MATIERES

11

LIST OF LEGAL INSTRUMENTS

A-NATIONAL INSTRUMENTS

1-LAWS:

- Law No, 96/06 of 18 January 1996 revising the 2 June 1972 Cameroon Constitution

- Law No, 2011/022 of 14 December 2011 Governing electricity supply in Cameroon.

- Law No. 2002/004 of the Cameroons' Investment Charter.

- Law No, 82-539 of 28 October 1982 governing International Telecommunications Corporation in Cameroon.

- Law No. 90/053 of 19 December 1990 relating to Freedom of Association in Cameroon.

- Law No,92/006 of 14th August 1992 relating to Cooperatives and Common Initiative Groups.

- Law No. 92/007 of 14 August 1992 relating to the Cameroon Labour Code.

- Law No.96/12 of August 1996 on Environmental Management.

- Law No.98/004 of 14 April 1998 on guidelines on General Education in Cameroon.

- Law No, 98/005 of 14 April 1998 to lay down the Water Code.

- Law No. 98/014 of 14 July 1998 governing Telecommunications in Cameroon.

- Law No, 99/014 of the 22nd of December 1999 governing Non-Governmental Organisations in Cameroon.

- Law No. 2006/012 of 29 December 2006 on the General Regime for Partnership Contracts.

- Law No. 2008/009 of 16 July 2008 setting the fiscal, financial, and accounting regime applicable to partnership contracts

- Law No. 2009/004 of 14 April 2009 to Organize Legal Aid in Cameroon

- Law No. 2010/001 of 13th April 2010 to promote Small and Medium Size Enterprises in Cameroon

- Law No.2010/001 of 13 April 2010 adopting an appropriate regulatory framework; promoting, collective and group entrepreneurship.

15

- Law No, 2010/013 of December 21, 2010 as amended and supplemented by law No 2015/006 of April 20, 2015 on Electronic Communications in Cameroon.

- Law No, 2010/012 of 21 December 2010 on Cybersecurity and Cybercrime in Cameroon.

- Law No. 2011/012 of 06 May 2011 on Consumer Protection in Cameroon

- Law No. 2013/004 of 18th April 2013 on Incentives in Cameroon.

- Law No. 2015/010 of 16th July 2015 amended and supplemented some of the past provisions of - - Law No. 2010/001 of 13th April 2010 relating to the promotion of Small and Medium Size Enterprises in Cameroon.

- Law No. 2016/008 of 12 July 2016 authorising the president of the republic to ratify the Paris Climate Agreement adopted in Paris on 12 December 2015.

- Law No.2016/014 of 14th December 2016 to fix minimum registered capital and conditions for using notaries public in the establishment of private limited Companies in Cameroon.

- Law No.2018/010 of 11 July 2018 governing Vocational Training in Cameroon.

- Law No. 2019/004 of 25th April 2019 on the Social Economy in Cameroon.

- Law No. 2019/021 of 24 December 2019 to lay down some rules governing credit activities in the Banking and Micro-Finance Sector in Cameroon.

- Law No. 2019/024 of 24 December 2019 bill to institute the General Code of Regional and Local Authorities in Cameroon.

- Law No, 2021/022 of 16 December 2021 to amend some provision of law No, 90 of 19 December 1990 relating to freedom of Association in Cameroon.

- Law No.2022 / 004 of 27 April 2022 relating to the protection of the National Road Assets.

2. DECREES:

- Decree N° 2008/0115/PM of 24 January 2008 specifying the modalities for the application of law N° 2006/012 of 29 December 2006 laying down the general regime for partnership contracts.

- Decree No 2004/320 of 8th December 2004 creation of the ministry of Environment and Protection of nature and Sustainable Development (MINEPDED).

- Decree No 2005/118 of 15th April 2005 organising the Ministry Agriculture and Rural Development.

- Decree No 2008/220 of 4th July 2008 creating MINEPAT in Cameroon.

- Decree No 2013/0399/PM of 27 February 2013 on the modalities of the consumers' protection in the electronic communication in Cameroon.

- Decree No 98/300/PM of 9th September 1998 laying down the procedure for the exercise of Savings and Credit Cooperatives activities.

- Decree No, 2008/035 of 23 January 2008 on the organisation and functioning of the Council for the Support of Partnership Contracts.

- Decree No,2022/523 of 28th November 2022 to ratifying loan agreement to finance agricultural production enhancement support programme in Cameroon.

- Decree No,76/165 of 27th April 1976 setting out conditions for obtaining land tittle in Cameroon, amended and supplemented by Decree No. 2005/481 of 16th December 2005 defined as the official certification of ownership on Land.

- Decree No. 2004/320 of 8 December 2004 Creating the Ministry of Women's Empowerment and the Family.

- Decree No. 2012/148 of 21 March 2012 amending and supplementing certain provisions of Decree No. 2008/035 of 23 January 2008 on the organization and operation of the Partnership Contracts Support Council.

- Decree No. 2013/092 of 3 April 2013 creating the SME Promotion Agency (APME).

- Decree No. 2019/0829/PM of 22 February 2019, a decree setting a general Decentralisation grant in Cameroon.

- Decree No. 2020/0301/PM of 22th January 2020, which sets out the terms and conditions for the fulfilment of the missions of the small and medium-sized enterprise incubation structures.

- Decree No. 78/263 of 1978 establishing prefect-level Commissions for resolving Agro-Pastoral Conflicts.

- Decree No. 88/1281 of 21 September 1988 merging the Ministries of Women's Affairs and Social Affairs.

- Decree No. 90/805/PR of 27 April 1990 creating the National Employment Fund in Cameroon.

- Decree No.2005/088 of 29 March 2005 to organise the Ministry of Women Empowerment and the Family.

- Decree No.98/198 of 08 September 1998 to create the Cameroon Telecommunication company in Cameroon.

3. ORDINANCES:

- Ordinance No. 74-1 of 6 July 1974 to establish rules governing land tenure.

- Ordinance No. 74-2 of 6 July 1974 to establish rules governing state lands.

- Ordinance No 81-02 of 29th June 1981 to organise civil statute registration

B. REGIONAL AND SUB- REGIONAL INSTRUMENTS:

- African Charter on Human and Peoples Right (1987)

- Central African Economic Union (UEAC) (1996)

- Central African monetary Union (UMAC) (1996)

- Economy Community of Central African State (CEMAC) (1994)

- OHADA Treaty signed on October 17, 1993 in Port – Louis (Mauritius Ireland) and revised in Quebec (Canada) on October 17, 2008.

- OHADA Uniform Act on Commercial Companies and Economic Interest Groups (1998).

- The declaration on freedom of expression in Africa (2002).

C. INTERNATIONAL INSTRUMENTS:

- International Covenant on Civil and Political Rights (1966).

- International Covenant on Economic, Social and Cultural Right (1966).

- International Labour Organisation (ILO) Convention 167.

- The 1984 International Convention against Torture and other Cruel, Inhumane and Degrading Treatment.

- the African Charter on Human and Peoples' Rights of (1981)

- The Beijing Platform for Action (1995).

- The Convention on the Elimination of all Forms of Discrimination against Women adopted by General Assembly Resolution 34/180 of 8 December 1979.

- The Monterrey Consensus (2002)

- The Rio Declaration on Environment and Development (1992).

- The Un Declaration on The Rights of Indigenous People (2007).

- The Un Millennium Declaration (1986)

- The Universal Declaration of Human Rights adapted by General Assembly of the United Nations on 10 December 1948.

- UN Committee on Economic, Social and Cultural Rights, The Right to Water, General Comment N° 15; UN DOC.E/C.12/11,29th Session, (2002).

- United Nation Framework Convention on Climate Change (UNOCCC) (1992).

LIST OF CASES

C. LOCAL CASES

- *Achu v. Achu Appeal No. BCA/62/86.*

- *Chibikom Peter Fru and 4 others v. Zamcho Florence Lum. Supreme Court Judgement No 14L of February 14 1993.SouthWest Court of Appeal. Suit No CASWP/17/931(CCLR),1997 ,213-223.*

- *Ngeh v Ngome (1962-64) WCLR321.*

- *Immaculate Wanga Vefonge v. Samuel Iyonga Yukpe (1981) CASWP/CC/81(unreported).*

- *Body Lawson v. Body Lawson, suit N° HCF/128Mc/86 (unreported).*

- *Debora S. Wara v. Dr. Ben Fru Wara and Justinan Atancho Neh. Suit No. HCB/59/97.*

- *Aforba Aloysuis Bougnyisi Elizabeth v. Nchari Mary Kinyuy. Suit No AE/06/96/IM/96.*

- *Boh Lucy v. kang Sume David. Suit No HCF/38/96.*

- *Njim William v. Njim Swiri Rose Saningong. Appeal No BCA/22/96.*

-

B. FOREIGN CASES:

- *Cobb v. Cobb (1955). EWCA CIV J0608-2*

- *Cumber v. Cumber (1974) W. L. R 1331.CA*

- *Midland Bank Green (1981) 2WLR 28. House of Lords.*

- *National Provincial Bank v. Ainsworth. (1965).AC 1175,1247-48(HL).*

- *Pettitt v. Pettitt (1970) AC 777 at 804.*

LIST OF ABBREVIATION / ACRONYMS

ACAFEJ: Cameroon Association of Women Lawyers

AEC: African Economic Community

AFCATA: African Continental Fund

AfDB: African Development Bank

AGOA: American Growth and Opportunity Act

ALVF: Association to Combat Violence Against Women

ANACLAC: National Association of Cameroonian Language

ANOR: Agency for Standards and Quality Control.

ASF: Avocat Sans Frontieres (Lawyers Without Borders)

AU: African Union

AWID: Association for Women's Rights in Development

PME: Small and Medium Sized Bank

BEAC: Bank of Central African States

CamCCUL: Cameroon Credit Union League

CAMERCAP-PARC: Research and Analysis Centre on the Economic and Social Policies of Cameroon

CAMNAFAW: Cameroon National Association for Family Welfare

CAMTEL: Cameroon Telecommunications Corporation

CARFIC: Agricultural Bank

CBD: Convention on Bio Diversity

CBF: Cameroon Business Forum

CCIMA: Chamber of Commerce, Industry, Mines and Handicrafts

CCJA: Common Court of Justice and Arbitration

CDC: Cameroon Development Corporation

CEDAW: Convention on the Elimination of all Forms of Discrimination against Women

CEFAN: Cameroon Education for all Network

CEMAC:	Economic Communities of Central African States
CFCE:	Decentralised Centres for Business Creation Formalities
CGCTD:	General Code on Regional and Local Authorities
CIGs:	Common Initiative Groups
CIMA:	Insurance Code of the Inter-African Conference on Insurance Market
CNEF:	National Economic and Financial Commission
CPD:	Country Program Document
CPE:	Country Portfolio Evaluation
CSO:	Civil Society Organisation
CSW:	Commission on the Status of Women
DRC:	Domestic Republic of Congo
DRTD:	Declaration of the Right to Development
ECOSOC:	Economic and Social Council
EMRIP:	Expert Mechanism on the Rights of Indigenous Peoples
ESCR:	Economic, Social and Cultural Rights
FAWECAM:	Forum for African Women Educationists Cameroon
FCE:	Femme Credit Epargne (Women Credit Union)
FGM:	Female Genital Mutilation
FIMAC:	Agricultural and Community Micro-Projects Investment Fund
FNE:	Fond Nationale d'Emploi
GDCF:	Gross Domestic Capital Formation
GDI:	Gender Related Development Index
GDP:	Gross Domestic Product
GEM:	Global Entrepreneurial Monitor
GESP:	Growth and Employment Strategy Paper
GPE:	Global Partnership for Education
GRPB:	Gender Responsive and Participatory Budgeting

HSR – CMR:	Human is Right Cameroon
IANWGE:	Inter-Agency Network on Women and Gender Equality
ICCPR:	International Covenant on Civil and Political Rights
ICESCR:	International Covenant on Economic, Social and Cultural Rights
ICTs:	Information and Communication Technologies
IFC:	International Financial Corporation
ILO:	International Labour Organisation
IMF:	International Monetary Fund
INTELCAM:	International Telecommunications Corporation of Cameroon
IP:	Industrial Policy
IPA:	Investment Promotion Agency
LLC:	Limited Liability Company
MAGZI: Authority	Industrial Zones Development and Management
MBOSCUDA:	Mbororo Social and Cultural Development Association
MDGs:	Millenium Development Goals
MFIs:	Micro-Finance Institutions
MINADER:	Ministry of Agriculture and Rural Development
MINDDEVEL:	Ministry of Decentralisation and Local Development
MINEPAT:	Ministry of Mines, Industry and Technological Development
MINEPDED:	Ministry of Environment and Protection of Nature and Sustainable Development
MINFI:	Ministry of Finance
MINPEESA:	Ministry of Small and Medium-Sized Enterprises, Social Economy and Handicrafts
MINPROFF: Family	Ministry for the Promotion of the Women and the
NCHRF:	National Commission for Human Rights and Freedom

NDS:	National Development Strategy
NEF:	National Employment Fund
NGO:	Non-Governmental Organisation
OAPI:	African Intellectual Property Organisation.
OAU:	Organisation of African Unity
OHADA:	Organisation for the Harmonisation of Business Law in Africa
ONZFI:	National Board Industrial Free Zones
OPAD:	Organisation for Poverty Alleviation and Development
PADC:	National Programme of Support to Community Development
PAEQUE:	Equity and Quality for Improved Learning
PAME:	Micro – Enterprise Programmes
PARPAC:	Agricultural Production Enhancement Support Programme in Cameroon
PNDES:	National Program for Development of Social Economy
PNDP:	National Participatory Development Programme
PNVRA: Programme	National Agricultural Extension and Research
PPP:	Public – Private Partnership
PRSP:	Poverty Reduction Strategy Paper
PSV:	Socially Vulnerable Persons
RECs:	Regional Economic Communities
SCHCL:	Southern Cameroon High Court Law
SDGs:	Sustainable Development Goals
SMEs:	Small and Medium Size Enterprises
SMIs:	Small and Medium-Sized Industries
SNFI:	National Strategy for Inclusive Finance
SNI:	National Investment Corporation.
TCC:	Trauma Centre Cameroon

UDHR:	Universal Declaration of Human Rights
UEAC:	Central African Economic Union
UMAC:	Central African Monetary Union
UN:	United Nations
UNCCD:	United Nations Convention to Combat Desertification
UNDP:	United Nation Development Program
UNDRIP:	United Nation Declaration on the Right to Indigenous People
UNESCO:	United Nations Educational, Scientific and Cultural Organisation
UNFCCC: Change	United Nation Framework Convention on Climate
UNICEF:	United Nations Children's Emergency Fund
UNO:	United Nations Organisation
UNPFII:	United Nations Permanent Forum on Indigenous Issues
UNSR:	United Nation Special Rapporteur
UWEP:	Uganda Women Entrepreneurship Programme
VAW:	Violence Against Women
VSE:	Very Small Enterprise
WEDEE:	Women's Entrepreneurship Development and Economic Empowerment
WIPO:	Intellectual Property Organisation.
WTO:	World Trade Organisation

CHAPTER ONE

GENERAL INTRODUCTION

1.1. Background to the Study

Women and development emerged as an issue on the international development agenda in the 1070s thanks to the activism and research by feminist economists and development practitioners. Prior to this period women had been perceived by most governments and international development agencies as mothers, housewives, men's dependants and passive recipients of welfare policies[1]. Women were not considered in development policies and planning because it was taken for granted that, they benefited automatically from economic development works through their male counterparts. Since the 1980s however, women and their economic concerns have become firmly established on the development agenda through a series of national, regional and international conferences particularly the fourth world conference on women held in Beijing-China in 1995.[2]

NGOs such as the UN, the Inter-Agency Network on Women and Gender Equality (IANWGE) and other international as well as national organisations[3] are not only working in synergy for the economic empowerment of women but equally promote the achievement of the Millenium Development Goals (MDGs) in rural areas with particular emphases on rural women.[4] The MDGs spurred up concerted actions across the globe, leading to impressive results in many areas, such as lifting more than a billion people out of extreme poverty. Goal 3 is out to promote gender equality and empowerment of women.[5]

---

[1] Dam Henk Van et al., (2000), Institutionalizing Gender Equality: Commitment, Policy and Practice, a global source book. KIT publishers.Vol.1, p.13.

[2] Ibid.

[3] We have several international organisations such as certain specialized agencies associated with the United Nations namely the UN Women, dedicated for gender equality and the empowerment of women, the United Nations Conference on Trade and Development (UNCTAD),which is out to empower women in information ,communication and technology .The Organization for Women Empowerment in Cameroon (AWEC),Rural women Center of Education and Development (RuWCED),a nationally accredited NGO that works to promote health, education ,livelihoods, human rights and development of the rural women.

[4] UN (2004), Inter-Agency Network on women and gender equality, Available at https://www.un.org. (Consulted on 14/08/2023).

[5] ILO (1996-2023). Millennium Development Goals. Available at https://www.ilo.org. (Consulted on the 14/08/2023).

The rural woman in Cameroon is that woman who lives and works only in the rural communities, that is the villages in Cameroon[6]. Unlike their fellow women in the urban areas, these women are either less educated or illiterates and rely basically on agricultural activities to sustain their home, meet their needs and educate their children[7].

The rural population of Cameroon stood at 41.27% of the country's population in 2022[8] with women constituting 55% of the rural population. [9] The empowerment of rural women is indispensable to fight against hunger, stimulate economic growth and sustainable development, given that women constitute one third of the global labour force, work as farmers, wage earners and entrepreneurs. Though they represent an important percentage of the agriculture work force, their contribution to the rural economy is widely underestimated[10].They are concentrated in the informal economy, low-skilled, low productivity and low unpaid jobs with long working hours.[11]

In most developing countries, particularly in Africa, though women constitute more than 70 % of the total agricultural labour force and are accountable for over 80% of food production[12], they are still economically weak and make up about 70% of the world's poor.[13] Very few women have succeeded in becoming economically empowered to the extent of developing economic activities such as creating SMEs. This hinders their opportunity to be economically empowered by enjoying their basic rights to work as previewed by both national law[14] and international instruments. The International Covenant on Economic, Social and Cultural Rights (ICESCR), which provides that ''States parties to the present covenant undertake to ensure the equal rights of men and

[6]Narayan M. et al., (2018), Rural Entrepreneurship in India: An Overview, International Entrepreneurship and Management Journal Vol.8, pp. 280-284.
[7] Interview with two rural women, all farmers, Mrs. Nchotu Magret from Mambu Bafut, (Interviewed on the 6th December 2022 at 9:00am) and Mrs. Azenui Lilian from Mendankwe village (Interviewed on the 9th September 2023 at 1:00pm). All these interviewees are based in the North-west region (Bamenda) of Cameroon.
[8] World Bank, Cameroon: Rural population (% of total population) :(2022). Available at https://www.data worldbank.org. (Consulted on the 11/08/2023).
[9] Ibid.
[10] International Labour Organization (1996-2024), Rural Women at work: Bridging the gaps. Available at https://www.Ilo.org.(Consulted on (22/02/2024).
[11] Ibid.
[12] Team S. and Doss C., (2011), The Role of Women in Agriculture, Available at <www.fao.org.> (consulted on the 14/02//2022).
[13] ILO (1996), ''Women Swell Ranks of Working Poor'', Available at <www.ilo.org> (consulted on 14/02/2022).
[14] Section 2 (1) of Law No.92/007 of 14th August 1992 on Cameroon Labour Code.

women to the enjoyment of all Economic, Social and Cultural rights set forth in the present convention''[15]

Women's economic empowerment means, ensuring women can equally participate in and benefit from decent work and social protection; access to market and have control over resources, their own time, lives, and bodies; and increased voice, agency, and meaningful participation in economic decision-making at all levels from the household to international institutions.[16]

1.1.1. The Development of women economic empowerment at the International Level

It could be argued that the 1948 Universal Declaration of Human Rights did not only advocate for equality of sexes amongst others, but empowered women to grow and develop businesses and entrepreneurial skills thus economically empowering them. The declaration applies to all rights and freedom, equality of men and women and prohibits discrimination on the basis of sex. These freedoms and rights include equal pay for equal work, the right to health and the right to education for all[17]. The 1948 DHR could be considered to have spurred the economic development of women since many female entrepreneurs developed after 1948. This was the case of Lillian Vernon whose enterprise was launched in 1951 and later became Lillian Vernon Corporation in 1965 and gained popularity in 1987.[18] It is worth noting that, Lillian Vernon's Corporation was the first company founded by a woman to be publicly traded on the American Stock exchange.

During the mid-18th Century, it was popular for women to own certain businesses like brothels, alehouses, taverns, and retail shops. Though most of these businesses were not perceived with good reputations, and were considered shameful and contrary to morals,[19] they nevertheless showed the desire of the female folk to be economically empowered by involving in entrepreneurial activities. By the end of the 19th centuries, women diversified their forms of

---

[15] Article 3 of the ICESCR 1966.

[16] UN WOMEN (2024). Facts and figures: Economic empowerment. Available at https//www.unwomen.org. (Consulted on 23/04/2024)

[17] Article 2 of the 1948 Universal Declaration of Human Rights.

[18] Freeman V. (2021), History of Women Entrepreneurs, Available at https://www.linkeden .com/pulse/history -women-entrepreneurs-valerie-freeman (Consulted on the 1/12/2022)

[19] Sujay M. K., (2015) Problems and prospects of women entrepreneurs, Scholarly Research Journal for Interdisciplinary studies. Available at <wwwoaji.net> (consulted on the 6/02/2020). Women such as Madame CJ Walker, took advantage of the changing times and was able to market her hair-care products, becoming the first African-American female millionaire.

businesses. They developed interest in iron work and nail factories, savings and loan schemes as well as textile industry.[20] Women were also involved in the hair care industry as was the case with Lillian Westropp the first African American female millionaire[21]. The women's movements in the 1960's gave women renewed purpose and a sense of power to pursue more entrepreneurial ventures.[22] By 1980 the public was also becoming more receptive and encouraging to female entrepreneurs, acknowledging the valuable contribution they were making to the economy. These led to the enactment of laws such as Women's Business Ownership Act in 1988 which gave the women the possibility to obtain loans and create competitive businesses Despite the interest of women in entrepreneurial ship activities, it is reported that women are still lagging behind men in terms of the number of female business owners, the size of women-owned businesses, and their access to economic resources. It was certainly for this reason and to promote the participation of women in entrepreneurial activities that gender and equality and Women's economic empowerment are cornerstones of the 2030 and 2063 Agenda for Sustainable Development.[23]

The Convention on the Elimination of All Forms of Discrimination against Women (CEDAW)[24] is one of the most widely ratified human rights treaties in history. CEDAW has inspired feminist activism around the world and helped raise women's legal consciousness.[25] Apart from the UDHR[26] which promotes human

---

[20] A woman took over the family business, Brandywine iron works and Nail Factory, and turned it into a profit generating steel business in the 1900s. started the Institution of women's saving and Loan as a way of empowering women. Female entrepreneurs became more influential with the boom of the textile industry and the development of the railroad and telegraph system. See generally Sujay M. K., (2015) Problems and prospects of women entrepreneurs, (note 19).

[21] Women such as Madame CJ Walker, took advantage of the changing times and was able to market her hair-care products, becoming the first African-American female millionaire. See generally Sujay M. K., (2015) Problems and prospects of women entrepreneurs, (note 19).

[22] For instance, in 1967, Muriel Siebert established the first woman-owned brokerage firm in New York city and the first woman to own a seat on the New York Stock Exchange. Mary Kay Ash founded Mary Kay cosmetics in Dallas in 1963 and it became the 6th largest direct firm in the world in 2018. See generally Sujay M. K., (2015) Problems and prospects of women entrepreneurs, (note 19).

[23] While the scope of Sustainable Development Goal 2030 is limited to social, economic and environmental dimensions, Agenda 2063 is broader in scope and includes social, economic and sustainability considerations in a broad context, political, cultural and other African priorities.

[24] Marta R.V., and Lisa R. P., CEDAW and Rural Development: Empowering Women with Law from the top-down, activism from the bottom-up. Available at www.law.ubalt.edu (consulted on the 7/02/2020 at 8:45am).

[25] Article 14 of the 1981 CEDAW Law.

[26] The 1948 UDHR.

rights as a whole, CEDAW recognises rural women as a particularly disadvantaged group in need of additional rights. Article 14 addresses rural women exclusively and specifically. It stipulates that", States Parties shall take into account the particular problems faced by rural women and the significant roles which rural women play in the economic survival of their families, including their work in the non-monetized sectors of the economy, and shall take all appropriate measures to ensure the application of the provisions of the present Convention to women in rural areas. (2), States Parties shall take all appropriate measures to eliminate discrimination against women in rural areas in order to ensure, on a basis of equality of men and women, that they participate in and benefit from rural development and, in particular, shall ensure to such women the right: (a) To participate in the elaboration and implementation of development planning at all levels; (b) To have access to adequate health care facilities, including information, counselling and services in family planning; (c) To benefit directly from social security programmes; (d) To obtain all types of training and education, formal and non-formal, including that relating to functional literacy, as well as, inter alia, the benefit of all community and extension services, in order to increase their technical proficiency; (e) To organize self-help groups and co-operatives in order to obtain equal access to economic opportunities through employment or self-employment; (f) To participate in all community activities; (g) To have access to agricultural credit and loans, marketing facilities, appropriate technology and equal treatment in land and agrarian reform as well as in land resettlement schemes; (h) To enjoy adequate living conditions, particularly in relation to housing, sanitation, electricity and water supply, transport and communications."[27]

They like their urban counterparts should enjoy panoply of rights such as the rights to education, health care, and an array of civil and political rights. It could be argued that the above cited provision is an indication of the international commitment to promote the economic development of the rural women.

The OHADA Treaty was signed on the 17th of October 1993 at Port Louise and amended by the Treaty of 17 October 2008 at Quebec,[28] amongst others promotes the economic development of the rural women. The Treaty is out to harmonize business law in Africa. Two Uniform Acts of this treaty are of great concern to us, that is the Uniform Act on General Commercial Law and The Uniform Act on Commercial Companies and Economic Interest Groups which

---

[27] Article 14 (1) and (2) of the 1981 CEDAW Law.
[28] OHADA Treaty signed on October 17, 1993 in Port – Louis (Mauritius Ireland) and revised in Quebec (Canada) on October 17, 2008.

deals with commercial matters. Under the uniform Act on general commercial law, provision is made for every trader to be subjected under the OHADA Law applicable in the States parties where the business is located.[29] It holds that, traders are persons whose usual occupation is to carryout commercial transactions.[30] Minors according to its provisions shall not have the status of a trader and equally that the spouse of a trader is not a trader unless he or she carries out the transaction of a trade.[31] These provisions boast women economic empowerment especially in the rural sector since the women will see the necessity to own their businesses by themselves and benefit from the protection given by this Act. They are encouraged not to be second figures in businesses as is often the case since they are often contented to be assisting their husbands in their businesses but now to own their own businesses and be economically empowered.

The OHADA Uniform Act on Commercial Companies and Economic Interest Groups on its part promote rural women economic development when it states that, "all economic interest groups shall also be subject to the provisions of this Uniform Act applicable in the States Parties in which their registered office is situated, provided that such laws are not contrary to the provisions of this Uniform Act."[32] The rural women as we know are most viable to create common initiative groups which play a very important part in rural economic development.[33] When the Uniform Act states that "any person wishing to engage in a commercial activity in the form of a company, on the territory of one of the States parties to the treaty, shall choose a form of company which suits the activities envisaged form among those provided for by the Uniform Act"[34] This provision further empower the women especially the rural women economically for it covers every person without distinction as to sex.

The rural women have thus benefit from these OHADA provisions and are becoming more economically empowered since its provisions are of general application to all without discrimination. It brings in a uniform law to govern all business transactions within the region thus spurring up economic growth at all levels.

---

[29] Article 1 of the 1993 OHADA Treaty on General Commercial Commer Law
[30] Ibid Article 2.
[31] Ibid Article 7.
[32] Article 1 of the 1993 OHADA Uniform Act on Commercial Companies and Economic interest groups
[33] Kengne Fodouop (2003), Developpement rural dans la province du Centre au Cameroun. Available at https://www.researchgate.net.(Consulted on the 31/05/2024).
[34] Article 3 of the 1993 OHADA Un4iform Act on Commercial Companies and Economic interest groups.

1.1.2. Historical Development at the National Level

In Cameroon, several entrepreneurship friendly policies which targets the youth including girls who are the most affected by unemployment are being implemented. The conception and implementation of these policies are motivated by the fact that entrepreneurship creates jobs, improve the welfare of the population and accelerates the growth and development impact of the whole economy. In fact, the economic empowerment of women through the promotion of entrepreneurship necessitates a good knowledge of the relationship between policy, economic indicators and entrepreneurial activity. Cameroon since independence has been one of the most peaceful and prosperous countries in Central Africa sub- region. However, Cameroon faced economic crises in the mid-1980s like other developing economies. This depressed the economy and increased the problem of unemployment. Since the beginning of 2000, the country's growth has steadily improved to a point that the country envisaged through the growth and employment strategy paper to be an emerging economy by 2035.[35] The economic circumstances in the early 1980s led Cameroon into an economic crisis, mainly as a result of the fall of export income due to the price decrease of products such as coffee, cocoa and oil in the international market. With a rise of approximately 40% in real effective exchange rate of the local currency in 1994 and the increase of external and the budgetary deficit prompted the government to withdraw from economic activities and a conducive environment was created that favoured the emergence of the private sector.[36]

The private sector is focused on the development of business activities and industrial production in the agricultural, natural resources and mining sectors while the government is concerned with the development of strategic sector such as infrastructure, energy and policies.

To boast the private sector, the law[37] on small and medium size enterprises in Cameroon were enacted which governs very small enterprises (VSE), small enterprises (SE), and medium Size enterprises (MSE) to boost the private sector in Cameroon. Since 2011 the number of companies in Cameroon has been rising every year (Over 80% are SMEs). In 2019, it was revealed that there were about 209 companies in the country as opposed to about 93 in 2009.[38]. Small Scale

---

[35] Cameroon: (2016) Creating Opportunities for inclusive growth and poverty reduction. Available at www.worldbank .org (Consulted on the 28/02/2023).
[36] CIA World Fact Book, (2020) Economy of Cameroon. Available at <, https://www.en.wikipedia.org> (consulted on the7/20/2020).
[37] Law no. 2010/001 of 13th April 2010 to promote Small and Medium Size Enterprises in Cameroon.
[38] National Institute of Statistics, (2019).

enterprises represent 75% of the total number of enterprises in the country[39]. The law creating these SMEs acts as a push to rural women economic development since the nature of activities of these rural women which is agriculture acts as fertile soil for small business unit to spring up thus boasting the rural section of the economy. The facilitation of procedure in the creation of SMEs through the creation of the one-stop-shop facilitates the creation of SMEs by these rural women which helps them to be economically empowered.

In Cameroon nowadays, there is a growing emphasis in the policy debate on rural women's economic empowerment as a poverty alleviation strategy and a preferred tactic to spur economic development. The poverty agenda comes into play largely because women invest earnings in children and the community, thus producing a positive ripple effect that does not manifest in the same way as men's income[40] Gender situation in Cameroon vary by regions, ethnic groups or religions. There is a persistent value of gender division of labour in which men take the productive and public roles and woman take domestic roles especially in the rural areas. Women labour force participation rate is high and they contribute to the household income. However, women's work tends to be undervalued as it is perceived as supplementing income of the husband, regardless of actual content of the task or the income. [41]

If women are now able to act and change things in the country, it is thanks to the State which reinforced institutional mechanisms and implemented strategic guidelines in this direction. Additionally, there is the growing attractiveness of the economy and increasing number of companies and investors found in Cameroon. Women in Cameroon just like others all around the world are fighting to get a place in a society where men are still privileged. Though these rural women in Cameroon are mostly active in the agricultural sector, the government, through adequate measures, established a dedicated ministry MINPROFF which even if yet to be at full check, strives to empower these rural women in the economic spheres by encouraging their presence in the entrepreneurial domain. It is

---

[39] African Development Bank Group, (2012), African Economic Outlook Available at <https://www.afdb.org> (consulted on the 7/02/2020).

[40] Guloba, M., et al., (2017), Rural Women Entrepreneurship in Uganda: A synthesis report on policies, evidence and stakeholders, Research series No. 134 p. 6.

[41] Efroymson D. et al., (2010), Women, Work and Money: Studying the Economic value of Women's unpaid work and using the results for advocacy, Available at<https//www.healthbridge.ca> (consulted on the 28/02/2020).

certainly thanks to such institutional[42] and legal mechanisms[43] that some women have been involved in entrepreneurial activities in Cameroon.[44]

In Cameroon's rural north, a career in science is a rarity for most women. Two young women have bucked the trend, winning a prestigious science award. Sabine Adeline Fanta Yadang, 32, a doctor of neuroscience, and Hadidjatou Daïrou, 33, a doctor of cellular physiology, overcame societal prejudice by winning the L'Oréal-Unesco Young Talent Award for Women in Science for their work on the power of medicinal plants. These two young scientists were chosen from among 30 scientists in sub-Saharan Africa to win an award in Botswana. Fanta and Hadidjatou were praised for their work on the potential of traditional medicinal plants in Cameroon for treating cardiovascular disease and Alzheimer's. The two young scientists work together in the laboratory of the Institute for Medical Research and the Study of Medicinal Plants (IMPM) in Yaoundé, the capital where traditional, ancestral medicine is recognised as a health sector in its own right in the country. Hadidjatou believes that the bark of the kola nut (Garcinia Kola) could improve cardiovascular health.

Fanta is banking on tigernut milk, widely consumed in Central Africa, extracted from a plant that has been renowned locally for its medicinal properties for thousands of years. In the face of expensive conventional treatments to slow Alzheimer's, the researcher hopes to prove that this plant will make it possible "to combat the degeneration of neurons and reduce stress in the affected brain.[45]

---

[42] We see institutions such as MINPROFF, Academy for Women Entrepreneurs (AWE), both national and international institutions respectively put in place in Cameroon for the promotion of female entrepreneurship.

[43] Legal mechanisms such as the 1948 UDHR, the UN Sustainable Development Goals, the African Charter on Human and People's Rights, the Cameroonian Constitution, the Social Economy law in Cameroon, the National Plan of Action for Development are among some of the several international and national legal mechanisms put in place by the Government of Cameroon for the promotion of female entrepreneurship.

[44] This is for instance the case of women such as Gwendoline Abunaw who since May 2017 is the managing Director of the Local Subsidiary of the pan African banking group Ecobank, Melissa Bime, Wins Cartier Women's Initiative Award for her digital blood bank start up infusion. Nadine Tinen a 45-Years old Cameroonian is a Regional Senior partner of Price Water house coopers (PWC). Fein Rosette founded 'Kayvey Mixed cereals. The lack of healthy nutritive food for her baby made Fien to seek for and provide solution to all babies suffering from malnutrition. She equally runs an NGO (Dovic Relief Cameroon), founded in 2010, a non-profit organization dedicated to women economic empowerment. Through this organization, she has worked with more than 23 rural communities and positively affect the lives of over 3000 women.

[45] Olomo Daniels B (2023). Women in science, two Cameroonians win prize. Available at https://africanews.com.(Consulted on (23/04/2024).

9

The unbalanced distribution of enterprises across the country has a negative impact on the economic development in other parts of the country particularly in rural areas. There is need therefore for the government to promote the development of entrepreneurial activities within the country. The adoption of the Investment Code in 2002[46] stressed on the Characteristics of investments and investors which also include some fiscal advantage to private investment according to given categories of the firms. Recent reforms such as the creation of the enterprise registration center (one-stop shop) in 2010 to facilitate the official procedures of all licenses needed for entrepreneurs to acquire a legal statute[47] has been created. Cameroon government created the Cameroon Business Forum in 2010[48] to improve dialogue between public sector and private sector. The government also created small and Medium Size Bank, National Agency of SMEs promotion and Agricultural Bank in 2013[49] to support economic activities. Despite government effort to promote economic development, the number of women involved in entrepreneurial activities in rural area is growing at a very slow rate as compare to their male counterparts despite the fact that they represent 53% of the population. This work is out to look at the effectiveness of the regulations in place in for the economic empowerment of the rural women in Cameroon.

1.2. The Problem of the Study

In 2020, statistics from the Ministry of Agriculture and Rural Development (MINADER) showed that Cameroonian rural women constitute more than 70% of the rural work force. They produce almost 90% of the food crop and only 3% of the industrial sector is occupied by these rural women.[50] As reported by the world Bank in 2022, the rural communities in Cameroon makes up 41.27% of the

---

[46] See Section 2 of Law No. 2002-004 of 19-04 2002, Instituting the Cameroon Investment Code.

[47] Business News (2014) Company Formation in Cameroon now possible in 72 hours, Available at <https://www.camerounweb.com> (consulted on the 7/02/2020 at 2:16pm).

[48] Patrick P. (2018), Cameroon Business Forum: Government and Private Sector Talk Business, Available at <www.crtv.cm> (consulted on the 7/02/2020 at 2:37pm).

[49] As reported in 2013, the government has released the capital of two new banks, benefiting from 10 billion XAF each. The" *Banque Camerounaise des PME*" which will be dedicated to Small and Medium-Sized financing and the Cameroon Rural Financial Corporation to meet the financing needs of the private sector in Cameroon, where 60 per cent of the population lives from agriculture; see generally, Making Finance Work for Africa. Available at https://www.mfw4a.org.(Consulted on the 24/02/2024).

[50] Boris Andzanga. N and Kouam Jean. C (2023), Cameroon, promoting Rural Development to reduce gender Inequalities. Available at https://www.on policy.org. (Consulted on the 27/07/2023).

country's population, majority of whom are women, who constitute 55% of the rural population.[51]

Though these women are involved in economic activities, they still face a lot of economic difficulties. Rural women concentrate in low-skilled, low-productivity and low or unpaid jobs with long working hours, poor working conditions and limited social protection.[52] In times of crisis, they are disproportionately pushed out of employment and forced to stay at home[53]and more likely to work as unpaid contributing family members which means their work is largely unrecognised or undervalued. In most cases, they depend on their husband's income for economic problems.[54] These situations cause injustice and negatively affect the rural women's right to economic development.

To resolve this and ensure the economic empowerment of women generally and the rural women in particular, both national and international regulations such as, the Cameroonian Constitution, the Social Economy law, the African Charter on Human and People's Rights, the CEDAW[55], amongst others have been put in place. Institutions both at national and international levels such as the Ministry of Women Empowerment and the Family, the UN Women in Cameroon just to name these few, have equally been put in place to facilitate the economic empowerment of the rural women.

Notwithstanding the above measures aimed at empowering rural women economically, the financial stability of the rural women still seems to be very weak. Most of them are unable to financially ensure the education of their children[56], pay their hospital bills,[57]afford quality food, just to name these few[58].

---

[51] World Bank, Cameroon: Rural population (% of total population), (2022), Available at https://www.data worldbank.org. (Consulted on the 11/08/2023).

[52] UN Women, (2022) Main Problems and Priority needs in CEE Countries. Available at https://www.unwomen.org>feature-story>2022/10> (Consulted 26/08/2024).

[53] UN Women,(2022),Three challenges for rural women amid a cost-of-living crisis. Available at https://www.unwomen.org>feature-story>2022/10(Consulted 26/08/2024)

[54]UN Women, (2022) Main Problems and Priority needs in CEE Countries. (note 57)

[55] Legal mechanisms such as the 1948 UDHR, the 2030 UN Sustainable Development Goals, the 1979 CEDAW law, the 1981 African Charter on Human and People's Rights, the 1996 Cameroonian Constitution, the 2019 Social Economy law in Cameroon, the 2015 National Plan of Action for Development are among some of the several international and national legal mechanisms put in place by the Government of Cameroon for the economic empowerment of the rural women

[56] Interview with two rural women, all farmers, Mrs. Nchotu Magret from Mambu Bafut (Interviewed on the 6th December 2022 at 9:00am) and Mrs. Azenui Lilian from Mendankwe village (Interviewed on the 9th September 2023 at 1:00pm).

[57] Ibid.

[58] Interview with Mrs. Rose Nying Head of Women's Empowerment Centre Santa sub-division in the North west Region of Cameroon on the 05/12/2023 at 10:00am.

It is worth pointing out that, from 2011 to 2023 only 594 small and medium sized enterprises have been created by women as opposed to 2,425 created by men.[59]

The authors are thus worried and wonders the effectiveness of the law in ensuring and promoting the economic empowerment of rural women in Cameroon. This worry sis based on the assumption that, the regulations towards the economic empowerment of the rural women in Cameroon are not satisfactorily effective. This study will endeavour to address the extent to which the existing regulations effectively empower rural women economic development in Cameroon.

To understand and appreciate the effectiveness of the law in promoting the economic empowerment of rural women, this research made use of the typical doctrinal and non-doctrinal or empirical research methodologies. Based on the doctrinal method both primary and secondary data was collected. Primary data was generated from national legislations such as Laws, Decrees, Ordinances, and Orders and case law. International treaties to which Cameroon is a signatory were also explored.

Secondary data was collected from text books, journal articles, conference reports from both governmental and non-governmental institutions, newspaper commentaries, policy papers, theses, dissertations and materials from internet websites and libraries. Through content analyses of primary and secondary data, the research questions and analytical frameworks were developed, the research sites chosen and the question guide designed.

Next was a field trip to collect more primary data because simple reliance on written literature would not have achieved the expected results. In this light, visits were scheduled to some local communities precisely within Mezam division due to security challenges. The regional delegations of women empowerment and the family as well as well that of small and medium size enterprises were visited.

In the course of these visits, oral interviews with the help of a question guide making use of qualitative approaches to data collection were carried out.

---

[59] Statistics from the regional delegation of small and medium size enterprises (SMEs) in the northwest region of Cameroon shows that from 2011 to 2023 only 594 small and medium sized enterprises have been created by women as opposed to 2,425 created by men.

This approach enabled the use of both closed-ended questions when precise answers were required and open-ended questions permitting respondents to explain their perceptions the economic empowerment of rural women. The research ended with an analysis phase in which both the SWOT (strength, weaknesses, opportunity and threat) method was used.

CHAPTER TWO

RATIONALE FOR THE ECONOMIC EMPOWERMENT OF THE RURAL WOMEN IN CAMEROON

2.1. Introduction

This chapter is grounded on the Utilitarian theory of Jeremy Bentham[60] which requires that public decisions and laws should be aimed at increasing the overall happiness of the greatest number of people thus maximising welfare. The chapter is thus out to show the relevance of economic empowerment of the rural women.

Women in developing countries generally bear the burden of poverty.[61] This is experienced not just as material deprivation, but also as marginalisation. Those living in poverty often have little or no opportunity to influence the political, economic and social process and institutions which control and shape their lives. They also lack the ability to enjoy some basic rights accorded to humanity as a whole due to poverty. Women's participation and leadership in decision making processes at every sector fundamentally attempt to eliminate gender-based poverty[62]and in so doing economically empowers women. It is certainly due to the indispensable contribution of rural women in the development of the economy that, Pope Francis prays for the recognition of role rural women play in the economy and that these women should be encouraged to develop SMEs.[63] The need to economically empower rural women is thus, not limited to economic perspectives but will also go a long way to enhance the enjoyment of their human rights.

2.2. Human Rights Perspective

Rural women have the right to benefit from all human rights in the same way as their male counterparts. This is clearly stated in the preamble of the Cameroon constitution which makes provision for equally of all thus prohibiting

---

[60] Jeremy Bentham. (2023). Theory of Utilitarianism. Available at https://study.com.(Consulted on 10/09/2024)

[61] UN Women. World Bank Group (2024) Gender Differences in Poverty and Household Composition through the life cycle. Available at https://wwwUN Women .org. (Consulted on the 26/08/2024).

[62] Hoare Joanna and Gell Fiona (2009). Women's leadership and participation: Case Studies on learning for action. Practical Action Publishing ltd in association with Oxfam GB. P.1.

[63] Our Lady of Fatima Parish Ntaafi, (found in the city of Bamenda, Cameroon), (2024). Sunday newsletter. 6, No13, PP.2.

discrimination of all forms against women[64].The human rights perspective brings out the various avenues in which upholding or enforcing the women's rights will render her economically empowered and thus will excel in the economic domain thus developing the rural communities and the national economy as a whole.

2.2.1. The Respect of Human Rights in the community

Rural women economic empowerment upholds the respect of human right in the community.[65] The Rural women in Cameroon are portrayed as key elements to national growth. The various challenges they face in the economic domain, for instance in their entrepreneurial activities has opened up so many areas where these women are discriminated against thus violating their Human Rights. Cameroon is a signatory of many international convention aimed at promoting and protection human rights. Some of these rights include the rights to an adequate standard of living, the rights to clothing, education, health, food, water, and housing just to name these few. These rights cannot be respected and implemented if the people don't have a means of subsistence. Consequently, economically empowering these women by promoting entrepreneurships for instance, government is not only aimed at improving the living standard of the population and women in particular but equally ensures the respect of international engagements. Economic empowerment of the rural women will bring forth rural development which will go a long way to address gender discrimination. This can be done through inclusion, improving life expectancy and improving knowledge of these rural women in Cameroon.[66]

A deeper commitment by the Ministry of Agriculture and Rural Development (MINADER) to promote the development of women led agricultural projects in the rural areas would help not only reduce poverty but also the gender inequality that exist. Economic empowerment of these women through entrepreneurship ventures for instance is a great method of inclusiveness of the rural women, for it provides opportunities for women who are considered the underrepresented group to participate in economic activities. These ventures such as SMEs create jobs across the sector. These jobs include low skilled jobs. SMEs

---

[64] Article 1 of the 1972 Cameroon's constitution.
[65] Acquah Kofi Nana (1991-2024). Women's Economic Empowerment Available at
https://www.gatesfoundation.org.
[66]Law No2019/014 of July 19 2019 make provision for the Cameroon Human Rights Commission (CHRC) Which is in charge of the promotion of the promotion and protection of Human Rights including also the prevention of Torture

provide opportunities for skill development .and help support employees' access to health care services and more.[67]

In 2015 all the countries of the UN adopted the 2030 Agenda for sustainable Development. These goals aim to transform our world. They are a call to action to end poverty and inequality, protect the planet and ensure that people enjoy health, justice and prosperity. It's a critical call and no one is left behind[68] especially the women.

2.2.2. The Right to Work

Economic empowerment of the rural woman fosters her right to work which enhances her development and that of her community. Under the 2006 Equality Act, the commission for equality and human Rights has as function encouraging and supporting the development of a society in which people's ability to achieve their potential is not limited by prejudice or discrimination, there is respect for and protection of each individual's human rights, respect for the dignity and worth of each individual and that each individual has an equal opportunity to participate in society and there is a mutual respect between groups based on understanding and diversity and on shared respect for equality and human rights.[69] The 2010 Equality Act goes further to harmonise all laws on discrimination and produces a uniform approach .It identifies those principles aimed at equality and prohibited conducts.[70]Goal 8 of the SDGs[71] promotes inclusive and sustainable economic growth, employment and decent work for all. Sustained and inclusive economic growth can drive progress, create decent jobs for all and improve living standard.

The preamble of the Cameroonian constitution[72]upholds and gives a legal backing of the SDGs when it states that ''Human person without distinction as to race, religion, sex or belief possesses inalienable and sacred rights.''

The Cameroon Labour Code equally upholds Goal 8 of the SDGs when it states that 'the right to work shall be recognised as a basic right of each citizen.

---

[67] Gurria Angel (2020): SMEs are key for more inclusive growth. Available at <https://www.oecd-ilibrary.org> (consulted on 11/03/202

[68] Sustainable Development Goals. Available at https://www.Unodo.org (consulted on the11/03/2023

[69] Lauterburg Dominique (2010). Core Statutes on Employment Law. Palgrave Macmillan.P.192.

[70] Turner Chris. (2012). Key Facts. Employment Law. Hodder Education.3rd edition. P.58

[71] Goal 8 of the 2015 Sustainable Development Goals.

[72] Law No 96/6 of 18 January 1996 to amend the constitution of 2 June 1972.

The state shall therefore make every effort to help citizen to find and secure their employment[73]'

The rights to work constitute human rights which have to be enforced by the State. It is a concept based on the fact that people have a human right to work, or engage in productive employment, and may not be prevented from doing so. The right to work,[74] through the economic empowerment of the rural women assist the government to ensure that its citizens meet their needs in terms of employment.

The government remains the largest employer in the country followed by the Cameroon Development Corporation (CDC),however, it is worth noting that Cameroon has so far lost CFA6bn in tax and 269 bn in turnover with 6,434 job cut as a result of the ongoing Anglophone Crisis[75]. An indicator which is not a good signal for an economy aspiring to join the ranks of "emerging nations" by 2035 or forecasting strong economic. This situation makes the need for the economic empowerment of the rural women in rural areas indispensable considering that women and children are always the most affected in almost all crises' situations.

Empowering the rural women to be their own boss and pay their own salaries, enable them to define how to work, thus making a balance between career and family life easier. The Universal Declaration of Human Rights states that everyone has the right to work, to free choice of employment, to just and favourable condition of work and to protection against unemployment [76] It further states that everyone without any discrimination has the right to equal pay for equal work[77] , This protects the vulnerable class in the society of which the women especially the rural women are part. Encouraging these rural women to develop economically, upholds these articles of the 1998 UDRH thus making these women financially independent to take care of themselves and their families. According to the international Covenant on Economic, Social and Cultural Rights, states parties to the present covenant recognises the right to work which includes the opportunity to gain his or her living by work which she or he freely chooses or accepts and will take appropriate measures to safeguard this right [78].It further states that , parties to the present covenant recognises the right to everyone to the

---

[73] Section 2 of the 1992 Labour code
[74] See Article 7 of the ICESCR and also section 2 of the 1992 labour code.
[75] GICAM: Business in Cameroon (2018). Available at http://www.businessincameroon.com.(Consulted on 12/03/2023).
[76] Article 23 of the 1998 UDHR.
[77] Article 23(2) of the 1998 UDHR.
[78] Article 6(1) of the International Covenant on Economic, social and cultural Rights.

enjoyment of just and favourable condition of work.[79] The right to work is a foundation for the realisation of other human rights and for life with dignity. It includes the opportunity to earn a livelihood by work freely chosen or accepted. In progressively realising this right, States are obliged to ensure the availability of technical and vocational guidance, and take appropriate measures to develop an enabling environment for productive employment opportunities. States must ensure non-discrimination in relation to all aspects of work[80].

Several national instruments upholding the right to work which is a gate way to economic empowerment are in place in Cameroon. These provisions make no discrimination as to sex, thus the women especially the rural women are not excluded from benefiting from these rights. The Cameroon labour code.[81]holds that the right to work is a fundamental right of all its citizens. It goes further to state that it is to this effect that work is a national right for every adult and valid citizen[82]. The preamble of the Cameroon constitution holds that everyone has the right and duty to work[83]

Even the African charter on Human and Peoples Right complement this constitutional arena when it states that everyone shall have the right to work under the equitable and satisfactory conditions and shall receive equal pay for equal work.[84]Thus in economically empowering these rural women in Cameroon, her Human Right to work is upheld. This in turn goes a long way to boast the national economy as a whole.

2.2.3. Gender Balance

Economic empowerment of the rural women promotes gender balance. The 1995 Beijing Platform for Action advocated for equality of women and men in law and in practice[85].This is the same stance held by the CEDAW law when it states that States should take all appropriate measures to fight discrimination against women[86].This gender balance will help these rural women fight poverty, for they will be able to excel in all aspects of life especially in the domain of entrepreneurship. Economic empowerment of the rural women improves their

---

[79] Article7 of the International Covenant on Economic, social and cultural Rights.
[80] ESCR-Net. The Right to work and workers' Rights. Available. http://www.escr-net.org.
[81] Article 2(1) of the 1992 Cameroon Labour code.
[82] Ibid. Article 2(2) of the 1992 Cameroon Labour code.
[83] Preamble of the Cameroon's constitution of 12 June 1972 as amended by law of 18 January 1996.
[84] Article 15 of the African Chater on Human and Poeples' Rights, 1979.
[85] UN Women. World Conference on Women (1995). Available on https://www.unwomen .org. (consulted on 15/09/2023).
[86] Article 14 (2) of the African Chater on Human and Poeples' Rights, 1979.

financial situations. This will enable them to take care of their health and that of their families. They will be able to educate themselves and improve their standards of living. Thus, it is quite imperative that the women be treated equally with the men to uphold the 1948 UDHR's provision of equality of all.

These women will also be able to reduce child immortality since they will have means to take care of themselves. They will be able to improve their own health especially when they are pregnant through maternity visits.

2.2.4. The Right to Subsistence

Economic empowerment of the rural women enhances the rural women right to subsistence. Subsistence rights are rights to those things humans need to live minimally decent lives. These include enough food, shelter, clean water, medical care and unpolluted surroundings to lead a decent life. It targets the basic welfare of human beings rather than their flourishing. Defenders of subsistence rights regards them as Universal Human Right.[87] Developing the rural women economically through the creation of economic activities such as SMEs for instance will enable her achieve all her subsistent needs as listed above. It is for this reason that the Universal Declaration of Human Right as incorporated in the Cameroons' constitution [88]upholds the rights of subsistence when it holds that everyone has the right to a standard of living adequate for the health and well-being of himself and of his or her family including feeding, clothing housing and medical care and necessary social services. The right to subsistence for all is equally guaranteed by the Cameroon 1992 labour code where it states that the law recognizes the right of workers and employers without distinction whatsoever to set up freely trade unions or employer's association for the promotion and protection of their interest particularly those of an economic, industrial, commercial or agricultural nature and for the social, economic, cultural and moral advancement of their members.[89]

2.2.5. Property Rights

Another Human Right upheld through the economic empowerment of the rural women is property rights. The Human Right Covenant upholds property right which influences the right to subsistence[90]According to the 1998 Human Rights Act under its first protocol,[91]every natural or legal person is entitled to the

---

[87] Encyclopaedia of Global Justice. Pg.1042-1045).
[88] Article 25(1) of the 1998 UDHR.
[89] Section 3 of the 1992 Cameroon Labour code.
[90] Article 1(2) of the 1966 Human Right Covenant.
[91] Smith J. Roger (2016). Property Law, Cases and Materials. Longman law series.5th edition.PP.28

peaceful enjoyment of his possession. No one shall be deprived of his possessions except in the public interest and subject to the conditions provided for by the law and the general principles of international law.[92] Economically empowering these rural women for instance through entrepreneurship goes a long way to uphold her property right which interns enhances her right to subsistence. The preamble of the Cameroons' constitution[93] also uphold the right to own properties, when it holds that ownership shall mean the right to every person by law to use and dispose of property. Her business is the property and she can acquire further property for her subsistence. In addition to the constitution, guaranteeing these women their rights. The Administration of Estate Act for instance holds that if the intestate leaves no issue, the residuary estate shall be held in trust for the surviving spouse.[94] Land Tenure system in Cameroon equally provides women with equal rights to property ownership.[95]

Cameroonian case laws are not left out in upholding these women property rights: The land mark case of Zamcho Florence Lum v. Chibikom Peter Fru[96] decided by the supreme court lends credence to the fact that women's' right to inheritance is protected in Cameroon. In overturning the court of Appeal's decision, held that the customary principle denying a female the right to inherit her father's property or to be declared next of kin is contrary to natural justice, equity and good conscience,[97] the women were economically empowered since they can now land and landed property for her development and thus the development of the nation at large.

Property rights of a woman was upheld in the case of Debora S. Wara v. Dr Ben Fru Wara and Justina Afancho Neh, where it was held that, there is community of property. One spouse cannot dispose it without the other's approval. As to conveyance when there is join property one arty cannot convey tittle to a 3rd party. Monogamous marriage gives the spouse equal interest in the property.[98]

In the case of Aforba Aloysius, Bougnyisi Elizabeth v. Nchari Mary Kinyuy, it was held that, where a Cameroonian dies intestate, the rules of succession applicable to his estate will depend on whether the marriage was

---

[92] Article 1 of the Human Right Act 1998.
[93] Preamble the 1972 Cameroon Constitution.
[94] Section 46(10 of the Administration of estate Act 1925.
[95] The 1974 Cameroon Land Tenure Ordinance.
[96] Supreme Court judgement No.14 L of February 14, 1993.South West Court of Appeal, suit No CASWP/17/931(CCLR),1997 213-223.
[97] Section 27(1) of the southern Cameroon's Hight Court Law ,1995.
[98] Debora S.Wara v. Dr Ben Fru Wara and Justina Afancho Neh.Suit No HCB/59/97.

monogamous or polygamous. As to whether applicants have a priority or can be included as beneficiaries of the estate, section 46(1) of the Administration of Estate Act 1925 clearly keeps them out. Whatever they get from the estate will depend on the good will of the beneficiaries. Thus, upholding the widow's right to her husband's property.[99]

In Mbokam Nya Rose Clarisse v. Tchouinjani Andre, the High court of Fako Division before her Lordship Justice Mba Acha (Mrs) upheld a letter of administration issued to Mbokam Nya Rose Clarisse, the Plaintiff and the daughter of the deceased and ordered the defendant against further meddling with the said estate.[100]

In Aboh Lucy v. Kang Sume David had among other issues whether a wife is entitled to property which she indirectly contributed during the subsistence of marriage. It was held that the wife is entitled in the share of the property.[101]

In Njim Williams v. Njim Swirri Rose Saningong, the court was called upon to determine when the tittle deed to property is clearly registered in the name of one spouse whether the courts can rightly infer a joint interest or joint property. As to implication of not haven mention types of ante nuptial settlement, the legislator considers marriage as a contract and requires parties to indicate their intention if the intend to avoid any equivoques .Since the parties failed to indicate clearly how property acquired during their marriage had to be considered, leave the court with no other interpretation than that the regime of such marriage is on joint property, and thus, held that any property acquired during the subsistence of the marriage form part of the mass or common property of the spouses and the disputed vehicle will constitute no exception.[102]

Foreign case laws from which the Cameroonian courts drew inspirations in upholding women property rights includes among others:

Pettitt v. Pettitt, Lord Morris held that, the indirect contribution of the wife should be taken into consideration. Indirect contribution should however be substantial and that case, the plaintiff was entitled to a share of the landed property.[103]

In Cumber v. Cumber where the parties had been married for long with only one child, it was held that the wife will receive 1/3 of the proceeds of the

---

[99] Aforba Aloysius, Bougnyisi Elizabeth v. Nchari Mary Kinyuy.Suit No AE/06/93/IM/96.
[100] Mbokam Nya Rose Clarisse v. Tchouinjani Andre.
[101] Aboh Lucy v. Kang Sume David.Suit No HCF/38/96.
[102] Njim Williams v. Njim Swirri Rose Saningong. Appeal No BCA/22/96.
[103] Pettitt v. Pettitt, (1970) AC 777 at 804.

sale of matrimonial home. This decision followed the earlier decision of Wachtel v. Wachtel.[104]

2.2.6. Protects her as a Vulnerable Group

Economic empowerment of the rural women protects her as a vulnerable group. Vulnerable persons in Cameroon include women especially widows, orphans and people with disabilities or chronic diseases.[105]Vulnerability is the quality of being easily hurt or attacked. The rural women under study can be considered a vulnerable group in Cameroon. Their rights are often being easily violated due to the presence of customary law rules in this sector of the economy. This hinders most often than not these rural women from benefitting from the provisions and protection offered by the laws in place for her development. Customary law practices regard women as second-class citizens making them stay in the back ground, taking care of the family while the male go to school and thus become economically empowered more than the women. They own properties, mostly through inheritance while the woman or girl child is regarded as property and thus cannot own property. The law sanctions this and upholds women's rights when it provides that practices that are repugnant to natural justice equity and good conscience which are incompatible to written law[106] will not be enforced as was held in the cases of Ngeh V. Ngome [107] and Immaculate Wanga Vefonge v. Samuel Lyonga Yukpe [108],thus protecting the vulnerable women in Cameroon.

Program 557 [109] which deals with Social protection of Socially Vulnerable Persons under the Ministry of Social Affairs is a Program, known under the acronym "Program 557", intends to guarantee Socially Vulnerable Persons (PSV) better protection against deficiencies, social maladjustment, social risks and scourges, in particular through the development of an appropriate strategic framework, the strengthening of awareness- raising and education actions, the establishment of strategies guaranteeing better protection of the elderly and persons with disabilities, improvement of the social protection system and promotion of the rights of PSVs .Based on the ministerial strategy, Program 557 intends, to contribute to the quantitative and qualitative strengthening of the

---

[104] Cumber v. Cumber (1976) WL 1331

[105] Mission 21 (2023). Help for particularly vulnerable people in Cameroon. Available at https://www.mission 21.org. (Consulted on 26/04/2024).

[106] Section 27(1) on the 1955 SCHCL.

[107] Ngeh v. Ngome (1962-1964) WCLR 321.

[108] Immaculate Wanga Vefonge v. Samuel Lyonga Yukpe (1981) CASWP/CC/25/81 (Unreported).

[109] Minas (2018). Program 557.Social Protection of socially Vulnerable persons. Available at https://www.minas.cm.(Consulted on 26/08/2024).

social protection mechanisms and actions of PSVs, taking into account emerging social phenomena and the specificities of each of the vulnerable targets. The strategic focus of the program is therefore prevention and social protection.

The main objective of this program is to "Strengthen the social protection of Socially Vulnerable Persons", through the improvement of the living conditions of populations, by protecting their rights and educating the populations to the prevention of deficiencies and social maladjustment.

By economically empowering these rural women through the implementation of mechanisms such as Program 557 provided by the Ministry of Social Affairs and strict implementation of section 27(1) of the SCHCL 1955, and more, the rural women will be capable of economically empowering themselves through business ventures such as the creation of SMEs in the rural sectors in Cameroon and will no longer be regarded as a vulnerable class to the Cameroonian economy.

2.2.7. Rights to Self-Determination

Economic empowerment of the rural women will improve their rights to self-determination. Economically empowering the rural women through activities such as the creation of SMEs is going to make these women assert their rights to self-determination. This right to self-determination is a conditional principle in Modern International law often referred to as jus cogens [110]self-determination can be examined from two angles. We have internal and external self-determination [111] internal is the right of people of the state to govern themselves without outside influence while external self-determination is the right to determine their own political status and to be free from alien domination.

Another interpretation which ties down to our point of view is the fact that self-determination is the right of people to freely choose their own political, economic and social system. The right to direct their future, have control over how they live their lives, where, and with whom, and have authority over the resources that support themselves[112]. The economic empowerment of the rural women gives these women the power and the right to determine how to run their lives. Empowering the rural women make them self-determined and will not be afraid to assert her rights since she will become more aware of what transpires in

---

[110] Jus Cogens are fundamental overriding principles of international law from which no derogation was ever permitted.

[111] Agbor Dicson A (2018). The Right to Self-Determination in Southern Cameroon. Public International Law and Human Rights. Bachelor Thesis.P.1.

[112] Connecticut (2023). Connecticut Self Determination Initiative. Available at https://portal.ct.gov.(Consulted on 18/09/2023).

the society. This is so because she must have left from her formal position of the housewife and a farmer to an entrepreneur who has gathered skills through training and guidance from both the government and NGOs. The right to self-determination is enshrined in the UN charter, the Universal Declaration of Human Rights, the African Charter on Human and People's Rights and the Preamble of the Cameroon Constitution. According to the UN Charter, the main purpose of the united nation is to develop friendly interactional relations based on respect for principles of equal right and self-determination of the people. According to the UDHR, all people have the right to self-determination. By virtue of that right, they freely determine their political status and freely pursue their economic social and cultural development[113].The preamble of the Cameroon constitution makes provision for freedom of communication, of expression of the press. With all these in place, the economic empowerment of the rural women will go a long way to promote her self-determination.

With this self-confident nature, she will increase her social interaction and even engage in political activity of her community and even the state. Empowering these rural women will equally improve her leadership skills for she will be trained to lead and manage her businesses. Empowering the rural women will equally boast her self-confidence since she will be financially independent to be able to intervene and solve problems in her family and to those related to other women in the community.

2.2.8. Right to Make Decision

Economically empowering the rural women will empower her make decisions in her family and the community at large. International Human Right laws protect people's right to decide how to spend their money, make their own health care decisions, work for a living and have a relationship with friends and family. The preamble of the Cameroonian Constitution contains inalienable rights of the human person among which includes freedom of communication, expression, and freedom of thoughts.[114]These provisions were drawn from the fundamental freedoms enshrine in the universal Declaration of Human Rights, The Charter of the United Nation, the African charter on Human and People's Right and all duly ratified international convention. [115]

---

[113] Article 1(1) of the International Covenant on Economic, Social and Cultural Rights. It was adopted and opened for signature, ratification and accession by General Assembly resolution 2200A(XXI) of 16 December 196 and entered into force 3 January 1976, in accordance with article 27.

[114] The preamble of the 18th January 1996 Constitution as amended by 2nd June 1972.

[115] Law number 96-6 of 18 January 1996 to amend the constitution of 2 June 1972.

With the right to make decision being a Universal Human Right, the rural women are not excluded so economically empowering them will go a long way to empower them to take decisions concerning their families and the communities at large. The law cannot change this reality by itself but we need a solid legislative framework that recognizes everyone's right to decide how to conduct their own lives without discrimination. Our lives are made up of choices and everyone should have full control over their decisions[116] Economically empowering these women through economic activities such as the Creation of SMS will empower her make decisions in her family and the community at Large.

2.3. The Economic Perspective

In economically empowering the rural women, they will be empowered to carry out economic activities which further develops her as a person, the community in which she lives and the nation at large. This will help Cameroon to attain emergence in 2035 as envisage by the Cameroon government[117]

2.3.1. Fosters Economic Development

Economic empowerment of the rural women fosters their economic development. Economic empowerment is the capacity of women to participate in, contribute to and benefit from the growth processes in ways that recognise the value of their contributions. Women economic empowerment is a prerequisite for sustainable development and for achieving the sustainable development goals.[118]

Empowering women in economic activities is key to achieving gender equality and boasting the growth of national economies[119]. The Convention on the Elimination of all Forms of discrimination against Women (CEDAW) is an international instrument adopted by Cameroon which highlights the need to promote the rural women in their person.[120] It holds that States parties should take

---

[116] Espinoza Carlos Rios. (2022). Everyone deserves the right to make decisions about their lives. Available at https://www.h.w.org (Consulted on the 18/09/2023).

[117] Republic of Cameroon (2024). Economic Emergence Action. Available at https://www.prc.cm.(Consulted on the 27/05/2024)

[118] The 8 Millenium Development Goals were identified in the year 2000 and they included the eradication of poverty and hunger (Goal 1), achieve universal primary education (Goal 2), the promotion of gender equality and empower women (Goal 3), reduce child mortality (Goal 4), improve maternal health (Goal 5), combat HIV/AIDS, malaria and other diseases (Goal 6), ensure environmental sustainability (Goal 7), and develop a global partnership for development (Goal 8).

[119] Care International (2023). Women Economic Justice. Available at https//www.care-internation.org. (Consulted on the 14/09/2023)

[120] The Convention of the Elimination of All forms of Discrimination Against Women was adopted and opened for signature rectification and accession by the general assembly

into account the particular problems faced by the rural women and the significant role they play in the economic survival of their families and should take appropriate measures to apply the present provisions of the contention to women in the rural areas.[121]

States should take appropriate measures to eliminate discrimination against women in the rural areas in order to ensure on a basis of equality women and men, that they both participate in, and benefit from rural development.[122] The economic empowerment of these rural women through the encouragement of activities such as entrepreneurship venture like the creation of SMEs for instance upholds these CEDAW's provisions of economic empowerment of the rural women and thus fosters economic development of the rural communities in particular and the nation at large.

2.3.2. Improves her Standard of Living

Economic empowerment of the rural woman improves her standard of living. Good living standard is a woman's right to subsistence and economically empowering these women through for instance, the creation of SMEs will help guarantee her right to subsistence, thus giving her a good standard of living. The government has facilitated empowerment through developments in the Cameroons' social and economy law and policy. In recent years the country has seen growing interest in the social economy as a means of eliminating poverty particularly in the rural and informal economies and in promoting balanced and sustainable economic growth.[123]. In 2004, the Ministry of Small and Medium-Sized Enterprises, Social Economy and Handicrafts (MINPEESA) was established. In 2009, the National Development Strategy for SMEs, social economy and Handicraft was equally launched. The strategy was out to improve knowledge on social economy among others. More recently, the MINPEESA and its departments of social economy commissioned a study on the formulation of the national program for development of social economy (PNDES). The most recent of these programs is aimed at 'improving the contribution of social economy organisation around value chains and sectors and better territorial anchoring to contribute to the local development, fight rural poverty and improve food, security[124].

---

resolution 34/180 of 18 December 1979 and entered into force on 3rd September 1981 in accordance with art 27(1).

[121] Article 14(1) of the 1981 CEDAW law.

[122] Article 14(2) of the 1981 CEDAW Law.

[123] The Frame work Law No 2019/004 on the Cameroon social Economy.

[124] The Frame work Law (note 36).

The rural reform that has been taking place in Cameroon since 1992 relating to cooperatives and common initiative Groups (CIG)[125],brought in liberalisation in the sector as it allowed cooperatives and CIGs to carry out their financial as well as administrative activities independently without government intervention. This is certainly a move by the government to economically empower the rural women. It equally introduced new operating methods in Community, agricultural, infrastructure and local forest management. There has been a proliferation of rural organisations, grouped under the "Groupes d'initiative Commune" (GICs), new corporative and forest management councils. These forms of organisations provide important opportunity for agronomic research, agricultural development and the local management of forest resources[126].which is certainly an important step towards the economic empowerment of the rural women who are highly engages in agriculture. This law will help these women to form economic groupings more where their voice as on person can be easily heard and their rights be easily defended as a group which will certainly improve their living standards

The Cameroon constitution in its preamble holds that the state has resolved to harness its natural resources in order to ensure the wellbeing of every citizen without discrimination, by raising standard of living and proclaiming right to development.[127] In promoting the right of improved living standard by the Cameroon government, our rural women are not left behind since the right are non-discriminatory so when the government goes further to economically empower the rural women through creation of SMEs for instance, it further improves these women's financial status which goes a long way to improve their living standards.

2.3.3. Promotes Community Development

Economic empowerment of the rural women promotes community Development. Cameroon has a population of about 11million.The population is largely rural than urban. The rural population is made up of about 7,542,000 and about 4,000.000 of whom are women. Thus, on a whole, women make up about 52% of the population[128],thus making women the greater proportion of Cameroon population.

---

[125] Law No 92/006 of 14th August 1992 relating to Cooperatives and Common Initiative Groups (CIG) in Cameroon.
[126] P.R Oyono and L. Temple (2003), Metamorphose des organisations rurales au Cameroun. Available at https://www.erudit.org.(Consulted on 09/06/2024).
[127] The preamble of the 1972 Cameroon constitution as revised in 2008.
[128] The 1987 Natonal Census.

Economically empowering these rural women will in turn empower these women to better develop their communities[129].The CEDAW law states that 'Parties shall take into account the particular problem faced by rural women and the significant roles which rural women play in the economic survival of their families including their work in the non-monetize sector of the economy and shall take all appropriate measures to ensure the application of the provisions of the convention to women in the rural areas'. The CEDAW equally holds that 'State parties shall take all appropriate measures to eliminate discrimination against women in the rural areas[130]in order to ensure on the basis of equality between men and women. That they participate in and benefit from rural development.

These women carry out diverse duties in their communities in the home, she carries out daily house hold chores, they fetch water, look for fuel, take care of food processing and preparation to add to, these women naturally perform their reproductive roles of child bearing naturally. Getting involved in food production and helping in some household chores is considered not appropriate for men because it is considered as a woman's job. The division of labour between sexes is mostly due to cultural and social norms of the different communities.[131] CEDAW knows the importance of these women and want them to grow beyond the boundaries set for the by these cultures and traditions [132] These roles attributed to women remain the same irrespective of the social class of these woman. Work done by these women have direct impacts on the community development since it helps in the development of human capital. Economic empowerment of these rural women such as in the creation of SMEs by these rural women will enable them better manage their homes thus further develop their communities since they will be empowered financially.

Apart from house hold management, these rural women are also mostly involved in education of their children. In polygamous homes which is very common in the rural settings for instance, the women are mostly the ones in charge of educating the children. The education of the children depends on the efforts of their mothers. This is so difficult because their income level is low and they cannot perform economically productive activities. It is for this reason that it is quite imperative to empower these women economically through the creation of economic activities such as SMEs which will empower them financially to take

---

[129] Article 14(1) of CEDAW.

[130] Article 14(2) of the CEDAW Law.

[131] Sikod Fondo (2007). Gender Division of Labour and Women's Decision-Making power n Rural Households in Cameroon. Africa Development.Vol.XXXII.No.3. PP 59-60.

[132] Ibid.

care of their children. Investment in the women especially the rural women mean more returns not only for the women but also to their families and their communities. If for instance effort is put for the education of these woman themselves, they will in turn empower their children especially the girl children. They will equally become more economically empowered and will generate income with ease to take care of the family.

The economic empowerment of the women through education is the development of their families and their communities at large. These women have the right to obtain all types of training and education, formal or informal as well as that relating to financial literacy as well as benefit from all community and extension services in order to increase their technical proficiency[133] Each added year of schooling for a mother result to 5-10% decrease in the mortality among children which is great for the development of their communities[134]. The creation of SMEs empowers these women financially and they can carry out educational programs and training for their empowerment and thus that of their families and the community as a large.

These rural women also engage in agriculture, providing about 90% of the food needed for the subsistence of the population.[135] The CEDAW saw the need to promote women and thus makes provision for access to agricultural credit and loans, marketing facilities appropriate technology and equal treatment in the land and agrarian reform as well as land resettlement schemes.[136] The rural women engage mainly in agriculture. They are mainly involving in food crop production and distributions. The involvement of the women in cash crop production is very low. These women produce deferent types of food crop. Encouraging these women to be economically empowered say through the creation of SMEs, that is moving from the informal mode of distributions of their food product to a formal mode will not only empower the women financially but will also go a long way to create positive impact in the communities. These enterprises will be able to create job opportunities for others since SMEs will need employees to work in the business for pay. These women will also be able to take good care of their families since they are financially viable. They can educate their children with ease, provide health care with ease and equally food and basic necessities with ease thus creating a positive impact in the community which she finds herself in. With

---

[133] Article 14(2)(d) of the CEDAW Law.
[134] Josiane Salu F.et al (2022). The Influence of mother's education and household's wealth on the use of prenatal health services in Cameroon. Revue Africaine des Science Economique et de Gestion Serie Science economique. No24 Janvier-Juin 2022. PP.7-13.
[135] Wikipedia. Rural Women. Available at https://en.wikipedia.org.
[136] Art 14(2)(g) of CEDAW.

money, these women can engage in cash crop production by renting hectares of lands. Although food crop production can be equally rewarding as cash crops production, the fact that women cannot freely choose which activity they like, reduces their earning and their participation in community development. Economically empowering the rural women by promoting the creation of SMEs will help these women expand their scope. Even in the domain of livestock which they engage timidly mostly helping their husbands to provide food and to feed the animals, these women need to be encouraged. Some women own small number of domestic animals such as pigs, goats and chicken. Some women in recent years in the South and Central regions of Cameroon have been trained in the domain of fishery. Promoting women create SMEs that deals in this domain will create a great impact in the lives of the women and the communities they find themselves. SMEs which are formal sectors will be recognised by the government and can easily receive government incentives[137]since they will be legally recognised as a registered company in the country. This law on incentive seeks to facilitate, promote and attract productive investment geared towards strong, sustainable and shared economic growth as well as job creation.

The Cameroon women as well as most African women have been contented with staying at home and taking care of their families. However, with the increase in cholerization and the economic hardship, these women have found it necessary to work out of home. They are thus present in both formal and informal sectors though more visible in the informal sectors.[138]

The rate of women involved in the formal sector in the business such as SMEs is very low. This is because they need education, finance, time and training in the domain which the rural women lack. Most of them are illiterates,[139] they lack finances and even the means of generating it since they cannot access financial institutions for loans due to lack of collateral security. This is so in spite of the fact that legal provisions make provisions for the facilitation of the creation of SMEs by all. According to the Cameroon investment Charter, the State shall oversee and promote small and medium-sized enterprises and industries (SMEs and SMIs)[140].It shall establish a financial services system that supports medium-sized economic operators through appropriate regulation and supervision. It shall

---

[137] Section 1(2) of law No 2013/004 of 18thApril 2013 on Incentives in Cameroon.
[138] OCHA (2023). Supporting Women's empowerment in rural areas of Africa. Available at https://reliefweb.int (Consulted on 26/08/2024).
[139]Ahl Helene et. al. (2023). Women's Contributions to rural development: Implications for entrepreneurship policy. International Journal of Entrepreneurship Behavior and Research. Volume 30 Issue 7.
[140] Article 38 of the 2002 Cameroon Investment Charter.

equally establish financing mechanisms for SMEs and SMIs that address various specific and sectoral needs through appropriate regulation and supervision.

Economically empowering these women through education, training and financing to create SMEs will enable these women make better decisions. At home, she can take better decisions on how to manage her house chores, she can install pipe borne water, electricity, prepare better meals for the children. She can even buy improved kitchen utensils and improve the standard of the kitchen to facilitate her cooking process. She can now decide to improve the standards of the meals, to change the wardrobes and equally improve in educational standard of her family. All these will go a long way to develop the community. These women opinion will count because they will be able to speak and execute projects in their cycles as female entrepreneurs. These women can easily advocate and support in the provision of school fees, water, electricity health care facilities for they know how vital it is for their children and the community at large.

At the national level, women's issues will be properly catered for. These empowered rural women will always be consulted on issues concerning them. These empowered women will be the ones to decide which project to be implemented and how to implement them in their communities. They will become enthusiastic to participate in the community projects because they are economically empowered which will go a long way to develop their community.

These women who become backbones of the economy by becoming economically empowered through for instance the creation of SMEs possess financial power as entrepreneurs, and thus have the ability to engage the state by lobbying for developmental projects through contracts to their communities. They can lobby for projects such as water, electricity, roads, health care facilities etc for the development of their communities.

In addition to all the above when the rural women are economically empowered financially through the creation of these SMEs, they can become educated and more aware, their girl children become educated equally and more aware. They become more aware of their rights and when these rights are violated. As such these women can bring up violation against their human rights before justice. So, when the laws are violated by any customary law practices, these women know when and where to cry out for remedies. Thus, economically empowering the rural women through development of economic activities such as the creation of SMEs is a great way to develop any rural community.

Equally, businesses run by rural women can be more flexible and can meet the changing needs of their communities. Rural SMEs for instance are usually a small enterprise and can be more flexible to meet the changing needs of their rural economy. This flexibility fosters confidence and loyalty among customers. In other words, as a rural business owner, you can make changes in your inventory, billing, offer new products, or change processes more easily. This is so because you are right there when the customer comes through the door and makes a request or shares feedback with you. You can make decisions or changes in the moment! That is customer satisfaction at its best. You do not have to consult multiple levels or parties to make changes or decisions. The ability to meet customer/client demands on the spot means customers are inclined to seek out your business services first.

Economically empowering the rural women through the creation of SMEs by rural women also improves Per Capita income of the community and the nation at large. Per capita income is the metric used to determine the amount earned by an individual in a nation or a geographical region. The Cameroon Labour code[141] states that the law shall govern relationship between wage-earners and employers as well as between employers and apprentices under their supervision.

Small and Medium Enterprises (SMEs) play a major role in most economies, particularly in developing countries in the creation of jobs which helps to increase the per capita income of the Rural women in particular and the rural community at large. SMEs account for the majority of businesses worldwide and are important contributors to job creation and global economic development. They represent about 90% of businesses and more than 50% of employment worldwide[142]. Formal SMEs contribute up to 40% of national income (GDP) in emerging economies. These numbers are significantly higher when informal SMEs are included. In emerging markets, most formal jobs are generated by SMEs, which create 7 out of 10 jobs.[143].

These SMEs created by rural women equally brings innovation to the community. Innovation is the key to entrepreneurship. It implies the commercial application of an invention. As an innovator, the entrepreneur assumes the role of a pioneer and an industrial leader. Entrepreneurs have contributed many innovations in the developing new products and in the existing products and services. Small businesses and start-ups provide more than just jobs for community members. More local small businesses mean new ways of thinking

---

[141] Section 1 of Law No 92/007 of 14 August 1992.
[142] The World Bank: Small and Medium Enterprises (SMEs) Finances. Available at <https://www.worldbank.org.(consulted on the 18/03/2023 at 8:00pm).
[143] The World Bank: Small and Medium Enterprises (SMEs) Finances. Available at <https://www.worldbank.org.(consulted on the 18/03/2023 at 8:00pm).

and fresh perspectives, almost like an entrepreneur mindset. For large businesses, trying fundamentally new approaches can be akin to turning a battleship, while it is relatively simple for small businesses to reinvent themselves.

Small businesses are generally more nimble than large businesses, with tighter-knit teams and simple communication channels. This enables them to quickly pivot and change their operations in major ways with minimal investment. As a result, early-stage entrepreneurs can act as laboratories of innovation, testing new ways of doing things and seeing if any of them pay off. And when they do, it can put the local community on the map.[144] Innovation creates disequilibrium in the present state of order. It goes beyond discovery and does implementation and commercialisation, of innovations. "Leapfrog" innovation, research, and development are being contributed by entrepreneurship.

Thus, entrepreneurship nurse's innovation that provides new ventures, products, technology, market, quality of good, etc. to the economy that increases Gross Domestic Products and standard of living of the people. It acts as an engine for innovation and job creation in Cameroon[145]Entrepreneurship is the nursing ground for new inexperienced adventurists. It is the field where a person can start his/her idea of the venture, which may be ended up in a giant enterprise. All the large industrial ventures started as a small entrepreneurial enterprise.

Therefore, entrepreneurship provides a wide spectrum of ventures and entrepreneurs in every economy. Entrepreneurship leads to the creation of SMEs, providing employment opportunities, income generation, uplifting of standard of living and utilisation of human, material, as well as financial resources of the country in the right direction[146]. The vast open arena of entrepreneurship thus acts as an incubator to entrepreneurs.

2.3.4. Create Social Change

Economic empowerment of the rural women Create Social Change. Through offering unique goods and services, entrepreneurs break away from tradition and reduce dependence on obsolete systems and technologies. This results in an improved quality of life, improved morale, and greater economic freedom. For example, the water supply in a water-scarce region will, at times, forces people to stop working to collect water. This will impact their business, productivity, and income. Imagine an innovative and automatic pump that can fill

---

[144] Treece Dock (2023): Why Small Businesses are Good for local Communities. Available at <https://www.businessnewsdaily.com>
[145] Ibid.
[146] Daniel M.T and Sophie N. N., (note 90).

people's water containers automatically. This type of innovation ensures people are able to focus on their jobs without worrying about a basic necessity like water. More time to devote to work translates to economic growth.

For a more contemporary example, smartphones and apps have revolutionised work and play across the globe. Smartphones are not exclusive to wealthy countries or people. As the growth of the smartphone market continues, technological entrepreneurship can have a profound, long-lasting impact on the world. Moreover, the globalization of technology means entrepreneurs in lesser-developed countries have access to the same tools as their counterparts in richer countries. They also have the advantage of a lower cost of living, so a young entrepreneur from an underdeveloped country can compete with a multi-million-dollar existing product from a developed country.

Economic vitality is a necessary condition for achieving social vitality which improves the standard of living of the citizens of nation. Important factors that make living attractive are flow of information, education, health, housing and transportation which are developed and sustained through entrepreneurship. The easiest approach to economic vitality is through women entrepreneurship. Developed women have been known for their ability to combine different activities that have the potential to enhance the standard of living and quality of life of the citizenries. Women are more likely to juggle their working time between the market sector and non- market production whether it involves subsistence crop production, water and fuel gathering, food preparation and house cleaning of care for the children and elderly is a crucial element in determining the quality of life.

By economically empowering these women say by helping them to become entrepreneurs through the creation of SMEs, these women will have access to and control over income and working conditions. This will empower them to be fully involved and participate in economic, social, and political policy making changes in gender inequality and discrimination especially in the labour market. It is believed that with self- employment and entrepreneurship, women gained confidence, self- esteem and decision-making experience leading to greater control over their lives in social, economic and political spheres.

On the business side, rural businesses offer intimate knowledge of the services and products needed in their geographic area. Business owners also know their customers' names and remember details about former transactions. Being local also gives you the inside track on what is happening in your immediate area. Being in tune with your immediate area can also help you adjust your stock availability and have a close 'handle' on your monthly cash flow key elements to a small business thriving.

On a social level, as a way of contributing to the sustainability of their community, many business owners often sponsor local events like ball tournaments and local festivals, also hold volunteer positions on town council demonstrating social accountability. In other words, rural business owners are not anonymous and absentee landlords. They directly contribute to the social fabric of the rural community and encourage strong viability, sponsoring population retention necessary to keep essential services available and operating full-time. They are an essential component of sponsoring a sense of community for rural residents.

2.3.5. Promotes the Growth of Entrepreneurship Initiatives

Economic empowerment of the rural women Promote the Growth of Entrepreneurship Initiatives[147]. The statistics reveal that in USA economy nearly half a million small enterprise is established every year.99.7 percent of U.S and 64 percent of net new private-sector jobs.[148] Our country is not an exception in this regard. Economic empowerment of the rural women through the creation of Small and Medium-sized Enterprises in Cameroon (SMEs) constitute the bulk of the country's enterprises. In fact, the law[149] and other legal and institutional instruments paved the way for the sector with many such enterprises being created. With other accompanying measures for a level playing ground created, the SMEs.[150] Going by the Research and Analysis Centre on the Economic and Social Policies of Cameroon (CAMERCAP-PARC), 61,366 SMEs were created in Cameroon between 2010 and 2016, with 59,200 being local enterprises and 2,166 foreign. 72.24 per cent of the enterprises, according to CAMERCAP-PARC are inexistent on the taxation department database as at May 2016. According to the 2016 annual statistics of the Ministry of Small and Medium-sized Enterprises, Social Economy and Handicraft, Cameroon SMEs considered as the main engine for economic growth, contribute only 36 per cent to the Gross Domestic Product

---

[147] Narayan Madhusudan et al (2018). Rural Entrepreneurship in India: An Overview. Available at https://www.researchgate.net.(Consulted on 26/08/2024).

[148] Advocacy (2012) The voice of Small Business in Government, Frequently Asked Questions, Available at <https://www.sba.gov> (consulted on the 18/02/2020).

[149] Law N° 2010/010 of 13 April 2010 on the promotion of SMEs in Cameroon.

[150] According to statistics from the Ministry of Small and Medium-sized Enterprises, (MINPMEESA), Social Economy and Handicraft, constitute 95 per cent of Cameroon's enterprises. The sectors concerned are; transformation, agriculture and animal husbandry, general commerce, construction and public works and most recently Information and Communication Technologies (ICTs).

(GDP) "Imagine that SMEs contribute 50 per cent to GDP, we would already be an emerging country". So, SMEs have to make an effort so that their contribution to the national economy can attain 50 per cent. The government expects SMEs to improve with all the accompanying structures at their disposal," Minister Laurent Serge Etoundi Ngoa, stated in one of his interviews with the national bilingual daily newspaper, Cameroon Tribune. Cameroon SMEs has one fundamental problem, a short life span. A good chunk of the SMEs dies naturally while still in the incubator stage. This, experts say, is as a result of poor or absence of market research as well as the good choice of area of specialty (niche). The Research and Analysis Centre on the Economic and Social Policies of Cameroon (CAMERCAP-PARC) in its 2016 study show that 66.43 per cent of SMEs in the transformation sector, 46.84 per cent in Agriculture, 31.64 per cent in general commerce, 28.16 in Associations and training and 25.86 per cent of enterprises in the construction and public works sectors survive the hurdles. [151]

Entrepreneurship is the advent of new venture particularly small ventures to materialise the innovative ideas of the entrepreneurs. Thus, the growth or establishment of small enterprises is the specific contribution of entrepreneurship in every economy of the world. SMEs have so many advantages which goes a long way to promote entrepreneurship. Rural business entrepreneurs have advantages that are often overlooked. They are smaller in size, which enables them to respond quickly to economic boom and bust cycles, and they also have the benefit of being near rural economic development. The advantages of being a rural entrepreneur in a small town are mutually beneficial to one another and create a strong partnership in the sustainability of rural life. There are three major advantages to starting your business in a rural area: you can access your customers immediately and directly, you can deliver niche market services, and your business can be flexible when shifting to meet new business needs. Entrepreneurship is innovation and hence the innovated ideas of goods and services have to be tested by experimentation. Therefore, entrepreneurship provides funds for research and development with universities and research institutions. This promotes the general development, research, and development in the economy.

Entrepreneurship is the pioneering zeal that provides events in our civilization. We are indebted to it for having prosperity in every arena of human

---

[151] Roland M., (2017) Small and Medium Sized Enterprises from 95 percent of the country's economic landscape, but its co. Cameroon business. Available at < https://www.cameroonbusinesstoday.cm>.(consulted on 18/02/2020 at 6:57am)

life- economic, technological and cultural.[152] New products and services created by entrepreneurs can produce a cascading effect, where it stimulates related businesses or sectors that need to support the new venture, furthering economic development.

2.3.6. Combat Poverty

Economic empowerment of the rural women combat poverty. The prevalence of poverty remains higher in the rural areas 66% in the rural area as opposed to 7% in the urban areas [153] Women represent the poorest portion of the population, though they contribute more than 55.8% of the national agricultural Production[154]. The Cameroon women constitute more than 70% of the rural work force. They produce almost 90% of the food crops and only represent 3% of the industrial agricultural sector.[155] This hinder the rural development which is essential for the achievement of development goals.

Rural development is not sufficiently financed in Cameroon by the public sector although it is one of the priorities of the strategic frame work for the fight against poverty. The fight against poverty is one of the major objectives of the national development strategy. It is out to reinforce the rural population access to quality education, land, natural resources, finance, and infrastructure to fight poverty, there must be equitable development and aspects which favours equitable development. They are, access to quality education for rural inhabitants irrespective of the sex.

Unfortunately, rural areas in Cameroon remain on the side-line when it comes to quality education especially in the far north and eastern region of Cameroon where the rural population still suffers from lack of educational infrastructures. This is accompanied by lack of teaching staffs and the few teachers who are assigned often abandon their post because of poor conditions in the area. You can find children in these areas being taught under trees sitting on the ground to study and the teachers looking so shabbily dressed and looking malnourished.[156]

Economically encouraging the rural women in areas such as the creation of SMEs will go a long way to generate income in the community and with money in the hands for the women the education of their children is certain. They will

---

[152] Valliere D., (note 100)
[153] Boris Andzanga .A and Kouam Jean-Cedric Dr (2023):Promoting rural development to reduce Gender inequalities.
[154] Ibid.
[155] 2020 statistics from the ministry of agriculture and rural development (MINDER).
[156] Equinox pidgin news on the 12th August 2022 at 1:00pm.

encourage through financing and creation of community schools, equally the living standards of their families will be improved thus that of the community at large.

Rural women can better fight Global warming which is a cause of poverty especially in the rural sectors in Cameroon since they are the backbone of the agricultural force of the economy which is highly affected by global warming. Cameroon has ratified more than 23 international agreements in the fields of forests and the environment among which can be cited the United Nation Framework Convention on Climate Change (UNFCCC) 1994, the Brazzaville Treaty on the Conservation and sustainable management of Forest Ecosystems in Central Africa in 2005.Several measures has equally been taken nationally by the government to combat this global warming. We have the law on environmental management[157],the law[158] authorising the president of the republic to ratify the Paris Climate Agreement adopted in Paris on 12 December 2015 and signed in New York on 22 April 2016.The creation of the ministry of Environment and Protection of nature and Sustainable Development (MINEPDED) [159] is another Government effort towards the creation of a healthy environment for the wellbeing of the population as a whole. An inter-ministerial committee on the environment has equally been created to facilitate the implementation of the sectoral programme on forest and the environment[160]. These notwithstanding, global warming still remains a major challenge especially to the rural population in Cameroon. The northern region of Cameroon especially the rural population are victims of global warming. Agricultural activities are affected particularly because of drying up water bodies. Equally the livestock sector is affected. The lack of pasture forces farmers to turn to alternative solutions that are not accessible to all to feed their livestock. It is thus important to economically empower the rural women by encouraging them create SMEs in these regions. In so doing these women will receive subventions and training from the government and other bodies to manage this global warming and develop the community.

These SMEs by Rural women facilitate financing of agricultural projects. Several agricultural projects are implemented by the ministry of agriculture and rural development (MINADER) to support and assist the rural population in other production process. Lack of communication however acts as a barrier in achieving this objective. Some farmers however manage to get information and benefit from

---

[157] Law No.96/12 of August 1996.
[158] Law No.2016/008 of 12 July 2016.
[159] Decree No 2004/320 of 8th December 2004.
[160] Order No.100/PM of 11 July 2006.

these projects. However, they are not sufficiently equipped and trained on the new agricultural techniques which makes their production below optimal. Furthermore, the agricultural programs do not necessarily take into account the needs of the rural women especially when it comes to access to finance. Between 2010 and 2020 of more than 112 agricultural projects and programs developed in Cameroon only 36.7% or 41% of them took gender into account in their conceptions while 63.3% remains gender insensitive and their conceptions are implementations.[161]

The creation of SMEs by these rural women will enable them to bring their resources together and create small formal businesses which are recognized by the government and thus with this government and other bodies can direct resources and man power to the further help them acquire skills to do their business. Communication can easily flow to these women since they will have fixed setting for their businesses.

2.3.7. Improve National Income

Economic empowerment of the rural women improves national income.[162] The economic empowerment of the rural women through the creation of SMEs in an economy especially the rural economy literally generates new wealth. The cascading effect of increased employment and higher earnings contribute to better national income in form of higher tax revenue and higher government spending. This revenue can be used by the government to invest in other struggling sectors and human capital. Although it may make a few existing players redundant, the government can soften the blow by redirecting surplus wealth to retrain workers. The Small and Medium Enterprises have the potential to create millions of jobs, improve per capital income and export earnings and enhance capacity utilisation in key industries.[163]

The creation of SMEs by rural women entrepreneurs can help women owned businesses generate more income which then can be used to support their households and improve their family welfare outcomes. This income can help women to start and grow their businesses which will in turn help them to offer employment to other in their community.

The bill governing the social economy in Cameroon makes provision for financial education, a process whereby consumers and of investors improve their

---

[161] Ibid note 16
[162] UN WOMEN (2024). Facts and Figures: Economic Empowerment Available athttps://www.unwomen.org.(Consulted on 26/8/2024).
[163] Awoyinfa Samuel (2020): SMEs can improve per capita income, (GDP),

knowledge of financial products, concepts and risk and through objective information, education and advice acquire the requisite skills and confidence to become more receptive.

The legal frame work bill governing social economy in Cameroon[164] which is the recent bill passed in Cameroon goes a long way to promote and empower the women entrepreneur in their financial transactions. Giving them the opportunity to know what it takes and how to manage their financial situation. With this knowledge on financial management, these women can easily fund an economy. There is financial sustainability in the economy especially the rural economy thanks to the financial education and development of these female entrepreneurs.

These SMEs by rural women also promote Capital formation. The Cameroons' Investment Charter holds that ''The present law establishes the framework for the promotion of investment in accordance with the overall development strategy, which is aimed at improving and sustaining growth, creating jobs in all sectors of economic activities and ensuring the social welfare of the population''[165]

SMEs play a crucial role in capital formation through expanding the components of gross domestic capital formation.[166] One of the most concerns in economic development is the expansion of a productive private sector in order to increase gross domestic capital formation (GDCF) for poverty reduction. Private sector development may take many different forms, and its outcome may be much different in terms of equitable development and social inclusiveness. One of the most efficient ways of private sector development is the promotion of SMEs instead of large firms. SME development contributes to render a more balanced industrial structure and income equality. There are ample kinds of literature concerning the importance of SMEs promotion policy and SMEs contribution in achieving the Sustainable Development Goals (SDGs), through promotion a comprehensive and sustainable economic growth, provision of employment and decent job opportunity for all, sustainable industrial development, encouraging innovation, supporting income equality. SMEs at least have three unique contributions to economic growth and development. First, and probably the most commonly stated claim is the role of SMEs in employment generation. SMEs

---

[164] Section 2 of Law no. 2019/004 of 25 April 2019 on Social Economy,

[165] Article 6 of Law No.2002/004 of the Cameroons' Investment Charter.

[166] Dr. Sultan Ahmad Taraki :(2019)'' The Role of SMEs in Capital Formation, Equitable Growth and Income Distribution in Developing Countries'' Volume 8. Available at <www.ijsr.net> (Consulted on the 25/03/2023)

provide a large percentage of the new generated job, particularly create employment opportunity at relatively lower capital cost than those generated by large firms. Therefore, SME development policy is more reliable with economic conditions of developing countries for employment generation and poverty reduction. Second, SMEs development is considered as the primary stage for future industrialization. Third, SMEs development advances competition and increase flexibility in the industrial structure of the economy. Consequently, SME development policy promotes a greater economic dynamism and makes faster and cheaper the adjustments process against the economic shocks.[167]

Currently, SMEs constitute the most significant percentage of total enterprises. Thus, this sector is considered as the major source of employment generation and economic growth in almost all economies, thus a strong instrument for rural women economic empowerment and further means to improve the national income.

2.3.8. Promotes the Growth of the National Economy

Economic empowerment of rural women promotes the Growth of the National Economy[168]. In Cameroon, the 1980s were marked by the economic crisis (falling export revenues) with the direct consequences of unemployment. Thus, many were retrenched from the public service, private companies and graduated students engaged in small- income generating activities which later became small businesses. It is in this context that the village palm grove started to bloom as an economic branch and contributes remarkably to the development of business activities in rural areas in Cameroon.[169]

Women entrepreneurship contributes more than 50% of Gross Domestic product (GDP) of most nations both developed and less developed. Its contributions to economic development have been predominant in the area of job creation, poverty alleviation, environmental vitality, wealth creation[170] Female entrepreneurs are top contributors to development and growth. One of the key advantages of empowering women to grow SMEs is that these SMEs act as major catalysts for development. These rural women often reinvest profits make from

---

[167] Ibid.

[168] Potters Charles (2024). Economic Growth: What it is and How it is measured. Available at https://investopedia.com.(Consulted on the 26/08/2024).

[169] Zongabiro P. N. P., (2014) The Contribution of Village Palm Grove to the Cameroonian Rural Economic Development, Available at < https://www.researchgate.net> (consulted on the 14/02/2020).

[170] Agu E. O (2015) An Assessment of the Contribution of Women Entrepreneur toward Entrepreneurship Development in Nigeria, International Journal of Current Research and Academic Review vol. 3.

SMEs in children's health, nutrition and education, promoting human capital both today and for the next generation as well as improving the potential for economic growth[171].

Several Ministries have been charged by the government to address issues related to women, notably the ministries responsible for SME, women and the family and employment and professional training, (MINPROFF). Units dealing with questions linked to women's entrepreneurship is found in the ministries responsible for Agriculture Husbandry, Labour, Professional training and social security. The government has created other organisations such as the FNE (Fond Nationale L'emploi) and chambers that support entrepreneurship including women's entrepreneurship. Support policies for the development of women's economic activities include: project to support diary formers, the pig industry, and non- animal breeding. The FNE in particular supports programmed that integrate the training needs of women entrepreneurs at each stage of the business development process[172]

2.4. Conclusion

Economic empowerment of the rural women through economic activities such as Promoting the growth of SMEs by rural female entrepreneurs helps to development the national economy as a whole as seen in the role it plays towards the community, the state and the family for their development. It is because of the importance of these rural women entrepreneurship in Cameroon that the government protects and promotes the women to be economically empowered through encouraging them to carryout economic activities such as the creation of SMEs in the rural settings since this domain is focused on agricultural production and thus SMEs will certainly succeed making these women become economically empowered. Several laws and institutions both national and International have been put in place to ensure these rural women carry out their businesses successfully. Equally guiding principles are in place to guide these women towards economic empowerment for her development and that of the national economy. This will take us to the next chapter where we will be examining the concept or guiding principles of women's economic empowerment in Cameroon.

---

[171]Patricia G. Q., (2016) Female Entrepreneurs, adding a New Perspective to Economic Growth, Available at <https://espacioinvestiga.org> (consulted on the 18/02/2020).
[172] Lois S. and Annette S., (2011) Assessment of the Environment of Women's Entrepreneurship in Cameroon, Mali, Nigeria, Rwanda and Senegal Employment, Report No. 15, Available at <https://www.africabib.org> (consulted on the 18/02/2020).

CHAPTER THREE

GUIDING PRINCIPLES TOWARDS THE ECONOMIC EMPOWERMENT OF RURAL WOMEN IN CAMEROON

3.1. Introduction

Supported by the pure theory propounded by Hand Kelson. According to Kelson's theory, law must be free from ethics, politics, sociology, history etc. The concept of women's right to development is grounded on the guiding principles of the right to development.[173] The rural women in Cameroon have a right to economic development, but they find it so challenging to become economically empowered. This chapter is to illustrate those guiding principles fostering women's right to development which if implemented will help these rural women become economically empowered.

The right to development is an inevitable human right by virtue of which every human person and all peoples are entitled to participate in, contribute to and enjoy economic, social, cultural and political development in which all human and fundamental freedoms can be fully realized.[174] The declaration of the right to development further states that human rights to development also implies a full realization of the right of people to self-determination which includes amongst others the exercise of their inalienable right to full sovereignty over all their natural wealth and resources. Therefore, as beneficiaries of the right to development, all human persons should be included and fully consulted in any development which affects them. It is the duty of the State to ensure that they have equal and adequate access to essential resources and it falls upon the international community to promote fair development policies and effective international cooperation. Despite efforts by the UN to promote effective cooperation for the realisation of the right to development, it is evident that minorities all over the world, particularly from developing countries, still suffer as a result of poverty stemming from violation of their right to development

This applies mostly to the women and especially the rural women whose right to economic development in particular are often violated due to the existence of repugnant traditions and customs of the rural people. Because these women have the right to development, the guiding principles or provisions put in place by various bodies be it international, regional, national or otherwise as examined

---

[173] UN Human Rights (1986), Declaration on the Right to Development. Available at htttps://www.unwomen.org. (Consulted on 26/08/2024).
[174] Article 1(1) of the United Nations declaration of the right to Development 1986.

43

below, will go a long way to promote these rural women's rights to development thus encouraging them to become economically empowered for their development and the development of the national economy.

3.2. Guiding Principles of Women's Right to Development at the International Level

3.2.1: Guiding principles by the UN Sustainable Development Goals for 2030[175]

The UN Sustainable Development Goals for 2030 [176]has not only set high standards for human society but presents an effort to guide society toward being more accessible and just by conveying a strong dimension of social development, human dignity and demanding justice at all stages. This agenda for sustainable development has 17 sustainable development goals (SDGs) which are urgent call for action by all nations.[177] These goals act as guiding principles for development[178]. It should be noted that in as much as all the 17 goals go a long way to empower the women, Goal 5 makes specific emphasis to gender equality and empowerment of all women and girls.

Rural women are in most need of such principles since they are the ones who suffer marginalisation the most due to the presence of discriminatory customary laws and practices. In spirit of the Universal Declaration of Human Rights and its Principles on Development, everyone is "entitled to participate in, contribute to, and enjoy economic, social, cultural and political development, in which all human rights and fundamental freedoms can be fully realized[179]. The Declaration requires that development be carried out in a manner "in which all human rights and fundamental freedoms can be fully realised."[180] The contents of

---

[175] United Nations (2024) About the 2030 Agenda on Sustainable Development. Available at https:///www.ohchr.org.(Consulted on 26/08/2024).

[176] ibid

[177] United Nations. Department of Economic and Social Affairs. (2023). Sustainable Development. Available at https://sdgs.un.org (Consulted on the 18/01/2024).

[178] They include, Goal 1, end poverty. Goal 2, no hunger. Goal 3, Good health and well-being, Goal 4, Quality education. Goal 5 Gender equality. Goal 6, clean water and sanitation. Goal 7, affordable and clean energy. Goal 8 decent work an economic growth. Goal 9, Industrial innovation and infrastructure. Gold 10 reduce inequality. Goal 11 sustainable cities and communities. Goal12, responsible consumption and production. Goal 13, Climate action. Goal 14, Life below water. Goal 15 Life on land. Goal 16, peace, Justice and strong institutions. Goal 17, Partnerships to achieve the goals. All government of member states to the UN has as obligation to implement all these 17 guiding principles in order to achieve all the sustainable development Goals by 2030.

[179] States the ground breaking UN Declaration on the Right to Development, proclaimed in 1986.

[180] Ibid Article 1.

these principles are not only explained but instruments have been enacted advocating the respect of these principles.[181]

3.2.1.1: Contents of the Principles

These principles which have been expressly outline in the 2 Agenda 2023 as well as could be inferred from other legal instruments such as DHR are coined around concepts such as development, accountability, non-discrimination, empowerment, collaboration, sustainability, self-determination amongst others.

3.2.1.2. Development Centered principle

The Declaration identifies "the human person" as the central subject, participant and beneficiary of development[182]. People-Centred Development is an approach to international development that focuses on the express needs of local communities for the necessities of life, clean water, health care, income generation that are often disrupted by conventional development assistance. A people-centred approach is needed for equity in access for everyone, everywhere to access the quality health services they need, when and where they need them, quality, Safe, effective and timely care that responds to people's comprehensive needs and are of the highest possible standards, responsiveness and participation, Care is coordinated around people`s needs, respects their preferences, and allows for people's participation in health affairs.

Ensuring that services are provided in the most cost-effective setting with the right balance between health promotion, prevention, and in- and-out patient care, avoiding duplication and waste of resources, Strengthening the capacity of health actors, institutions and populations to prepare for, and effectively respond to, public health crises.[183]

All human beings have a responsibility for development, individually and collectively, taking into account the need for full respect for their human rights and fundamental freedoms as well as their duties to the community, which alone can ensure the free and complete fulfilment of the human being, and they should therefore promote and protect an appropriate political, social and economic order for development.[184]

States have the right and the duty to formulate appropriate national development policies that aim at the constant improvement of the well-being of

---

[181] Article 1(1) of the 1986 UN Declaration on the Right to Development.
[182] Article 2 of the 1986 UN Declaration on the Right to Development.
[183] Community keepers (2015). People centered Development in South Africa. Available at https://www.community.keepers.org .
[184] Article 2 (1) of the 1986 UN Declaration on the Right to Development.

the entire population and of all individuals, on the basis of their active, free and meaningful participation in development and in the fair distribution of the benefits resulting therefrom.[185]This principle helps women especially the rural women to be economically empowered in Cameroon.

3.2.1.3. Human Rights-Based

Human rights-based approaches are about turning human rights from purely legal instruments into effective policies, practices, and practical realities. Human rights principles and standards provide guidance about what should be done to achieve freedom and dignity for all. A human rights-based approach emphasises how human rights are achieved. Human Rights principles include, Participation, Accountability, Non-discrimination and equality, Empowerment, Legality which all go a long way to foster women economic empowerment in Cameroon.

3.2.1.4. Principle of Participation

This principle holds that, everyone has the right to participate in decisions which affect their human rights. Participation must be active, free and meaningful, and give attention to issues of accessibility, including access to information in a form and a language which can be understood. The Declaration insists on the "active, free and meaningful participation" of individuals and populations in development[186]

The human person is the central subject of development and should be the active participant and beneficiary of the right to development.[187]All human beings have a responsibility for development, individually and collectively, taking into account the need for full respect for their human rights and fundamental freedoms as well as their duties to the community, which alone can ensure the free and complete fulfilment of the human being, and they should therefore promote and protect an appropriate political, social and economic order for development.[188]

States have the right and the duty to formulate appropriate national development policies that aim at the constant improvement of the well-being of the entire population and of all individuals, on the basis of their active, free and meaningful participation in development and in the fair distribution of the benefits resulting therefrom.[189]

---

[185] Ibid Article 2 (2).
[186] Article 2 of the 1948 UN Declaration of Human Rights
[187] Ibid Article 2 (1).
[188] Article 2 (2).
[189] Article 2 (3) of the 1986 UN DRTD

3.2.1.5. Principle of Accountability

Accountability requires effective monitoring of compliance with human rights standards and achievement of human rights goals, as well as effective remedies for human rights breaches. For accountability to be effective, there must be appropriate laws, policies, institutions, administrative procedures and mechanisms of redress in order to secure human rights.

Effective monitoring of compliance and achievement of human rights goals also requires development and use of appropriate human right indicators. Accountability comprises four core principles; participation, evaluation, transparency, and feedback mechanisms. This means accountability is achieved when goals exist, ownership is delegated, transparent evaluation occurs, complete transparency ensues, and regular feedback exist[190]

3.2.1.6. Principle of Non-discrimination and equality

A human right-based approach means that all forms of discrimination in the realisation of rights must be prohibited, prevented and eliminated. It also means that priority should be given to people in the most marginalised or vulnerable situations who face the biggest barriers to realising their rights.[191] All States should co-operate with a view to promoting, encouraging and strengthening universal respect for and observance of all human rights and fundamental freedoms for all without any distinction as to race, sex, language or religion.[192]

All human rights and fundamental freedoms are indivisible and interdependent; equal attention and urgent consideration should be given to the implementation, promotion and protection of civil, political, economic, social and cultural rights[193].

States should take steps to eliminate obstacles to development resulting from failure to observe civil and political rights, as well as economic social and cultural rights.[194]

3.2.1.7. Principle of Empowerment

Everyone is entitled to claim and exercise their rights and freedoms. Individuals and communities need to be able to understand their rights, and to participate fully in the development of policy and practices which affect their

---

[190] Finkelstein Darren (2022), What are the 4 core components of Accountability? Available at https://www.tickhoseboxes.com. (consulted on the 20/01/2024).
[191] Article 6 of the 1986 UN DRTD.
[192] Ibid Art 6 (1).
[193] Ibid Art 6 (2).
[194] Art 6 (3) of UN DRTD.

lives. Empowerment for sustainable development means giving to people and communities the true capacity to cope with the changing environment, for increased social awareness and for a higher level of social and economic participation. Human empowerment principles include;

3.2.1.8. The principle of collaboration

This principle holds that, the setting and achieving objectives must be done in a collaborative environment. There should be collaboration between all stakeholders.

3.2.1.9. The principle of Equitable Partnership

It holds that, all stakeholders take on the roles of both learners and teachers. All stakeholders should have different and diverse skills and all have a part to play in setting meeting objectives.

3.2.1.10. The Principle of Support

All stake holders should support one another in an environment that fosters independence and self-empowerment

3.2.1.11. The Principle of Sustainability

Holds that, all stakeholders should walk towards a sustainable outcome, ensuring that the positive impact made today continues long after the project has ended.

3.2.1.12. The Principle of Representation

Stakeholders must be fairly represented in conceptualising and implementing the work. All stakeholders must be conscious and respectful of how they portray each other. This will include visual, written and verbal communication.

3.2.1.13. Principle of Self-determination

The Declaration requires the full realisation of the right of peoples to self-determination, including full sovereignty over their natural wealth and resources[195] The right to development is an inalienable human right by virtue of which every human person and all peoples are entitled to participate in, contribute to, and enjoy economic, social, cultural and political development, in which all human rights and fundamental freedoms can be fully realized.[196]

---

[195] Article 1 1986 UN DRTD
[196] Ibid Article 1(1).

The human right to development also implies the full realization of the right of peoples to self-determination, which includes, subject to the relevant provisions of both International Covenants on Human Rights, the exercise of their inalienable right to full sovereignty over all their natural wealth and resources.[197]

3.2.2. Other Legal Instrument Advocating the Principles

Apart from DHR and Agenda 2030 already discussed, there are a host of other instruments that advocate for the implementation of these principles at the international level.

3.2.2.1. Declaration of the Right to Indigenous People

Indigenous Peoples are distinct social and cultural groups that share collective ancestral ties to the lands and natural resources where they live, occupy or from which they have been displaced. The land and natural resources on which they depend are inextricably linked to their identities, cultures, livelihoods, as well as their physical and spiritual well-being. They often subscribe to their customary leaders and organizations for representation that are distinct or separate from those of the mainstream society or culture. Many Indigenous Peoples still maintain a language distinct from the official language or languages of the country or region in which they reside; however, many have also lost their languages or on the precipice of extinction due to eviction from their lands and/or relocation to other territories. They speak more than 4,000 of the world´s 7,000 languages though some estimates indicate that more than half of the world's languages are at risk of becoming extinct by 2100.[198] There are an estimated 476 million Indigenous Peoples worldwide. Although they make up just 6 percent of the global population, they account for about 19 percent of the extreme poor.[199]

Indigenous Peoples' life expectancy is up to 20 years lower than the life expectancy of non-Indigenous Peoples worldwide.[200] Indigenous Peoples often lack formal recognition over their lands, territories and natural resources, are often the last to receive public investments in basic services and infrastructure and face multiple barriers to participate fully in the formal economy, enjoy access to justice, and participate in political processes and decision making. This legacy of

---

[197] Ibid Article 1(2).
[198] The World Bank (2023, Indigenous people. Available at https://www.worldbank.org. (consulted on the 20/01/2024).
[199] Ibid.
[200] Australian Bureau of Statistics (2023). Aboriginal and Torres Strait Islander life expectancy. Available at https:/www.indigenoushpf.gov.au. (Consulted on 26/08/2024).

inequality and exclusion has made Indigenous Peoples more vulnerable[201] to the impacts of climate change and natural hazards, including to disease outbreaks such as COVID-19.

While Indigenous Peoples own, occupy, or use a quarter of the world's surface area. Indigenous Peoples conserve 80 percent of the world's remaining biodiversity and recent studies reveal that forestlands under collective IP and local community stewardship hold at least one quarter of all tropical and subtropical forest above-ground carbon They hold vital ancestral knowledge and expertise on how to adapt, mitigate, and reduce climate and disaster risks.

Much of the land occupied by Indigenous Peoples is under customary ownership, yet many governments recognize only a fraction of this land as formally or legally belonging to Indigenous Peoples. Even when Indigenous territories and lands are recognized, protection of boundaries or use and exploitation of natural resources are often inadequate. Insecure land tenure is a driver of conflict, environmental degradation, and weak economic and social development. This threatens cultural survival and vital knowledge systems loss in these areas increasing risks of fragility, biodiversity loss, and degraded Health (or ecological and animal health) systems which threaten the ecosystem services upon which we all depend.

Improving security of land tenure, strengthening governance, promoting public investments in quality and culturally appropriate service provision, and supporting Indigenous systems for resilience and livelihoods are critical to reducing the multidimensional aspects of poverty while contributing to sustainable development and the Sustainable Development Goals (SDGs). The World Bank works with Indigenous Peoples and governments to ensure that broader development programs reflect the voices and aspirations of Indigenous Peoples.

Over the last 30 years, Indigenous Peoples' rights have been increasingly recognised through the adoption of international instruments such as the United Nations Declaration on the Rights of Indigenous Peoples (UNDRIP) in 2007, the American Declaration on the Rights of Indigenous Peoples in 2016, the Regional Agreement on Access to Information, Public Participation and Justice in Environmental matters in Latin America and the Caribbean (Escazú Agreement) in 2021 and the Indigenous and Tribal Peoples Convention from 1991. At the same time, global institutional mechanisms have been created to

---

[201] UNESCO (2020). Indigenous Peoples: Vulnerable, yet resilient. Available at https://www.unesco.org. (Consulted on the 26/08/2024).

promote Indigenous peoples' rights such as the United Nations Permanent Forum on Indigenous Issues (UNPFII), the Expert Mechanism on the Rights of Indigenous Peoples (EMRIP), and the UN Special Rapporteur on the Rights of Indigenous Peoples (UNSR).[202]

Indigenous peoples have the right to determine and develop priorities and strategies for exercising their right to development. In particular, indigenous peoples have the right to be actively involved in developing and determining health, housing and other economic and social programmes affecting them and, as far as possible, to administer such programmes through their own institutions.[203]

3.2.2.2. Vienna Declaration and Program of Action

This Convention which was adopted in June 25 1993 by consensus by the representatives of the 171 States attending the World Conference on Human Rights and subsequently endorsed by the United Nations General Assembly on 20 December 1993, amongst others, affirms the right to development as a fundamental human right and the recognition of the interdependency of democracy, development and respect for human rights.

The Declaration calls for increased coordination of human rights within the United Nations system and requests the Secretary-General and the General Assembly take immediate steps to substantially increase the financial resources for the human rights programme and to strengthen the United Nations Centre for Human Rights to assure adequate means for the system of thematic and country rapporteurs, experts, working groups and treaty bodies. At the same time, the Declaration recognizes the important roles played by national institutions, "regional arrangements" and non-governmental organizations in the promotion and protection of human rights.

The Declaration makes recommendations and requests on a number of pressing human rights issues including racism, torture and enforced disappearance and the rights of minorities, indigenous peoples, migrant workers, women, children and disabled persons. Recommendations are also made for additional measures to strength human rights including a new programme within the United Nations to help States build adequate national structures to protect human rights

---

[202] Ibid.
[203] Article 23 of the UN Declaration on the Rights of Indigenous Peoples states.

and to maintain of the rule of law. There are also recommendations with respect to human rights education and implementation and monitoring methods.[204]

This provision acts as a guide for the economic empowerment of the rural women in Cameroon since their Human Rights is being guaranteed under this convention.

3.2.2.3. Rio Declaration on Environment and Development

The three Rio Conventions on Biodiversity, Climate Change and Desertification derive directly from the 1992 Earth Summit. Each instrument represents a way of contributing to the sustainable development goals of Agenda 21. The three conventions are intrinsically linked, operating in the same ecosystems and addressing interdependent issues.[205].These sustainable development goals should be noted are guiding principles to economic development which are very essential for the rural women economic empowerment in Cameroon.

3.2.2.4. Convention on Bio Diversity

The convention advocates for sustainable use of its components and the fair and equitable sharing of the benefits arising from commercial and other utilization of genetic resources. The agreement covers all ecosystems, species, and genetic resources.

This provision of the convention as we can see acts as a guiding principle on which the rural women can dwell and be economically empowered since they suffer too much discrimination in all domain of life. The principle talks of sustainability, fairness and equitability in the sharing of benefits arising from business without discrimination

3.2.2.5. United Nations Convention to Combat Desertification (UNCCD)

This Convention aims to combat desertification and mitigate the effects of drought in countries experiencing serious drought and/or desertification, particularly in Africa, through effective actions at all levels, supported by international co-operation and partnership arrangements, in the framework of

---

[204] Article 1 and 2 of the Vienna Declaration and Programme of Action was adopted on June 25, 1993 by consensus by the representatives of the 171 States attending the World Conference on Human Rights and subsequently endorsed by the United Nations General Assembly on 20 December 1993.

[205] Cultural Rights (2010). Rio Declaration on Environment and Development 1992.Available at https://culturalrights.net .(Consulted on 22/01/2024)

an integrated approach which is consistent with Agenda 21, with a view to contributing to the achievements of sustainable development in affected areas.

3.2.2.6. The Rio Declaration's principles.

It states that;

"Human beings are at the centre of concerns for sustainable development. They are entitled to a healthy and productive life in harmony with nature."[206]

The right to development must be fulfilled so as to equitably meet developmental and environmental needs of present and future generations.[207]

All States and all people shall cooperate in the essential task of eradicating poverty as an indispensable requirement for sustainable development, in order to decrease the disparities in standards of living and better meet the needs of the majority of the people of the world.[208]

States shall enact effective environmental legislation. Environmental standards, management objectives and priorities should reflect the environmental and development context to which they apply. Standards applied by some countries may be inappropriate and of unwarranted economic and social cost to other countries, in particular developing countries.[209]

Warfare is inherently destructive of sustainable development. States shall therefore respect international law providing protection for the environment in times of armed conflict and cooperate in its further development, as necessary.[210].All these acts as a guide to Cameroon's rural women economic empowerment.

3.2.2.7. ILO Convention Concerning indigenous and Tribal Peoples in Independent Countries

This Convention applies to tribal peoples in independent countries whose social, cultural and economic conditions distinguish them from other sections of the national community, and whose status is regulated wholly or partially by their own customs or traditions or by special laws or regulations;[211] peoples in independent countries who are regarded as indigenous on account of their descent from the populations which inhabited the country, or a geographical region to

---

[206] Principle 1 of the 1992 Rio Convention on Biological Diversity
[207] Ibid Principle 3.
[208] Ibid Principle 5.
[209] Ibid Principle 11.
[210] Ibid Principle 24.
[211] Article 1(a) of the 1989 Indigenous and Tribal Peoples Convention, (No. 169).

which the country belongs, at the time of conquest or colonisation or the establishment of present state boundaries and who, irrespective of their legal status, retain some or all of their own social, economic, cultural and political institutions[212]

The peoples concerned shall have the right to decide their own priorities for the process of development as it affects their lives, beliefs, institutions and spiritual well-being and the lands they occupy or otherwise use, and to exercise control, to the extent possible, over their own economic, social and cultural development. In addition, they shall participate in the formulation, implementation and evaluation of plans and programmes for national and regional development which may affect them directly.[213]

The improvement of the conditions of life and work and levels of health and education of the peoples concerned, with their participation and co-operation, shall be a matter of priority in plans for the overall economic development of areas they inhabit. Special projects for development of the areas in question shall also be so designed as to promote such improvement.[214]

Governments shall ensure that, whenever appropriate, studies are carried out, in co-operation with the peoples concerned, to assess the social, spiritual, cultural and environmental impact on them of planned development activities, the results of these studies shall be considered as fundamental criteria for the implementation of these activities.[215]

Governments shall take measures, in co-operation with the peoples concerned, to protect and preserve the environment of the territories they inhabit.[216]The rural women in Cameroon are indigenous people and so benefit from these provisions as a guide to her economic empowerment.

3.2.2.8. The UN Millennium Declaration

The right to development embodies an entitlement to participate in and contribute to as well as to enjoy development. This necessitates the participation of the beneficiaries of development in the articulation of policies and in the implementation of development plans, thus empowering these beneficiaries at all levels. The participation of all sectors strengthens the political legitimacy of plans as well as the scope and effectiveness of implementation mechanisms.

---

[212] Article 1(b) of the 1989 Indigenous and Tribal Peoples Convention, (No. 169)
[213] Ibid Article 7(1).
[214] Ibid Article 7(2).
[215] Ibid Article 7(3).
[216] Ibid Article 7(4).

The entitlements of rights holders require a corresponding duty to respect, protect and fulfil, which in turn brings the requirement of accountability of those involved in and responsible for implementation mechanisms. This implies the need for specific national and international mechanisms to ensure accountability of funders and development planners (both Government and civil society) to the beneficiaries themselves, or the rights holders. Consequently, participation in identifying mechanisms of accountability is also important. Participation at both national and international levels is a core entitlement of the right to development[217]

The Declaration on the Right to Development reaffirms international human rights standards and norms. The Declaration defines the right to development as "an inalienable human right by virtue of which every human person and all peoples are entitled to participate in, contribute to and enjoy economic, social, cultural, and political development, in which all human rights and fundamental freedoms can be fully realized".[218]

The Declaration on the Right to Development highlights the importance of international cooperation and, by implication, global partnership in the realization of the right to development.[219]With the postulation of this principle, the rural women in Cameroon stand a chance to be economically empowered.

3.2.2.9. The Monterrey Consensus

Since its adoption, the Monterrey Consensus has become the major reference point for international development cooperation. The document embraces six areas of financing for Development:

- Mobilising domestic financial resources for development;
- Mobilising international resources for development: foreign direct investment and other private flows;
- International Trade as an engine for development;
- Increasing international financial and technical cooperation for development;
- External Debt;

---

[217] Article 1 the 1986 UN Right to Development and the Millennium Development Goals.
[218] Ibid.
[219] Section III the 1986 UN Right to Development and the Millennium Development Goals.

- Addressing systemic issues: enhancing the coherence and consistency of the international monetary, financial and trading systems in support of development.[220]

In a common pursuit of growth, poverty eradication, and sustainable development, a critical challenge is: to ensure the necessary internal conditions for mobilizing domestic savings, both public and private; sustaining adequate levels of productive investment; and increasing human capacity. A crucial task is to enhance the efficacy, coherence, and consistency of macroeconomic policies. An enabling domestic environment is vital for mobilizing domestic resources, increasing productivity, reducing capital flight, encouraging the private sector, and attracting and making effective use of international investment and assistance.

Efforts to create such an environment should be supported by the international community. Good governance is essential for sustainable development. Sound economic policies, solid democratic institutions responsive to the needs of the people, and improved infrastructure are the basis for sustained economic growth, poverty eradication, and employment creation. Freedom; peace and security; domestic stability; respect for human rights, including the right to development and the rule of law; gender equality; market-oriented policies; and an overall commitment to just and democratic societies are also essential and mutually reinforcing.

Fighting corruption at all levels is a priority. Corruption is a serious barrier to effective resource mobilization and allocation and diverts resources away from activities that are vital for poverty eradication and economic and sustainable development. An effective, efficient, transparent, and accountable system for mobilizing public resources and managing their use by Governments is essential.

The consensus recognises the need to secure fiscal sustainability, along with equitable and efficient tax systems and administration, as well as improvements in public spending that do not crowd out productive private investment. They also recognize the contribution that medium-term fiscal frameworks can make in that respect. Investments in basic economic and social infrastructure, social services and social protection, including education, health, nutrition, shelter, and social security programs, that take special care of children and older persons and are gender sensitive and fully inclusive of the rural sector and all disadvantaged communities are vital for enabling people, especially people living in poverty, to better adapt to and benefit from changing economic

---

[220] Monterrey Consensus. Available at https://www.en.m.wikipedia.org. (Consulted on the 22/01/2024)

conditions and opportunities. Active labour market policies, including worker training, can help to increase employment and improve working conditions.

Economic crises also underscore the importance of effective social safety nets. There is a need to strengthen and develop the domestic financial sector, by encouraging the orderly development of capital markets through sound banking systems and other institutional arrangements aimed at addressing development financing needs, including the insurance sector, debt and equity markets, which encourage and channel savings and foster productive investments. This requires a sound system of financial intermediation, transparent regulatory frameworks, and effective supervisory mechanisms, supported by a solid central bank.

Guarantee schemes and business development services should be developed for easing the access of small and medium-sized enterprises to local financing. Microfinance and credit for small and medium-sized enterprises, including in rural areas, particularly for women, as well as national savings schemes, are important for enhancing the social and economic impact of the financial sector. Development banks and commercial and other financial institutions, whether independently or in cooperation, can be effective instruments for facilitating access to finance, including equity financing, for such enterprises, as well as an adequate supply of medium-term and long-term credit. It is critical to reinforce national efforts in capacity-building in developing countries and countries with economies in transition in such areas as institutional infrastructure, human resource development, public finance, mortgage finance, financial regulation and supervision, basic education in particular, public administration, social and gender budget policies, early warning and crisis prevention, and debt management. In that regard, particular attention is required to address the special needs of Africa, the least developed countries, small island developing states, and landlocked developing countries

To attract and enhance inflows of productive capital, countries need to continue their efforts to achieve a transparent, stable, and predictable investment climate, with proper contract enforcement and respect for property rights, embedded in sound macroeconomic policies and institutions that allow businesses, both domestic and international, to operate efficiently and profitably and with maximum development impact investment flows to developing countries.

These issues are of particular concern to developing countries and countries with economies in transition: international trade to enhance their capacity to finance their development, including trade barriers; trade-distorting subsidies and other trade-distorting measures, particularly in sectors of special export interest to developing countries such as agriculture; the abuse of anti-dumping measures; technical barriers and sanitary and phyto-sanitary measures; trade liberalization in labour intensive manufactures; trade liberalization in agricultural products; trade in services; tariff peaks, high tariffs, and tariff escalation, as well as non-tariff barriers; the movement of natural persons; the lack of recognition of intellectual property rights for the protection of traditional knowledge and folklore; the transfer of knowledge and technology; the implementation and interpretation of the Agreement on Trade-Related Aspects of Intellectual Property Rights in a manner supportive of public health; and the need for special and differential treatment provisions for developing countries in trade agreements to be made more precise, effective, and operational.

Financing for Development Multilateral assistance is also needed to mitigate the consequences of depressed export revenues of countries that still depend heavily on commodity exports. In this connection, the recent review of the International Monetary Fund Compensatory Financing Facility will continue to assess its effectiveness. Further cooperation is also necessary between bilateral donors and multilateral aid agencies to strengthen their support to export diversification programs in those countries. In support of the process launched in Doha, immediate attention should go to strengthening and ensuring the meaningful and full participation of developing countries, especially the least developed countries, in multilateral trade negotiations. In particular, developing countries need assistance in order to participate effectively in the World Trade Organization work program and negotiating process through the enhanced cooperation of all relevant stakeholders, including the United Nations Conference on Trade and Development, the World Trade Organization, and the World Bank. To those ends, we underscore the importance of effective, secure, and predictable financing of trade-related technical assistance and capacity-building.

Effective partnerships among donors and recipients are based on the recognition of national leadership and ownership of development plans and, within that framework, sound policies and good governance at all levels are necessary to ensure official development assistance (ODA) effectiveness. A major priority is to build those development partnerships, particularly in support of the neediest countries and to maximize the poverty reduction impact of ODA. The goals, targets, and commitments of the Millennium Declaration and other internationally agreed development targets can help countries to set short- and medium-term national priorities as the foundation for building partnerships for external support. Recipient and donor countries, as well as international institutions, should strive to make ODA more effective.[221`]

3.3. Guiding Principles on Women's Right to Development at the Regional Levels

At the regional level some four instrument are very relevant for the promotion of the guiding principles for the economic empowerment of women. These are the following.

3.3.1. African Charter on Human and People's Rights as a guide to Economic empowerment.

This charter holds that,' all peoples shall have the right to their economic, social and cultural development with due regard to their freedom and identity and in the equal enjoyment of the common heritage of mankind, and that States shall have the duty, individually or collectively, to ensure the exercise of the right to development.[222]

New standards have been set, particularly on economic, social and cultural rights as well as the rights of women and children. The African Court on Human and Peoples' Rights has been established to provide an effective enforcement mechanism for the Charter. The African Union (AU) replaced the Organization of African Unity (OAU) in 2000 and has explicitly committed itself to protecting and promoting human rights.[223]

Since 1948, the human rights and fundamental freedoms recognized in the UDHR have been developed and further defined in treaties, declarations and resolutions adopted by UN and regional bodies, including the OAU/AU. Contributing to this process were many of the formerly colonized countries in Africa and elsewhere that had been denied a voice in defining the nature of human rights and fundamental freedoms. One of the regional treaties to emerge was the African Charter, drawn up in 1981 by African countries through the OAU. All of these treaties, declarations and resolutions reinforce the universally held belief that every government is obliged to protect the rights of the people within its borders. Despite this, governments continue to violate human rights and often try to justify their actions on grounds of "security" or "sovereignty". It is therefore

---

[221] Bouab Abdel H. (2004), Financing for Development, the Monterrey Consensus Achievements and Prospects, Michigan Journal of International Law. Vol 26, issue 1.
[222] Article 22 (1) and (2) of the African Charter of Human and Peoples' Rights 1981.
[223] Okafor Chinedu Obiora A, Regional perspective: Article 22 of the African Charter on Human and People's Rights. Available at https://www.ohchr.org. (Consulted on 25/01/2024).

up to the international community as a whole to protect these rights on behalf of people all over the world an aim central to the work of Amnesty International.[224]

This lack of an effective enforcement mechanism led to calls for the establishment of an African Court on Human and Peoples' Rights, and in June 1998 the OAU adopted a protocol to establish such a court.

Other Protocols have been adopted to expand specific rights guaranteed by the African Charter such as the Protocol to the African Charter on Human and Peoples' Rights on the Rights of Women in Africa (Women's Protocol), which entered into force in November 2005, the AU Convention on Preventing and Combating Corruption of 2003, the African Charter on the Rights and Welfare of the Child of 1999.[225] The African Commission itself has adopted several guidelines and declarations to expand the human rights and fundamental freedoms under the African Charter. These include:

3.3.2. The Principles and Guidelines on the Right to a Fair Trial and Legal Assistance in Africa in 2003

The African charter stipulates that, every individual shall have the right to have his cause heard. These rights comprise: The right to an appeal to competent national organs against acts violating his fundamental rights as recognized and guaranteed by conventions, laws, regulations and customs in force, the right to be presumed innocent until proven guilty by a competent tribunal, the right to defence, including the right to be defended by counsel of his choice and the right to be tried within a reasonable time by an impartial court of tribunal.[226]

According to this Charter, no one may be condemned for an act or omission which did not constitute a legally punishable offence at the time it was committed. No penalty may be inflicted for an offence for which no provision was made at the time it was committed. Punishment is personal and can be imposed only on the offender.[227]

This Charter on Human and Peoples' Rights represent a turning point in Africa's efforts to fully ensure justice in terms of equality, Rule of Law, and development. The position of the Charter has been reinforced by the growing recognition in Africa that human-cantered and sustainable development cannot be

---

[224] Amnesty International (2006), A guide to the African charter on Human and people's Rights. International Secretarial Peter Benenson House Eastern street London, Available at https://www.amnesty.org (Consulted on 25/01/2024).

[225] Ibid.

[226] Article 7(1) (a) (b) (c) and (d) of the African Charter on Human and Peoples' Rights.

[227] Ibid Article 7(2).

realised without ensuring human rights, democracy and the rule of Law. The African Charter on Human and Peoples' Rights spells out rights to be guaranteed by all States Parties to it. Capital, if not the most important, among these rights is the right to fair trial. Without ensuring this right, there would be no real guarantee against any violation of the rights contained in the Charter, nor would the individuals have the sense of security that encourages them to participate fully in the life of the society.[228]

As per the African charter, every child has an inherent right to life. This right shall be protected by law. States Parties to the present Charter shall ensure, to the maximum extent possible, the survival, protection and development of the child[229] Death sentence shall not be pronounced for crimes committed by children.[230] Every child shall have the right from his birth to a name. 2. Every child shall be registered immediately after birth. 3. Every child has the right to acquire a nationality. 4. States Parties to the present Charter shall undertake to ensure that their Constitutional legislation recognize the principles according to which a child shall acquire the nationality of the State in the territory of which he has been born if, at the time of the child's birth, he is not granted nationality by any other State in accordance with its laws[231].Every child who is capable of communicating his or her own views shall be assured the rights to express his opinions freely in all matters and to disseminate his opinions subject to such restrictions as are prescribed by laws[232]

3.3.3. The Declaration of Principles on Freedom of Expression in Africa in 2002

The Declaration of Principles of Freedom of Expression and Access to Information in Africa was adopted by the African Commission on Human and Peoples' Rights at its 65th Ordinary Session which was held from 21 October to 10 November 2019 in Banjul, The Gambia[233]. Which requires the African Commission to promote human and peoples' rights, among others, by formulating and laying down principles and rules to solve legal problems relating to human

---

[228] Ibrahim Ali Badawi E. Preliminary Remarks on the Right to a Fair Trial Under the African Charter on Human and Peoples' Rights. Available at http://www.hrlibrary.umn.edu/fairtrial/wrft-bad.htm. https://www.achpr.au.int/ (Consulted on the 25/01/2024).

[229] Article 5 (1) and (2) of the African Charter Human and Peoples' Rights

[230] Ibid Article 5 (3).

[231] Ibid Article 6 (1), (2) and (3).

[232] Ibid Article 7.

[233] The Declaration was prepared pursuant to Article 45 (1) of the African Charter on Human and Peoples' Rights.

and peoples' right and fundamental freedoms upon which African States may base their legislation. The Declaration establishes or affirms the principles for anchoring the rights to freedom of expression and access to information[234] The Declaration therefore forms part of the soft-law corpus of Article 9 norms developed by the African Commission, including the Model Law on Access to Information for Africa as well as the Guidelines on Access to Information and Elections in Africa, adopted by the Commission, respectively, in 2013 and 2017.

This Declaration replaces the Declaration of Principles on Freedom of Expression in Africa which the African Commission had adopted in 2002. The 2002 Declaration elaborated on the scope and content of Article 9 of the African Charter. Yet, over the last two decades, major pertinent issues emerged which were addressed insufficiently. This was notably the case in relation to access to information and the interface between Article 9 rights and the internet.

Consequently, initially in 2012 and then again in 2016, the African Commission decided to modify the 2002 Declaration to include access to information while also taking note of developments in the internet age. Hence, this Declaration consolidate developments on freedom of expression and access to information guided by hard-law and soft-law standards drawn from African and international human rights instruments and standards, including the jurisprudence of African judicial bodies. Preparation of this Declaration was led by the Special Rapporteur on Freedom of expression and Access to Information in Africa, who worked closely with stakeholders from State and non-State actors to generate the concept for and to prepare the Declaration. [235]

3.3.4. Guidelines and Measures for the Prohibition and Prevention of Torture, Cruel, Inhuman or Degrading Treatment or Punishment in Africa in 2002

In October 2002, at its 32nd Ordinary Session, the African Commission on Human and Peoples' Rights, adopted the Guidelines and Measures for the Prohibition and Prevention of Torture, Cruel, Inhuman or Degrading Treatment or Punishment in Africa.[236]

---

[234] Article 9 of the African Charter which guarantees individuals the right to receive information as well as the right to express and disseminate information.
[235] Lawrence Murugu Mute (2019). Declaration of Principles on Freedom of Expression and Access to Information in Africa 2019.Available at https://www.achpr.au.int/ (Consulted on the 25/01/2024)
[236] To elaborate on Article 5 of the African Charter on Human and Peoples' Rights of 1981 which prohibits torture, cruel, inhuman or degrading treatment or punishment.

The Robben Island Guidelines seek to prevent and eradicate torture and other ill-treatment in Africa. It is an essential tool which States may use in fulfilling their national, regional and international obligations to strengthen and implement the prohibition and prevention of torture and other ill-treatment.

The African Charter is a set of rules, called Articles, guaranteeing certain human rights and fundamental freedoms for individuals. It also guarantees certain rights of entire peoples. The Charter is a human rights treaty. When a state ratifies a treaty, it becomes a state party to the treaty. It is then legally obliged to protect the rights specified in the treaty. It is also obliged to submit itself to scrutiny of its human rights record. All AU member states have ratified the Charter and must therefore respect and fulfil in good faith all the human rights and obligations contained in it. The majority of the human rights and fundamental freedoms in the African Charter are the same as those contained in international human rights treaties adopted by the UN.

Many African states have ratified these treaties and have therefore agreed to be bound by their provisions. Among the most important international human rights treaties are the International Covenant on Civil and Political Rights and its two Optional Protocols the First Optional Protocol (1976) created an individual petition procedure for complaints; the Second Optional Protocol (1991) aims at abolishing the death penalty , the International Covenant on Economic, Social and Cultural Rights, the Convention against Torture and Other Cruel, Inhuman or Degrading Treatment or Punishment and its Optional Protocol that established an individual complaints procedure, the Convention on the Prevention and Punishment of the Crime of genocide, the Convention relating to the Status of Refugees and its 1967 Protocol, the International Convention on the Elimination of All Forms of Racial Discrimination, the Convention on the Elimination of All Forms of Discrimination against Women and its Optional Protocol, the Convention on the Rights of the Child and its two Optional Protocols and the International Convention on the Protection of the Rights of All Migrant Workers and Members of Their Families .There are, in addition, many international human rights standards developed.

3.4. Guiding Principles on Women's Right to Development at the National Level

Apart from international and regional commitments, Principles as well as instruments promoting the economic empowerment of rural women at the national or local level include the following amongst other.

3.4.1. The Cameroon Constitution and its Guiding Principle on Women development

The Cameroon constitution is the highest law of the country. The institutional and political organisation of the Republic of Cameroon derives its legitimacy and basis from the constitution.[237]

The Cameroonian people, proud of its linguistic and cultural diversity, solemnly proclaimed that it constitutes a single and one Nation, engaged in a common destiny. It affirms "its firm will to build the Cameroon fatherland on the ideological base of brotherhood, justice and progress". The preambles also proclaim the adhesion of the Republic of Cameroon to fundamental universally recognized democratic principles, the principle African unity and to that formulated by the United Nations Charter. Cameroon's people affirm its attachment to fundamental liberties inscribed in the Universal Declaration of Human Rights, the UNO Charter, African Charter for Human and Peoples Rights and all international conventions related to it, and dully ratified.[238] The Preamble to the constitution postulated the following principles which are guiding principles to women's development.

3.4.2. Principle of Non-Discrimination

According to the Constitution, the state shall guarantee the right to education. Primary education in Cameroon as per the Constitution is compulsory and the state shall guarantee the organization and supervision at all levels[239] With regards to employment rights and protection, everybody shall have the right and obligation to work.[240]

The Constitution further states that Human persons without distinction to race religion sex or believes possess inalienable rights and believes. All shall have equal rights and obligation which are conditions necessary for their development and the state has the duty to guarantee all citizens of either sex the right and freedom as stated in the Constitution. The state as per the Constitution has to recognize and protect traditional values that conform to democratic principles of human rights and the law. It has to ensure equality of all citizens before the law.[241]

---

[237] Law No.c96/06 of 18 January 1996 on the revision of the Constitution of June 1972.
[238] The preamble of the Cameroon Constitution.
[239] Preamble of the 1996 Cameroon Constitution as revised in 1972.
[240] Preamble of the Constitution.
[241] Article 1 of the 1996 Constitution.

The Constitution further states that, the state shall ensure the protection of minorities and shall preserve the rights of indigenous people in accordance with the law.

With regards to marriage and family life the Constitution holds that it is the state that shall be responsible to protect and promote the family which is the foundation of human society. It shall protect especially the young, the elderly and disabled.[242]

As per the Constitution ownership shall mean the right guarantee to all by the law to use, enjoy and dispose of property. Concerning protection from violence the Constitution holds that everyone has a right to life and to physical and moral integrity and no one should be subjected under no circumstances to torture, Cruelty or in humane and degrading treatment. No person should be harassed on grounds of his origin, sex, religion or political opinion.[243]

3.4.3. Principle of Liberty and security

Human right and criminal law dispositions has given responsibilities to the State of Cameroon in ensuring the protection of this right by preventing their violations which in return will pose an adverse effect on the fundamental human of those living in the territory when issues of liberty and security is concerned. The application of this right by Cameroon will go a long way in conforming with the dispositions and provision put in place by International Standard guaranteeing and safeguarding the protection and implementation of this right by Cameroon. Issues of human right protection has been the sole responsibility of the government of Cameron as they enact credible laws and institutions in ensuring the proper implementation of this right through its legal mechanisms. Respecting and enforcing these provisions will go a long way acquiring and maintaining Justice at all levels of the criminal proceedings.[244]

3.4.4. The Principle of Inviolability of Correspondences

With the advent of globalisation, electronic communications are now the order of the day. This poses a serious threat to the privacy of individuals. In this regard in order to preserve the private life of individuals against attacks in the electronic communication sector, Cameroon legislator had to sign laws protecting privacy. One of such laws is that relating to cyber security and cyber criminality

---

[242] Preamble of the Constitution.

[243] Ibid.

[244] Nana Charles Nguindip et al., (2021), Ensuring the Right to Liberty and Security of Person: An Application or Nightmare in Respecting Human Right Standard in Cameroon. International Journal of law Management and Humanities, Volume 4, issues 2, pp. 424-435.

in Cameroon[245]. This law is to the effect that, every individual shall have the right to the protection of their privacy. Also, a decree on the modalities of the consumers' protection in the electronic communication has been put in place to guarantee consumers' protection in the electronic communication sector in Cameroon.[246]The provisions of these legal instruments are complemented by those of the 2010 law on electronic communications which punishes anyone who intercepts and discloses a private conversation, be it voluntarily or involuntarily without the consent of the author.[247]

Cameroon has ratified some international instruments which equally protect privacy. These include CEMAC Directive[248] the directive is to the effect that member states shall ensure the protection of the privacy of users by ensuring the confidentiality of electronic communications. As such everyone is forbidden from listening, intercepting or storing communications and data, or enabling such interception or surveillance without the author's consent.[249]

3.4.5. Principle of non-retroactivity of the law

The principle of non-retroactive application of law, prohibits the application of law to events that took place before the law was introduced. The application of this principle has become particularly controversial as states adopt stricter regulations to tackle climate change with retroactive effect, and investors challenge such regulations before international courts and tribunals. In the context of criminal law however, the principle is widespread and has become a binding norm of international law[250].

3.4.6. The Cameroon Social Economy Law and its guiding principle on Women Development

The social Economy law in Cameroon is a new framework law that establishes structures and instruments to promote the development of social economy enterprises and organizations, as a means of promoting balanced and sustainable economic growth in Cameroon. This law in recent years have seen

---

[245] Law no. 2010/012 of 21 December 2010 relating to rights to privacy in Cameroon.
[246] Decree No 2013/0399/PM of 27 February 2013 on the modalities of the consumers' protection in the electronic communication in Cameroon.
[247] Vigiline Tise Esq. (2021), Privacy protection in electronic communications under Cameroon. Available at https://www.hallelaw.com (Consulted on 26/01/2024).
[248] Directives No 07/08-UEAC-133-CM-18 laying down the legal framework for the protection of the rights of users of the electronic communication services in the CEMAC region.
[249] Article 3 of Directive No 07/08-UEAC-133-CM-18.
[250] Yarik Kryvo and Shaun Matos (2021), Non-Retroactivity as a General Principle of Law. Article. Volume: 17 Issue: 1 pp: 46–58,

growing interest in the social economy as a means of alleviating poverty particularly in the rural and informal economies and in promoting balanced and sustainable economic growth.[251]

This 2019 framework law defines the standards, principles and forms of social economy units and establishes structures and instruments that advance their development. Specifically, the social economy units are defined as enterprises and other organizations which meet the following criteria, irrespective of their legal forms: primacy of individuals and social objectives over capital; freedom of membership; transparent, democratic and participatory governance; collective or social utility of their project; search for collective interest and fair distribution of surpluses: pooling of members' resources; and compliance with their original legal status.[252]

The Ministry of Small and Medium-sized Enterprises, Social Economy and Handicrafts (MINPEESA) was established in 2004. In 2009 the National Development Strategy for Small and Medium-sized Enterprises, Social Economy and Handicrafts (2010-2014) was launched. The Strategy included the following social economy components: improving knowledge on the social economy; adopting an appropriate regulatory framework; promoting collective and group entrepreneurship; and facilitating access to finance by social economy enterprises and organizations, among others.[253]

3.4.7. The National Plan of Action and its Guiding Principles on Women Development

The overall objectives of the National strategy 2020-2030 for structural transformation and inclusive development are to establish favourable conditions for economic growth and the accumulation of national wealth and to ensure that the structural changes essential for the industrialisation of the country are obtained, to improve the living conditions of the populations and their access to basic social services by ensuring a significant reduction in poverty and underemployment, to strengthen climate change adaptation and mitigation measures and environmental management to ensure sustainable and inclusive economic growth and social development, and to improve governance to

---

[251] The Framework Law No. 2019/00 of 25th April 2019 on the Social Economy in Cameroon.
[252] Ibid.
[253] Law No.2010/001 of 13 April 2010.

strengthen the performance of public action with a view to achieving developmental objectives. [254]

3.5. Conclusion

These are general guiding principles which applies indiscriminately to all the citizen in Cameroon irrespective of their sex. The rural women being our main focus has equal right to benefit from these guiding principles to become economically developed. As has been noted, the achievement of the 2030 emergence plan can be achieved if and only if these principles are applicable to a great extend especially across the national territory with the rural areas being the main focus and the rural women the point of concern for as we have discovered, they constitute the backbones of the rural economy. Economically empowering the rural women is tantamount to developing the rural economy which will go a long way to develop the national economy thus facilitating the 2030 vision of emergence in Cameroon. Thus, both the ratified international, regional guideline adopted should be implemented together with our national provisions as have been stated above for the economic empowerment of the rural women in Cameroon.

---

[254] Climate change laws. (2019) National strategy 2020-2030 for structural transformation and inclusive development. Available at https://climate-laws.org.(Consulted on the 26/01/2024).

CHAPTER FOUR

POLICY STANDARDS FOR THE ECONOMIC DEVELOPMENT OF THE RURAL WOMEN IN CAMEROON

4.1. Introduction

Supported by the Natural Law theory postulated by Aristotle which holds that "there is a social injustice when equals are treated unequally and conversely", this chapter examines the various policies put in place by the Cameroon government in Cameroon for the economic empowerment of the rural women. The rural women who are the backbone of the national economy since they produce most of the food crop still remain less developed economically. These policies as will be seen are out to promote economic development of the national economy as a whole of which the rural women are part and since the terms of these policies are of general application without distinction as to gender, the rural women are all covered under the provisions. They are meant to benefit from the terms of the provisions in the same manner as their male counterparts. However, we shall equally examine those instruments that are specific for women empowerment with particular focus to the rural women.

A modernising nation's economic prosperity requires at least a modest legal infrastructure centred on the protection of property and contract right. The essential legal reform required to create that infrastructure maybe the adoption of a system of relatively precise legal rules.[255] Economic development is defined as an increase in the country's wealth and standard of living for instance improve productivity, higher literacy rates, and better public education are all consequences of economic development in a country. Cameroon developed rapidly from 1978 thanks to its oil wealth, agricultural diversity and well-

---

[255] Posner Richard A (1998), Creating a legal framework for economic development. The world Bank Research Observer.Vol.13. No. 1. Pp 1-11. Oxford University Press.

developed agro-industries. However, after the mid-1980s. the economy decline and debt rose.[256]

The strategy of the government in its fight against poverty is based on policies such as the promotion of strong, sustained and equitable growth, strengthen the supply and quality of essential social services such as education, health and drinking water, increase access of the poor to them. Promote Community-based development, implement specific actions for groups at risk and in difficulties and equally ensure the increased involvement of women in economic and social development [257]

The government policies of economic development include economic objectives such as price, high employment and sustainable growth. Such efforts include monetary and fiscal policies, regulations of financial institutions, trade and tax policies. It equally includes provisions of infrastructure and services such as highways, parks, water, electricity etc. It also includes job creation and retention such as small business development.[258]

Recognising the necessity of increasing the involvement especially of the rural women in economics spheres for economic growth of the nation, the government has put in place several policies which protect and promote these women to be economically empowered. Policies put in place by the Cameroon government include both national, regional and international policies for the economic empowerment of the women, especially the rural women

4.2. Policy Standards Established by National Legal Instruments for the Economic Empowerment of Rural Women

These policies include general policies for economic growth such as the social economy law, the finance law, the investment law, the industrial policies, and, the regional economic planning policies, and specific policies such as, the labour code, and the National Gender policy.

4.2.1. General Policy Standards for the Economic Empowerment of the Rural Women

---

[256] Common Wealth Governance (2015), Economy of Cameroon. Available at https://www.commonwealthgovernance.org. (Consulted on 01/05/204).

[257] International Monetary Fund (1999), Cameroon enhanced structural adjustment facility, Medium-term economic and financial policy framework paper, (1999/2000-2001/02). Available at https://ww.inf .org. (Consulted on 01/05/2024).

[258] Wikipedia. Economic development. Available at https://www.en.m.wikipedia.org (Consulted on 01/05/2024).

The general policy standards aimed at empowering rural women economically can be deduced from some national legal instruments such as those dealing with social, investment, industrial as well as economic issues.

4.2.1.1. The Cameroon's Social Economy Law and its provisions on Economic Empowerment

The government adopted a new framework law in 2019[259] that establishes structures and instruments to promote the development of social economy enterprises and organizations, as a means of promoting balanced and sustainable economic growth in Cameroon. In Cameroon, recent years have seen growing interest in the social economy as a means of alleviating poverty particularly in the rural and informal economies and in promoting balanced and sustainable economic growth. Thus, empowering the rural women economically since these provisions are not gender biased. They are applicable to all and the fat that the social economy law targets the rural and informal economies in particular simply means the rural women will equally benefit more from its provisions.

Since 2010, Cameroon has been endowed with a Law on the promotion of SMEs, thus materialising the desire to provide a framework for this vital sector of our economy.[260] This has had the merit of laying the foundations for the development of SMEs in Cameroon. It defines micro enterprise as one having 1-5number of workers with less than 15 million fcfa as turnover, a small enterprise as one comprising 6-20 workers with equal to 15million, but less than 100 million fcfa turnover, a medium enterprise as one with 21-100 workers and a turnover of equal to 100 million, but less than 1billion fcfa and a large enterprise as one comprising above 100 workers and a turnover of at least 1 billion fcfa. SME are thus defined based on two elements: the turnover and the number of people employed. In addition to the definition, the Law sets out the mechanisms for supporting SMEs, including support for their creation, the incubation strategy, their development, support for financing and their regrouping. SMEs are subject to some obligations which non-compliance is liable to sanctions. In order to take into account, the evolution of the SME sector and to consider local realities, the 2010 Law has been revised in 2015[261]. SME was redefined as any company, whatever its sector of activity, which employs no more than one hundred (100)

---

[259] Law No 2019/004 of 25th April 2019. A framework bill governing the social economy in Cameroon.

[260] The Law No. 2010/001 of 13th April 2010 on the promotion of small and medium-sized enterprises.

[261] Law No. 2015/010 of 16th July 2015 amended and supplemented some of the past provisions.

people and whose annual turnover excluding taxes does not exceed three (03) billion.

Within the framework of the improvement of the business climate and, in a concern for harmonising procedures in the OHADA area, the Cameroonian legislator has set the minimum share capital and the modalities of recourse to the services of the Notary within the framework of the creation of an LLC[262]. Thus, the minimum share capital for the creation of an LLC is set at 100,000 CFA francs, divided into equal shares whose nominal value cannot be less than CFA francs five thousand (5000) and recourse to a Notary is now optional.

As for the SME incubation strategy, the Prime Minister, Head of Government, in application of the provisions of the 2010 Law, signed a Decree[263] In the same vein, Implementing Orders of the said Decree have also been signed. On the one hand, they concern the form, elements contained in the Act of Approval of private structures of incubation and the conditions of its renewal, on the other hand on the content of the Partnership Agreements between MINPMEESA and the public incubation structures as well as the specifications relating thereto. To further facilitate the operationalisation of the modalities enacted by the Prime Minister, Head of Government, the Minister of SMEs took on 17th August 2021, the decision setting up the list of documents required for the constitution of application files for validation of training modules and support mechanisms of incubation structures.[264]

The implementation of these social economy laws will go a long way not only to develop the national economy but also to economically empower the rural women since their provisions facilitate the creation of small businesses by these rural women.

4.2.1.2. Cameroon's Investment Law and the Economic Empowerment of the Rural Women

In its efforts to build a competitive and prosperous economy through the development of investment and savings, and performance objectives of its economic and social action, the Republic of Cameroon has put in place several guidelines amongst which we can cite; the promotion of social and economic

---

[262] Law No. 2016/014 of 14th December 2016.

[263] Decree No. 2020/0301/PM of 22th January 2020, which sets out the terms and conditions for the fulfilment of the missions of the small and medium-sized enterprise incubation structures.

[264] MINPMEESA (2019), Sound Normative Framework for Small and Medium-Sized Enterprises in Cameroon. Available at https://www.minpmeesa.cm. (Consulted on 01/05/2024).

development, the acknowledgement of the entrepreneur's, investors and private company's key role as crucial factors of creation of wealth and jobs. This must be subject to particular attention from, not only the whole State machinery, but also from the entire society. The promotion of entrepreneurship as back bone of valorisation of the potential of creativity of Cameroon, a prior condition for the creation of viable and competitive companies and determinant factor to solve sustainably the problem of unemployment and poverty. The taking into account of specific or particular sectors which need measures, mindful of constraints tied to conditions of exploitation and valuing of local resources. The preoccupation to establish an appropriate institutional and regulatory framework that guarantees security of investment, support to investors and equitable rapid settlement of disputes on investment and commercial and industrial activities.[265]

The Cameroonian Government wants to build a competitive and prosperous economy by boosting investment and savings. To this end, Cameroon's National Assembly adopted an Investment Charter in April 2002 to attract international investors. The 2002 Investment Charter replaced the 1990 Investment Code[266]. The 2002 Charter does not discriminate with regard to equity ownership thus empowering the women especially the rural women to become economically empowered by owning property under the investment charter. Substantial local equity ownership may assist in the investment approval process. [267]

The law defines the investment promotion framework in accordance with the overall development strategy aimed at increased and sustainable growth, job-creation in all branches of economic activity and social well-being of the people. Thus, the investment charter provides opportunity for all to be economically empowered by developing strategies for sustainable growth and equally the creation of jobs.

The government under the investment code recognises the right of private ownership. The Ministry for Land Rights and Administration governs property issues. The procedures for obtaining land titles have been simplified and authority decentralized. These documents can now be obtained at Divisional levels within a timeframe of six months. Foreign and domestic individuals and firms are legally

---

[265] Section 2 of Law no. 2002/004 of 19th April 2002 instituting the investment charter in Cameroon.

[266] Law no 2002/004 of 19th April 2002 instituting the investment charter in Cameroon.

[267] US Department of states archives, Cameroon, (2001), 2007 investment climate statement-Cameroon openness to foreign investment. Available at http://www.state.gov. (Consulted on 15/02/2024).

entitled to establish and own firms; engage in remunerative activities; and establish, acquire and dispose of interests in business enterprises. Investors are permitted to dispose of their property via sale, transfer, or physical repatriation of moveable property. Thus, facilitating the procedure for the rural women to own land and become economically empowered.[268]

4.2.1.3. Cameroon's Industrial Policy and the Economic Empowerment of the Rural Women

Cameroon is a gateway country in central Africa and a commodity driven economy. The oil sector has historically played a dominant role, and there are substantial untapped mineral resources. Additionally, the nation's economic landscape is supported by the export of agricultural commodities, with a notable focus on cocoa, coffee, cotton, and bananas. To mitigate the impact of global commodity price fluctuations and enhance macroeconomic stability, it is imperative for Cameroon to foster economic resilience through diversification strategies.

To promote high and sustained growth and diversification, the country has put industrial policy (IP)[269] at the centre of its development strategy. The authorities build their IP mainly around import substitution policy to support domestic production of consumer goods, while working on addressing infrastructure gaps and institutional deficiencies. Over the longer term, the authorities aspire to expand domestic production, enable local producers to compete globally, and improve export performance. Thus, the current emphasis on import substitution is portrayed by the authorities as a transitional phase toward an export-oriented strategy. Additionally, certain measures promoting export have also been implemented. Globally, there has been a renewed interest in IP among policy makers who are driven by both economic and non-economic considerations. While debates surrounding the efficacy of IP persist, recent developments indicate a notable increase in its use, especially since 2018.

IP is defined as targeted government interventions to support domestic firms, industries, and economic activities to achieve certain national objectives.

---

[268] US Department of states archives, Cameroon, (2001).2007 investment climate statement- Cameroon openness to foreign investment. Available at http://www.state.go. (Consulted on 08/01/2024).

[269] IMF (2024). Industrial policy in Cameroon. Available at https://www.elibrary.imf.org.(Consulted on the 10/06/2024).

The traditional economic objectives of the IP are promoting growth, diversification, employment, and technological catch-up. This will for sure go a long way to promote and empower especially the rural women economically in Cameroon.

4.2.1.4. Cameroon's Regional Economic Policies and the Promotion of Women Economic Empowerment

The General Code on Regional and Local authorities (CGCTD) was put in place by the law in 2019[270].The regions in Cameroon are the heirs of the provinces, which could never be institutionalised as 'local authorities that are freely administered by councils.[271]. The recognition of the regions as fully-fledged territorial authorities is an institutional revolution that requires a reorganisation of relations between the various components of the political-administrative system i.e., the state, the administrative departments and the local authorities. In this reorganisation, the regions are at the heart of many issues such as the distribution of institutional resources; the structuring of regional political markets and the production of public action between the central administration and the regions.

As of January 22, 2021, all the regional councils resulting from the regional elections of December 2020 have been effectively installed, the offices of the councils elected and installed. However, the main thing is not to elect representatives at the regional level, but to have their consistent autonomy from the central state and its deconcentrated administrations. The region does not have legislative power but regulatory power, which allows for a territorial application of the norms enacted by the central government and the enactment of rules to facilitate territorial management. Its competences, although exclusively administrative, constitute the backbone of its actions in favour of economic development. [272]

The region is invested with a general mission of economic and social progress[273]. Within the framework of this mission, various competences have been transferred to it in terms of economic development, health and social development, and educational, sporting and cultural development. These include; economic action, management of the environment and natural resources,

---

[270] Section 1(1) of law No 2019/024 of 24 December 2019 bill to institute the general code of regional and local authorities in Cameroon.
[271] As per the 1960 Cameroon Constitution.
[272] Ngo Tong Chantal Marie (2023). Regions and Economic Development in Cameroon. Available at https://www.nkafu.org/regions-and -economic-development-in -Cameroon. (Consulted on 02/05/2024).
[273] Article 259 paragraph 2 of the CGCTD.

planning, land use, public works, urbanism and housing. The decrees setting out the terms and conditions for the exercise of these competences allow the regions to define their action plan for the next four years.

Since the first competences transferred to the regions are related to economic development, it can be said that the Cameroon State is clearly orienting its regional policy towards the promotion of economic policies. In this perspective, the regions in their deployment must work effectively to contribute to the harmonious, balanced, united and sustainable development of the territory. Among the tools they have at their disposal to achieve this, are regional development plans and the regional land use plan. Furthermore, without being a supervisory body over the municipalities, they must work in close collaboration with the latter, particularly in terms of urban planning, town planning and housing. The territory, a determining factor in the redefinition of development approaches, sets the relevant scales for reflection and economic action. [274]

With these regional economic policies in place in Cameroon, we realise that economic development is carried down to the regions and local municipalities where in the local population will benefit and become economically empowered, thus our rural women.

4.2.2. Specific Policy Standards for the Economic Empowerment of the Rural Women in Cameroon

These are national instruments that makes direct allusion to the economic empowerment of the rural women such as gender and labour related matters.

4.2.2.1. National Gender Policy and the Economic Empowerment of the Rural Women in Cameroon

The government's growth and employment strategy [275]recognize the promotion of gender equality as key to achieving inclusive growth and meeting the SDGs. The 2035 Vision of Emerging Cameroon states that "Cameroon, an emerging country, builds on the principles of good governance where women and men can enjoy the same rights and participate equally and in an equitable manner to the development.

With regards to the advancement of the status of women in the economic and socio-cultural areas is concerned, the policy declaration on the Integration of Women in Development, the Multi-sectoral Plan of Action on Women and

---

[274] Ibid.
[275] The 2010/2020 Growth and Employment strategy paper (GESP).

Development, and the National Plan of Action on the Integration of Women in Development were drafted and approved in 1997 and adopted by the Government in 1999. The advancement and protection of the girl child constitute one of the priority elements of those documents. Since the holding of the Fourth World Conference on Women in Beijing in 1995, women's concerns are increasingly taken into account in the major reforms being undertaken at national level. The participatory approach adopted in connection with the Poverty Reduction Strategy Paper (PRSP) has made it possible for 30 to 40% of Cameroon's women to become involved in that process. The Millennium Declaration served to a large extent as the inspiration for the PRSP. Element 6 of PRSP, that is to say the strengthening of human resources, the social sector and the integration of disadvantaged groups in the economic circuit, gives particular attention to Goal 3 on gender equality and women's empowerment, The Government is accentuating the democratization of education and non-discrimination between the sexes in terms of access to education by both girls and boys. With this in mind, primary education has been made free. Moreover, the Government has finalised its strategy for the advancement of women, which provides for women's education and training programmes. The following areas have been identified at national level in connection with the implementation of this part of the Beijing Plan of Action: agriculture, stockbreeding and fishing, forestry, environment, trade, industry, arts and crafts, tourism and employment. These areas also form part of the Government's poverty reduction policy. The Government has drawn up an integrated strategy of rural development whose principal elements include the following modernisation of production mechanisms, restructuring of the institutional framework, improvement of available incentives, and sustainable management of natural resources. The strategy places special emphasis on gender-based and participatory approaches.

The following programmes have been set up with a view to promoting local development and strengthening the capacity of communities to enable grass-roots actors to participate more actively in the development of their locality: National Participatory Development Programme (PNDP), National Programme of Support to Community Development (PADC).

The National Micro-Financing Programme sets out to improve the access of rural dwellers to micro-financing institutions and to strengthen the capacities of micro-financing institutions.

The Agricultural and Community Micro-Projects Investment Fund (FIMAC) forms part of the effort to achieve greater food security. Its goal is to increase the purchasing power of beneficiary groups and to encourage self-advancement among the rural population.[276]

The National Agricultural Extension and Research Programme (PNVRA) aims at raising farmers' productivity by improving their technical competence. The Decentralised Rural Credit Fund supports rural dwellers' economic initiatives.

In the area of animal husbandry, poultry keeping and pig-breeding are activities habitually performed by women. These occupations are now receiving better support through measures designed to reduce stock mortality.

A project for the installation of community tele-centres has been developed with the aim of promoting integrated development in rural areas and of facilitating rural dwellers' access to information on new technologies. The object is to provide information and communication services with a view to improving rural dwellers' quality of life, creating employment- and income-generating activities and preventing the drift from the countryside.

In the area of trade, activities have been undertaken in cooperation with businesswomen's organizations with a view to deriving greater benefit of new export opportunities provided by the American Growth and Opportunity Act (AGOA).

All these as we can see goes a long way to empower women specifically. The rural women are highly taken into consideration.

4.2.2.2. The Cameroon's Labour Code and Women Economic Empowerment

Women are victims of discrimination especially the rural women due to the presence of customary law rules that are prevalence in this sector of the economy. This discrimination equally existed in the employment sector in almost all States. In the wake of gender equality and non-discrimination, States began to adopt and established legislations which protected gender equality in all aspects of life. Cameroon as a State committed to the protection of human rights has ratified several human rights treaties protecting equality towards the enjoyment of the right to work. She has equally put in place laws guaranteeing equality in the enjoyment of the right to work; the main legislation is the Labour Code[277] The code provides that "The right to work shall be recognized as a basic right of each citizen"[278]. This code protects female workers as common workers and equally as

---

[276] Ibid.
[277] Law No. 92/007 of 14th August 1992, instituting the Cameroon Labour Code.
[278] Ibid Section 2.

special workers. Female workers as common workers enjoy the same rights as male workers some of which include the right to be paid damages for wrongful termination of the employment contract or specific reinstatement, the right to annual leave, the right to weekly rest, the right to join a trade union and so on. And as special workers they enjoy rights more than their male counterparts some of which include the right to maternity leave and nursing breaks. [279]

4.3. Policy Standards Established by Regional Legal Instruments for Women Economic Empowerment in Cameroon

Regional arrangement for which Cameroon is a party that promote the economic development of women include the OHADA treaty, the CIMA treaty CEMAC.

4.3.1. The OHADA Treaty and the Promotion of Women Economic Empowerment

OHADA's mission is to harmonize business Law in Africa in order to guarantee legal and judicial security for investors and companies in its member states. The Organization for the Harmonization of Business Law in Africa (OHADA) was established by the Treaty on the Harmonization of Business Law in Africa (OHADA)[280].To date, seventeen States are members of the Organization for the Harmonization of Business Law in Africa: Benin, Burkina Faso, Cameroon, Central African Republic, Côte d'Ivoire, Congo, Comoros, Gabon, Guinea, Guinea Bissau, Equatorial Guinea, Mali, Niger, the Democratic Republic of Congo (DRC), Senegal, Chad and Togo. The Treaty's main objective is to address the legal and judicial insecurity in Member States.

Indeed, it is undeniable that legal balkanization and judicial insecurity were the key impediments to the economic development of the continent. Harmonising economic laws and improving the functioning of judicial systems in Member States were therefore necessary to restore investor confidence, facilitate trade between countries and develop a vibrant private sector. Economic globalization requires the harmonization of laws and legal practices. Regarding developing countries like ours, this is a priority in order to create a favourable climate for legal and judicial security, a condition sine qua non to attract an inflow of foreign investment. This task is even more important considering that investment is in

---

[279] Pascal Nkwa Ayuk, (2021), The protection of Cameroon female Workers under the Labour code. International Journal of social sciences and Humanities Research. Vol.9, issue 3, pp 22-260.

[280] OHADA Treaty signed on October 17, 1993 in Port – Louis (Mauritius Ireland) and revised in Quebec (Canada) on October 17, 2008.

itself a risk, even if it is a calculated risk, it would therefore be much difficult to attract investors if they have to deal with an additional risk of legal norms that are changing, fluctuating and uncertain.

Twenty-two years after the creation of OHADA, the result is a huge work of legal unification in its Member States. OHADA is therefore an important tool for the development of business law, the creation of an integrated legal space conducive for a viable and lively economic space. OHADA can be a role model in Africa and beyond since the Caribbean countries have already implemented a similar project. Every commercial company, including those in which the state or a corporate person governed, whose registered office is located on the territory of one of the State parties to the Treaty on the Harmonisation of Business Law in Africa shall be subject to the provision of this Uniform Act.

The OHADA Uniform Act on Cooperatives defines a cooperative as an autonomous group of individuals who willingly join together to fulfil their aspirations and meet their common Economic, Social and Cultural needs so as to form a corporate body whose ownership and management are collective and where power is exercised democratically and according to the cooperative's basis.[281]

The OHADA Law on Cooperatives equally makes provision for the contribution in cash or kind towards the creation of cooperatives[282].

All economic interest groups shall also be subject to the provisions of this Uniform Act applicable in the States Parties in which their registered office is situated, provided that such laws are not contrary to the provisions of this Uniform Act.[283]The provisions of this Uniform Act are mandatory, except in cases where the Act explicitly authorizes the sole proprietor or members of a company to substitute contractual provisions between them for those of this Uniform Act or to supplement the provisions of this Uniform Act with their own provisions.[284] Any of the company on the territory of one of the State Parties, shall choose a form of company which suits the activity envisaged from among those provided for by this Uniform Act. Any persons, whatever their nationality, wishing to engage in a commercial activity in the form. The persons referred to in the

---

[281]Article 4 of the 1993 OHADA Law.
[282] Article 33 of the 1993 OHADA Law.
[283] Article 1 of the 1993 OHADA Law.
[284] Article 2 of the 1993 OHADA law

preceding paragraph may also elect, under the conditions provided for by this Uniform Act, to form an economic interest group.[285]

These provisions promote the Cameroonian rural women to emerge economically. By facilitating the procedure for the creation of cooperatives even through bringing together resources in kind, these rural women can easily belong to cooperatives. Since they become one body they can stand as one and seek their common good to be economically empowered.

As concerns the creation of companies, OHADA Law has equally made provision for limited liability companies (LLCs) which are companies ideal for small to medium sized businesses and requires at least one or two shareholders. This type of a company has less strict requirements for creation than that of the public limited companies. (SA). LLCs have flexible structure making them ideal for family-owned businesses or entrepreneurs like the rural women wishing to lunch a new company. Pursuant to the UA on Commercial Companies and Economic Interest Groups, the Cameroonian law seeks to facilitate the creation of LLCs which remains the most used form of companies. The Law reduces the minimum share capital of LLCs to 100.000frs and makes optional recourse to notarial deed when setting up LLC in case of sole proprietorship or where its capital does not exceed one million frs cfa.

For the rural woman to be economically empowered, they need to leave from informal sector to formal sector by creating SMEs and the simplified procedure given by the OHADA Law to create LLCs will help these women to easily realise their dreams in creating SMEs for their economic growth.

4.3.2. The CIMA Code and Economic Empowerment of the Rural Women

The CIMA Code, cornerstone of the sectorial integration project, coming into force in 1995, applies to all insurance companies operating in the 14 African member states. It regulates local insurers and branches of foreign insurers domiciled in the region in standardized fashion.

The initial legal framework has been subject to several updates and amendments with the int roduction of modifications aimed at adapting the regulations to the socio-economic environment, strengthening the legislation, increasing the retention capacity of insurers, improving the solvency of companies, and protecting the insured. Several provisions and articles of the CIMA Code have profoundly reformed the region's insurance landscape.

---

[285] Article 3 of the 1993 OHADA Law

The reforms introduced by the ministers of the organization's member countries at their 11 April 2011 meeting in N'Djamena are designed to put an end to a situation that threatens the very existence of insurers. Consequently, the new Article 13, introduced in 2011 and amended in 2014, now requires the payment of premiums to the insurer before the entry into force of the policy (Cash Before Cover) and before the renewal of coverage. This measure is introduced to address the significant level of outstanding premiums on the balance sheets of insurance companies at the time.[286]

The code equally covered activity governing microinsurance to cover low-income populations.[287] It equally covers the reinsurance business. This regulation is binding on all reinsurance companies established in the CIMA zone including foreign branches, representative or liaison offices[288] The code has increased the minimum share capital of joint stock insurance companies and the establishment fund of mutual insurance companies.[289] This code equally covers agricultural risk. Amended on 20 April 1995 by Decision of the Council of Ministers, the following shall be considered, for the application of this Code, as exhibiting the nature of agricultural risks:

- risks to which individuals or legal entities who exercise exclusively or principally a profession of agricultural nature or related to agriculture are exposed;

- risks to which the staff employed by these individuals or legal entities are exposed, as well as their agricultural good;

- risks to which the family members of the aforementioned individuals as well as their agricultural property are exposed, when they live with them in their establishment. [290]

Agriculture is the main activity of the rural sector of the economy and by making provision for insurance coverage by this code only goes a long way to economically empower the rural population especially the rural women who are so much engaged into agriculture.

4.3.3. The Central African Economic and Monetary Community (CEMAC) and the Economic Empowerment of Rural Women

---

[286] Article 13 of the 1995 CIMA code
[287] Book VII, of the 1995 CIMA Code, adopted in 2012.
[288] Book VIII, of the 1995 CIMA Code, adopted in 2015
[289] Articles 329(3) and 330(2) of the 1995 CIMA Code as amended in 2016, 2018, and 2020.
[290] Article 55 of the 1995 CIMA CODE.

The Central African Economic and Monetary Community (CEMAC) is made up of six States: Gabon, Cameroon, the Central African Republic (CAR), Chad, the Republic of the Congo and Equatorial Guinea. CEMAC aims to promote peace and the harmonious development of its member states, in the framework of establishing an economic union and a monetary union. In each of these two areas, the member states intend to move from cooperation to a situation of union to complete the process of economic and monetary integration and to improve mutual assistance to support less developed member states. CEMAC has as objectives:

- strengthen competitiveness of economic and financial activities by harmonising regulations that govern them;

- ensure the convergence toward sustainable economic and financial performance by coordinating economic policies and rendering national budgetary policies consistent with the common monetary policy;

- create a common market based on free mobility of persons, goods, capital and services;[291]

- assure coordination of national sector policies in the following areas: agriculture, livestock, fishing, industry, commerce, transport, telecommunications, energy, environment, research, education and professional training; implement common actions and adopt common policies.

The Commission of CEMAC is responsible for preparing the documentation necessary for the multilateral monitoring system. For this, reliable socio-economic data are necessary to evaluate national performances and to compare domestic situations in the sub-region. To this end, the Commission de la CEMAC aims at improving the quality and harmonisation of statistics of member states, as well as extending their scope.[292]

All this provision empowers Cameroon's economy since it's a member of the CEMAC Zone which goes a long way to promote the rural women economically for its provisions are universal and non-discriminatory to all African member states.

4.4. Policy Standard Established by International Instruments for the Economic Empowerment of Rural Women in Cameroon

---

[291] The 1994 CEMAC Law.
[292] The 1994 CEMAC Code.

These policy standards at the international level include some UN conventions and international covenants.

4.4.1. The Convention on the Elimination of All Forms of Discrimination Against Women (CEDAW)

On 18 December 1979, the Convention on the Elimination of All Forms of Discrimination[293] Against Women was adopted by the United Nations General Assembly. It entered into force as an international treaty on 3 September 1981 after the twentieth country had ratified it. By the tenth anniversary of the Convention in 1989, almost one hundred nations have agreed to be bound by its provisions

Among the international human rights treaties, the Convention takes an important place in bringing the female half of humanity into the focus of human rights concerns. The spirit of the Convention is rooted in the goals of the United Nations: to reaffirm faith in fundamental human rights, in the dignity, and worth of the human person, in the equal rights of men and women. The Convention explicitly acknowledges that "extensive discrimination against women continues to exist", and emphasises that such discrimination "violates the principles of equality of rights and respect for human dignity".[294] Discrimination according to the convention [295]is understood as "any distinction, exclusion or restriction made on the basis of sex...in the political, economic, social, cultural, civil or any other field".

The Convention thus gives positive affirmation to the principle of equality by requiring States parties to take "all appropriate measures, including legislation, to ensure the full development and advancement of women, for the purpose of guaranteeing them the exercise and enjoyment of human rights and fundamental freedoms on a basis of equality with men"[296] The wordings of the convention in its articles 10,11,13,14,15, and 16 makes provision for the economic empowerment of the women and particular reference is made in article 14 to the rural women for her economic empowerment.

The convention holds that, 'States Parties shall take all appropriate measures to eliminate discrimination against women in order to ensure to them equal rights with men in the field of education and in particular to ensure, on a basis of equality of men and women. It holds that, the same conditions for career

---

[293] The 1981 CEDAW Convention.
[294] Preamble of the 1981 CEDAW Convention.
[295] Article 1 of the 1981 CEDAW convention.
[296] Ibid Article 3.

and vocational guidance, for access to studies and for the achievement of diplomas in educational establishments of all categories in rural as well as in urban areas; this equality shall be ensured in pre-school, general, technical, professional and higher technical education, as well as in all types of vocational training. Access to the same curricula, the same examinations, teaching staff with qualifications of the same standard and school premises and equipment of the same quality. The elimination of any stereotyped concept of the roles of men and women at all levels and in all forms of education by encouraging coeducation and other types of education which will help to achieve this aim and, in particular, by the revision of textbooks and school programmes and the adaptation of teaching methods. The same opportunities to benefit from scholarships and other study grants. The same opportunities for access to programmes of continuing education, including adult and functional literacy programmes, particularly those aimed at reducing, at the earliest possible time, any gap in education existing between men and women. The reduction of female student drop-out rates and the organization of programmes for girls and women who have left school prematurely. The same Opportunities to participate actively in sports and physical education. Access to specific educational information to help to ensure the health and well-being of families, including information and advice on family planning.[297]

The Convention also upholds women's economic rights when it postulates that, States Parties shall take all appropriate measures to eliminate discrimination against women in the field of employment in order to ensure, on a basis of equality of men and women, the same rights, in particular, the right to work as an inalienable right of all human beings. It make provision for the right to the same employment opportunities, including the application of the same criteria for selection in matters of employment; the right to free choice of profession and employment, the right to promotion, job security and all benefits and conditions of service and the right to receive vocational training and retraining, including apprenticeships, advanced vocational training and recurrent training; the right to equal remuneration, including benefits, and to equal treatment in respect of work of equal value, as well as equality of treatment in the evaluation of the quality of work; the right to social security, particularly in cases of retirement, unemployment, sickness, invalidity and old age and other incapacity to work, as well as the right to paid leave. The right to protection of health and to safety in working conditions, including the safeguarding of the function of reproduction.[298]

---

[297] Article 10 of the 1981 CEDAW.
[298] Ibid Article 11(1).

In order to prevent discrimination against women on the grounds of marriage or maternity and to ensure their effective right to work, as per the convention, States Parties shall take appropriate measures to prohibit, subject to the imposition of sanctions, dismissal on the grounds of pregnancy or of maternity leave and discrimination in dismissals on the basis of marital status. The state should introduce maternity leave with pay or with comparable social benefits without loss of former employment, seniority or social allowances. It should encourage the provision of the necessary supporting social services to enable parents to combine family obligations with work responsibilities and participation in public life, in particular through promoting the establishment and development of a network of child-care facilities. Provide special protection to women during pregnancy in types of work proved to be harmful to them and make provision for protective legislation.[299]

When the convention goes further to state that, states Parties shall take all appropriate measures to eliminate discrimination against women in other areas of economic and social life in order to ensure, on a basis of equality of men and women, the same rights, in particular the right to family benefits; the right to bank loans, mortgages and other forms of financial credit; the right to participate in recreational activities, sports and all aspects of cultural life,[300] it is simply empowering the women economically for the growth of their communities and the nation at large.

The rural women which are considered as the marginalised group in the rural settings have been given special consideration by the code when it states that 'States Parties shall take into account the particular problems faced by rural women and the significant roles which rural women play in the economic survival of their families, including their work in the non-monetized sectors of the economy, and shall take all appropriate measures to ensure the application of the provisions of the present Convention to women in rural areas.[301]

The states Parties shall take all appropriate measures to eliminate discrimination against women in rural areas in order to ensure, on a basis of equality of men and women, that they participate in and benefit from rural development and, in particular, shall ensure to such women the right: to participate in the elaboration and implementation of development planning at all levels; to have access to adequate health care facilities, including information, counselling and services in family planning; to benefit directly from social

[299]Ibid Article 11(2).
[300] Ibid Article 13 CEDAW
[301] Ibid Article 14(1).

security programmes; to obtain all types of training and education, formal and non-formal, including that relating to functional literacy, as well as, inter alia, the benefit of all community and extension services, in order to increase their technical proficiency; to organize self-help groups and co-operatives in order to obtain equal access to economic opportunities through employment or self-employment; to participate in all community activities; to have access to agricultural credit and loans, marketing facilities, appropriate technology and equal treatment in land and agrarian reform as well as in land resettlement schemes; to enjoy adequate living conditions, particularly in relation to housing, sanitation, electricity and water supply, transport and communications[302]

The Convention equally accords legal protection to the women which is another form of asserting their rights thus empowering the economically. It holds that, states Parties shall accord to women equality with men before the law.[303] It further states that, states Parties shall accord to women, in civil matters, a legal capacity identical to that of men and the same opportunities to exercise that capacity. In particular, they shall give women equal rights to conclude contracts and to administer property and shall treat them equally in all stages of procedure in courts and tribunals.[304]As we know early and forced marriages for young girls is very common in Cameroon especially in the rural areas where young children are forced into early marriages. They cannot go to school and be educated so they remain less economically empowered. It is for this reason that the Convention has made provision for the fight against early marriage. It states that, "States Parties shall take all appropriate measures to eliminate discrimination against women in all matters relating to marriage and family relations and in particular shall ensure, on a basis of equality of men and women the same right to enter into marriage."[305]

4.4.2. The Universal Declaration of Human Rights and its Policies on Women Economic Empowerment

The 1948 Universal Declaration of Human Rights is a foundational text in the history of human and civil rights. The Declaration consists of 30 articles detailing an individual's "basic rights and fundamental freedoms" and affirming their universal character as inherent, inalienable, and applicable to all human beings.[306] Adopted as a "common standard of achievement for all peoples and all nations", the UDHR commits nations to recognize all humans as being "born free

---

[302] Ibid Article 14(2).
[303] Ibid Article 15(1).
[304] Ibid Article 15(2).
[305] Article 16 (1).
[306] Article 1 of the 1948 UDHR

and equal in dignity and rights" regardless of "nationality, place of residence, sex, national or ethnic origin, colour, religion, language, or any other status".[307]

The Declaration holds that, "everyone has the right to work, to free choice of employment, to just and favourable conditions of work and to protection against unemployment. Everyone, without any discrimination, has the right to equal pay for equal work and everyone who works has the right to just and favourable remuneration ensuring for himself and his family an existence worthy of human dignity, and supplemented, if necessary, by other means of social protection. It further holds that, everyone has the right to form and to join trade unions for the protection of his interests".[308]To this right to work it further makes provision for every one the right to rest and leisure309.It equally makes provision for high standard of living for all when it states "everyone has the right to a standard of living adequate for the health and well-being of himself and of his family, including food, clothing, housing and medical care and necessary social services, and the right to security in the event of unemployment, sickness, disability, widowhood, old age or other lack of livelihood in circumstances beyond his control. That motherhood and childhood are entitled to special care and assistance. All children, whether born in or out of wedlock, shall enjoy the same social protection.[310]

Everyone has the right to education. Education shall be free, at least in the elementary and fundamental stages. Elementary education shall be compulsory. Technical and professional education shall be made generally available and higher education shall be equally accessible to all on the basis of merit.

Education shall be directed to the full development of the human personality and to the strengthening of respect for human rights and fundamental freedoms. It shall promote understanding, tolerance and friendship among all nations, racial or religious groups, and shall further the activities of the United Nations for the maintenance of peace.

Parents have a prior right to choose the kind of education that shall be given to their children.[311]

The Declaration also states that everyone has the right to own property alone as well as in association with others. That no one shall be arbitrarily

---

[307] Ibid.
[308] Ibid Article 23 of the 1948 UDHR.
[309] Ibid Article 24.
[310] Ibid Article 2.
[311] Article 26.

deprived of his property.[312] Furthermore, everyone has the right to freedom of thought, conscience and religion; this right includes freedom to change his religion or belief, and freedom, either alone or in community with others and in public or private, to manifest his religion or belief in teaching, practice, worship and observance. Everyone has the right to freedom of opinion and expression; this right includes freedom to hold opinions without interference and to seek, receive and impart information and ideas through any media and regardless of frontiers.[313]

When the Declaration states all are equal before the law and are entitled without any discrimination to equal protection of the law. That all are entitled to equal protection against any discrimination in violation of this Declaration and against any incitement to such discrimination, [314]it is simply enforcing these rights which will all go a long way to economically empower the women especially the rural women.

4.4.3. UN Chater Policies on Women Economic Development

The Charter of the United Nations is the founding document of the United Nations. It was signed on 26 June 1945, in San Francisco, at the conclusion of the United Nations Conference on International Organization, and came into force on 24 October 1945.The UN has four main purpose:

- To keep peace throughout the world;

- To develop friendly relations among nations;

- To help nations work together to improve the lives of poor people, to conquer hunger, disease and illiteracy, and to encourage respect for each other's rights and freedoms;

- To be a centre for harmonizing the actions of nations to achieve these goals.[315]

The United Nations can take action on a wide variety of issues due to its unique international character and the powers vested in its Charter, which is considered an international treaty. As such, the UN Charter is an instrument of international law, and UN Member States are bound by it. The UN Charter codifies the major principles of international relations, from sovereign equality of States to the prohibition of the use of force in international relations.

---

[312] Ibid Article 17.
[313] Ibid Articles 18 and 19.
[314] Ibid Article 7.
[315] United Nations (2023), The UN General. Available at https://unis.unvienna.org. (Consulted on the 08/05/2024).

With regard to the creation of conditions of stability and well-being which are necessary for peaceful and friendly relations among nations based on respect for the principle of equal rights and self-determination of peoples, the United Nations shall promote: higher standards of living, full employment, and conditions of economic and social progress and development; solutions of international economic, social, health, and related problems; and international cultural and educational cooperation; and universal respect for, and observance of, human rights and fundamental freedoms for all without distinction as to race, sex, language, or religion[316].With this the nations states are empowered economically and since Cameroon is a member state, the nation will be empowered thus the rural women inclusive.

4.4.4. International Covenant on Civil and Political Rights

The International Covenant on Civil and Political Rights (ICCPR) was adopted by the United Nations General Assembly[317] As one of two international treaties that make the 'International Bill of Human Rights' along with the Universal Declaration of Human Rights. The ICCPR provides the legal framework to protect and preserve the most basic civil and political rights, including the right to life, freedom from slavery and the right to equality. For this reason, most of the rights contained in the ICCPR are related to tackling violence against Women (VAW), given that VAW is a cause and consequence of women's unequal enjoyment of their human rights when compared to men. Some of the ICCPR's articles most relevant to tackling violence against women include: right to non-discrimination and the right to an effective remedy[318], right to life [319] right not to be subjected to torture or to cruel, inhuman or degrading treatment or punishment,[320] right not to be subjected to slavery or forced labour[321] , right to recognition before the law,[322] right to marry with free and full consent; equality in marriage,[323] right to equality before the law and equal protection of the law and rights of individuals in minority groups.[324]

Under the General Reporting ICCPR Guidelines, countries must submit a detailed report including information on violence against women. When reporting

---

[316] Article 55 Article 23 of the 1948 UDHR.
[317] Resolution 2016 of 16 December 1966.
[318] Article 2 of the 1976 ICCPR.
[319] Ibid Article 6.
[320] Ibid Article 7.
[321] Ibid Article 8.
[322] Ibid Article 16.
[323] Ibid Article 26.
[324] Ibid Article 27.

under each Covenant right, States must provide information regarding the enjoyment of this right by women, addressing in particular:

-   The proportion of women in positions of responsibility in both the public and the private sector and the measures taken to promote the representation of women in Parliament and in senior positions in Government as well as in the private sector;
-   Measures to ensure equal pay for equal work for women and men. Whether the State party has adopted legislation which specifically criminalizes domestic violence and provide information on its scope and content;
-   What measures have been taken to ensure that acts of domestic violence are effectively investigated and perpetrators prosecuted and sanctioned.;
-   Other steps taken to combat domestic violence such as training for judges, prosecutors, police and health officers and awareness-raising campaigns for women on their rights and available remedies, as well as information on the number of safe shelters and the resources allocated to the assistance of victims of domestic violence;
-   Discrimination in minimum age of marriage;
-   Unequal rights in marriage;
-   Equality in divorce arrangements, including regarding custody of children;
-   School attendance by girls;
-   Legislation on rape, including spousal rape;
-   Measures taken to eliminate traditional practices and customs affecting the dignity and personal integrity of women and girls.[325]

With all these measures put in place by the ICCPR the rights of the women especially those of the rural women are protected which will go a long way to empower them economically.

4.4.5. International Covenant on Economic, Social and Cultural Rights

Economic, Social and cultural Rights (ESCR) are human rights concerning the basic social and economic conditions needed to live a life of dignity and freedom, relating to work and worker's rights, social security, health, education, food, water, housing, healthy environment and culture.[326]

---

[325] Resolution 2016 (note 1)
[326] ESCR-Net (1966) Introduction to Economic, Social and Cultural Rights. Available at https://www.escr-net. (Consulted on the 09/05/2024)

In 1948, the UN adopted the Universal Declaration of Human Rights (UDHR), outlining the basic civil, cultural, economic, political and social rights that all human beings should enjoy. In 1966, ESCR were expressed as legal rights in the International Covenant on Economic Social and Cultural rights.

The ICESCR outlines a number of important principles in the realisation of ESCR, which are often included in other ESCR sources as well. States must guarantee ESCR without discrimination on the basis of grounds specified in the ICESCR, including race, colour, sex, language, religion, political or other opinion, national or social origin, property, and birth. The articulation of ESCR in international law followed long-term demands for these basic rights by people worldwide, and reflects concern for the life of every individual, particularly the most vulnerable, as expressed in many philosophical, religious and other traditions.

In an era of increasing economic globalisation and growing inequality within and between states, there is an urgent need for grassroots groups, NGOs, academics, and other organisations and individuals to unite to recognise connections between continuing, localised struggles and to realise the human rights of all persons in practice. In understanding instances and patterns of poverty and deprivation as violations of ESCR rather than mere misfortune, events outside human control, or the result of individual shortcomings an obligation is placed on states and, increasingly, on corporations and other non-state actors, to prevent and address such situations.

Around the world, the ESCR framework is used to bolster actions for justice and against oppression, and amplify progressive alternatives to enhance the enjoyment of ESCR. Activists have brought legal cases before UN treaty bodies, courts and other dispute resolution bodies to demand change, documented and publicised recurring violations, mobilised communities, developed legislation, analysed domestic budgets and international trade agreements to ensure compliance with human rights, and built solidarity and networks between communities locally and across the globe. ESCR unite women and men, migrants and indigenous people, youth and elders, of all races, religions, political orientations, and economic and social backgrounds, in a common realisation of universal human freedom and dignity.[327]

Part III the Covenant recognize the right to work, which includes the right of everyone to the opportunity to gain his living by work which he freely chooses or accepts, and will take appropriate steps to safeguard this right. State Party to

---

[327] Ibid.

the present Covenant are to take appropriate steps to achieve the full realization of this right shall include technical and vocational guidance and training programmes, policies and techniques to achieve steady economic, social and cultural development and full and productive employment under conditions safeguarding fundamental political and economic freedoms to the individual.[328]

States parties to this covenant recognize the right of everyone to the enjoyment of just and favourable conditions of work and thus should provide all workers, as a minimum, with Fair wages and equal remuneration for work of equal value without distinction of any kind, in particular women being guaranteed conditions of work not inferior to those enjoyed by men, with equal pay for equal work. Provide decent living for themselves and their families in accordance with the provisions of the present Covenant; Safe and healthy working conditions; Equal opportunity for everyone to be promoted in his employment to an appropriate higher level, subject to no considerations other than those of seniority and competence and rest, leisure and reasonable limitation of working hours and periodic holidays with pay, as well as remuneration for public holidays.[329]

The right of everyone to form trade unions and join the trade union of his choice, subject only to the rules of the organization concerned, for the promotion and protection of his economic and social interests. No restrictions may be placed on the exercise of this right other than those prescribed by law and which are necessary in a democratic society in the interests of national security or public order or for the protection of the rights and freedoms of others is guaranteed by state parties. The right of trade unions to establish national federations or confederations and the right of the latter to form or join international trade-union organisations. It equally holds that trade unions should function freely subject to no limitations other than those prescribed by law and which are necessary in a democratic society in the interests of national security or public order or for the protection of the rights and freedoms of others.[330]

The convention holds that the widest possible protection and assistance should be accorded to the family, which is the natural and fundamental group unit of society, particularly for its establishment and while it is responsible for the care and education of dependent children. Marriage must be entered into with the free consent of the intending spouses. Special protection should be accorded to mothers during a reasonable period before and after childbirth. During such period

---

[328] Article 6 of the 1976 ICESCR
[329] Ibid Article 7.
[330] Article 8 of the 1976 ICESCR

working mothers should be accorded paid leave or leave with adequate social security benefits. Special measures of protection and assistance should be taken on behalf of all children and young persons without any discrimination for reasons of parentage or other conditions. Children and young persons should be protected from economic and social exploitation. Their employment in work harmful to their morals or health or dangerous to life or likely to hamper their normal development should be punishable by law. States should also set age limits below which the paid employment of child labour should be prohibited and punishable by law.[331]

The covenant also recognises the right of everyone to an adequate standard of living for himself and his family, including adequate food, clothing and housing, and to the continuous improvement of living conditions. The States Parties will take appropriate steps to ensure the realisation of this right, recognising to this effect the essential importance of international co-operation based on free consent. This covenant, recognises the fundamental right of everyone to be free from hunger, and shall take, individually and through international co-operation, the measures, including specific programmes such as, improve methods of production, conservation and distribution of food by making full use of technical and scientific knowledge, by disseminating knowledge of the principles of nutrition and by developing or reforming agrarian systems in such a way as to achieve the most efficient development and utilization of natural resources, taking into account the problems of both food-importing and food-exporting countries, to ensure an equitable distribution of world food supplies in relation to need.[332]

There is no doubt that this international instrument promotes the economic empowerment of states party to the convention. The ratification of this convention of Cameroon means the women, even the rural women who are our point of fucus will benefit and thus become economically empowered.

4.4.6. International Convention against Torture and other Cruel Inhumane and degrading Treatment

The term "torture" means any act by which severe pain or suffering, whether physical or mental, is intentionally inflicted on a person for such purposes as obtaining from him or a third person information or a confession, punishing him for an act he or a third person has committed or is suspected of having committed, or intimidating or coercing him or a third person, or for any reason

---

[331] Ibid Article 10.
[332] Ibid Article 11.

based on discrimination of any kind, when such pain or suffering is inflicted by or at the instigation of or with the consent or acquiescence of a public official or other person acting in an official capacity. It does not include pain or suffering arising only from, inherent in or incidental to lawful sanctions.[333]The rural women in Cameroon are most often than not abused both physically and psychologically. Domestic violence is mostly common in these areas. The women are often relegated to the background due to the presence of customary law rules that prevail in these regions. Women are considered in these regions as property thus are treated as such.

With the effective application of this convention, these women will no longer suffer from these cruel treatments. They will no longer be considered second class citizens and will be empowered to carry out their activities without hindrances emanating from customs and tradition and thus they will become economically empowered. Each State Party has to take effective legislative, administrative, judicial or other measures to prevent acts of torture in any territory under its jurisdiction[334]

4.5. Conclusion

Policy standards as we have seen are therefore those measures put in place by the government of Cameroon, those postulated at the national level, those ratified at the regional level and those ratified at the international level are those legal provisions available in Cameroon the economic development the Cameroon's economy in general and the Cameroonian rural women in particular. Our preceding chapter will now examine those institutions which are equally in place I Cameroon for the economic empowerment of the rural women.

---

[333] Article 1(1) of the 1984 International Convention against Torture and other Cruel, Inhumane and Degrading Treatment.

[334] Article 2 of the 1984 International Convention against Torture and other Cruel, Inhumane and Degrading Treatment.

CHAPTER FIVE

INSTITUTIONAL ARRANGEMENT TOWARDS RURAL WOMEN ECONOMIC EMPOWERMENT IN CAMEROON

5.1. Introduction

According to John Locke in his "Theory of Property", holds that "being all equal and independent no one ought to harm another in his life, liberty or possessions". This chapter has as objective to examine the role played by various institutions in the advancement of women's right to economic empowerment. These institutions include national institutions both government and NGO's institution and regionally and internationally ratified institutions by the Cameroon government which advocate for women's right to economic empowerment especially the rural women. These institutions help to implement the legal provisions in Cameroon that promote rural women economic development. However, these rural women in Cameroon still remain economically unempowered.

5.2. National Institutions Promoting Women Economic Development

There are various ministerial departments, which in addition to their specific duties equally promote the economic empowerment of rural women.

5.2.1. Ministry of Women Empowerment and the Family

The Ministry responsible for women's affairs was initially established by presidential decree in 1984. In 1987, with the worsening of the economic crisis, Cameroon adopted a structural adjustment plan, which entailed reducing public expenditures and restructuring the Government. In particular, the Ministries of Women's Affairs and Social Affairs were merged into a single Ministry[335]. In December 1997, the President of the Republic, aware of the special problems of women and anxious to improve their status, set up the new Ministry of Women's Affairs [336] The Ministry of Women's Affairs shall be responsible for drafting and implementing measures relating to respect of women's rights and strengthening guarantees of gender equality in the political, economic, social and cultural spheres.[337] So far as the advancement of the status of women in the economic and socio-cultural areas is concerned, the policy declaration on the Integration of Women in Development, the Multi-sectoral Plan of Action on Women and Development, and the National Plan of Action on the Integration of Women in

---

[335] Decree No. 88/1281 of 21 September 1988.
[336] Decree No. 97/205 of 7 December 1997 on the organization of the Government.
[337] Article 5(8) of the 1997 Decree.

Development were drafted and approved in 1997 and adopted by the Government in 1999.

The organization of the ministry in charge of women empowerment (MINPROFF)[338] was put in place by the Cameroon government to see into it that matters concerning the women especially the rural women should be specially handled by this Ministry. Its mission is to empower the women in general thus the economic empowerment of the rural women in Cameroon. It institutes a national machinery for gender equality and women's Empowerment. There is an inter-ministerial committee of gender at the Central level of the country headed by the Prime Minister. The committee is responsible for the coordination and supervision of implementation of the National gender policy. In collaboration with the gender focal points of the Ministers, civil organisations and development organisations, the technical committee has discussions with the stakeholders in quarterly meetings, assists the Ministries to secure budget and carryout monitoring and evaluation of the implementation of the National gender Policy. The gender focal points are responsible for gender mainstreaming of each Ministry's Policies and Projects. They conduct gender training for the staff and ensure that gender perspectives are incorporated by making sure that questions about gender are included in the questionnaires for project design. MINPROFF participates in the genders committees of each ministry, and checks the progress of the Ministry's Policies and projects from gender perspectives MINPPROFF's budget is 5% of the National budget. Each ministry is responsible for obtaining budget for its gender related activities. [339]

In the regions there are gender committees at every level from regions, Divisions to sub division. Each gender committee implements policies and projects at each level. All regions have its Appropriate Technology Center which runs training for women farmers about food processing and improvements of productivity.

The technical secretariat, placed under the supervision of the Ministry in charge of women's empowerment and gender promotion, the technical secretariat shall be presided over by the secretary General of the said Ministry and shall hold quarterly meeting. Organizing the steering committee secretariat for an effective coordination of activities, the technical secretariat shall establish collaboration protocols with the various stakeholders.

---

[338] Decree No.2005/088 of 29 March 2005 to organise the Ministry of Women Empowerment and the Family.
[339] Law No. 2000/011 of 10 July 2009 to law down the Financial Regime of the Regional and local Authorities.

In the regions general coordination will be overseen by the Governors while the Regional Delegates in charge of women's empowerment and gender promotion will be responsible for technical coordination. This ministry actually sees into it that policies in favour of women economic empowerment are implemented especially those concerning the rural women in Cameroon thus economically empowering these women.

5.2.2. Ministry of Decentralisation and Local Development (MINDDEVEL)

This Ministry was created by the presidential Decree of March 2, 2018[340]. This Ministry is responsible for the development, monitoring, implementation and evaluation of the Government's policy on decentralization as well as the promotion local development. With regard to its mission on Decentralisation, the ministry has as mission, the development of legislation and regulations relating to the organization and functioning of Decentralized Territorial Communities; the evaluation and monitoring of the implementation of decentralization; monitoring and control of Decentralized Territorial Communities; application of legislation and regulations on civil status; under the authority of the President of the Republic, the exercise of State supervision over the Decentralized Territorial Collectivities.

MINDDEVEL mission in the field of local development includes the Promotion of the socio-economic development of Decentralized Territorial Communities and the Promotion of good governance within Decentralized Territorial Communities. With a Decree setting a general Decentralisation grant in place[341],this Ministry can better carry out its functions which goes a long way to economically empower the rural women since their mission is local development and the rural women form part of the rural communities in Cameroon.

5.2.3. The Ministry of Small and Medium Size Enterprises (MINPMEESA)

Supporting small or medium scale enterprise development has become popular among planners and policy makers in poor countries everywhere. The advancement of this strategy is in capitalising on the entrepreneurial instinct of people for economic growth of the country.[342]The rural women have entrepreneurship instinct through their various agricultural and petit trading activities. Capitalising on these women entrepreneurial instincts and encouraging

---

[340] Decree No. 2018/190 of March 2, 2018, modifying and supplementing certain provisions of Decree No. 2011/408 of December 9, 2011 on the organization of the Government.
[341] Decree No. 2019/0829/PM of 22 February 2019.
[342] Creevey Lucy E. (1996). Changing Women's Lives and Work.IT Publications vol 1. p.1.

them to create SMEs will certainly make them to become economically empowered.

The Ministry of Small and Medium-sized Enterprises, Social Economy and Handicrafts (MINPMEESA) was created in December 2004[343]. It shall be responsible for the elaboration, implementation and evaluation of Government policy with regard to the development of small and medium sized enterprises, social economy and handicrafts. It is responsible for promoting and supervising small and medium-sized enterprises and handicrafts, developing Social Economy, in collaboration with professional organisations, a data and projects bank for investors in small and medium-sized enterprises and handicraft sectors ,promoting the spirit of entrepreneurship and private initiative, monitoring the activities of bodies offering assistance to small and medium sized enterprises and handicrafts, promoting small and medium sized enterprises and handicrafts products, in collaboration with the professional organisations concerned, monitoring professional organisations of small and medium sized enterprises and handicrafts, monitoring the evolution of the informal sector and studies related thereof, identifying and studying possibilities of the migration of informal sector actors towards handicrafts and micro-enterprises; and studying all measures aimed at informing and training informal sector actors.

The ministry is made up of the minister in charge of SMEs, a general secretariat, technical directions. Related structures under the ministry supervision include mission team members, organizational chart and Decentralised services. Under the ministry we have SMEs, which are created at the regional levels headed by Regional Delegates of SMEs. We have SMEs created at all the 10-regional headquarters in the 10 regions of the country. In the North West region, the regional delegate heads the SMEs. He heads all the other units operating under the SMEs. These sub-units include Bank of SMEs, the Department of Social Economy, the one- stop -shop center for the creation of businesses, the support center for building and facilitating the growth of SMEs. This is what obtains in all the 10 regions of Cameroon. With this structural setup, it is easy for the implementation of the law on SMEs and thus the economic empowerment of the rural women.

The one stop shops and business support centers under the SMEs are bodies put in place for the creation and financing of businesses. They equally provide assistance both financially and giving technically, giving advice to those who

---

[343]Presidential Decree No. 2004/320 to lay down the organisation of the Government, amended and supplemented by Decree No. 2011/408 of 09 December 2011 and recently supplemented by that of 27 May 2013 No. 2013/169.

want to develop enterprises. This help to further encourage and promote the rural women in their entrepreneurship venture since they can receive advice on how to go about developing their own businesses and even receive financial aids to develop her business thus becoming economically empowered.

A 2020 Decree[344] appointed officials in the Ministry of Small and Medium-sized Enterprises, Social Economy and Handicrafts for the effective functioning of this Ministry. The SME Promotion Agency (APME) was created by a Presidential Decree[345]. This Agency is a public administrative body with legal personality and financial autonomy, placed under the technical supervision of the Ministry of SMEs and under the financial supervision of the Ministry of Finance. It has as missions Supporting and monitoring SMEs, facilitating enterprise creation procedures, Supervising and advising idea and project holders, competences capacity building, setting up a data and project database, promoting technological innovation, developing a SME observatory, Start-up incubation and mentoring in partnership with large Enterprises.

MINPMEESA, a ministry in Cameroon that is out to implement government measures to boast its economic domain through the creation of SMEs goes a long way to promote the rural women to grow economically since the facilitation in the creation of enterprises by bringing the to the regional levels and further creating a one-stop-shop at every level for the facilitation of the creation of these small enterprises will obviously be a motivating factor for these rural women to create small businesses and thus become economically empowered.

5.2.4. Ministry of Economy, Planning and Regional Development in Cameroon (MINEPAT)

A 2008 decree[346] created MINEPAT in Cameroon. MINEPAT is responsible for land use planning at the national level, public investments and the control and evaluation of development programs. This Ministry has a strong mandate and is able to carry out activities that require inter-ministerial collaboration. It also coordinates industrial, commercial and trade matters and liaises with various public and private sector organisations to facilitate the implementation of government sector policies related to trade and industry. This is in line with the Ministry's mission statement. To facilitate and promote the growth, development and competitiveness of commercial, trade and industrial sectors in order to enhance socio-economic development.

---

[344] Decree No. 2020/1036/PM of 31 March 2020.
[345] Decree No. 2013/092 of 3 April 2013.
[346] Decree No 2008/220 of 4th July 2008.

Through this goal, the MINEPAT will articulate policies, develop legislation and create an environment that will focus on making the Cameroon commercial, trade, and industrial base sustainable and globally competitive. The Ministry is responsible for the following portfolio functions[347],investment Promotion Policy, Trade Licensing Policy, Privatization Policy, Commercial, Industrial and Trade Policy, Companies and Business names, Foreign Trade Policy and Agreements, Industrial Research, Patents, Trade Marks and Designs, Weights and Measures, Competition and Fair Trade, Medium and Small-Scale Enterprises (SMEs) Development, Standardization, Standards and Quality Assurance.[348]

This ministry makes sure government developmental projects are implemented by carrying out evaluations on its implementation at the regional levels in Cameroon. Thus, economically empowering these rural women through the implementation of these measures.

5.2.5. Ministry of Mines, Industry and Technological Development (MINMIDT)

According to the presidential Decree,[349] the ministry of Mines, Industry and Technological Development is in charge of the elaboration of the government mining and industrial policy and technological development strategies within the various sectors of the national economy. Among its several duties includes local transformation of mining, agricultural and forestry products, in conjunction with the Ministry of Agriculture and Rural Development, the ministry of forestry and wildlife. This ministry is in charge of the elaboration of the mining map; geological prospection and mining activities; the valuation of mining, oil and gas resources; the management of mining and gaseous natural resources; the monitoring of the upstream oil sector, the promotion local industry; the development of industrial zones; the promotion of private investment; the promotion of investment in the mining, industry and technological development sector, in conjunction with the Ministry of the Economy, Planning and Regional Development; the elaboration and implementation of the country's industrialisation plan; the elaboration, dissemination and follow up of the implementation of instruments provided for by the Investment Charter; local transformation of mining, agricultural and forestry products, in conjunction with the Ministry of Agriculture and Rural Development, the Ministry of Forestry and Wildlife and the other administrations concerned; technological development, in

---

[347] As contained in Government Gazette Note Number 547 of 2004.
[348] Ibid.
[349] Decree No 2012/432 of 1 October 2012.

conjunction with the Ministry of Scientific Research and Innovation; technological industrial monitoring, in conjunction with the authorities concerned; the promotion and defence of a quality label for products meant for the local market and for export, in conjunction with the administrations concerned; the follow up of activities of the National Board of Industrial Free Zones and the Mission for the Development and Management of Industrial Zones, the follow up of standards and quality, in conjunction with the relevant administrations.

It liaises between the Government and the World Intellectual Property Organization (WIPO), the African Intellectual Property Organization (OAPI), as well as the United Nations Industrial Development Organization (UNIDO) in conjunction with the Ministry of External Relations. It has supervision over public or semi-public corporations involved in its sector of competence, organizations that provide advocacy and assistance to industries and companies in charge of supervising the mining sector, notably: National Investment Corporation (SNI); The Agency for Standards and Quality control (ANOR) Investment Promotion Agency (IPA); National Board Industrial Free Zones (ONZFI) ; the Chamber of Commerce, Industry, Mines and Handicrafts (CCIMA) and the Industrial Zones Development and Management Authority (MAGZI).The implementation by these measures by this ministry will certainly promote the rural women economically.

5.2.6. Ministry of Post and Telecommunication

The Ministry of Posts and Telecommunications shall be placed under the authority of a Minister. A presidential Decree[350]creates the Cameroon telecommunication company. The Minister of Posts and Telecommunications shall be responsible for the development and the implementation of the government's Posts, Telecommunications and Information and Communication Technologies policy. In this regard, he shall: Study, set up or make it possible to be set up infrastructure and equipment corresponding to the Posts and Telecommunications sectors; ensure the development of Information and Communication Technologies (ICTs), as well as electronic communications in all their forms, in conjunction with the Administrations concerned. He shall also ensure the promotion of investments in the sector, in conjunction with the Ministry of the Economy, Planning and Regional Development and the bodies concerned. The implementation by this government measure by this ministry will economically empower the rural women it will ensure communication flows to

---

[350] Decree No.98/198 of 08 September 1998 to create the Cameroon Telecommunication company in Cameroon.

all sector of the national economy enabling the rural women to benefit from information flow which will enable her to be more informed on the activities they carry out and strategies to use in order to become economically empowered.

5.2.7. Ministry of Agriculture and Rural Development

Created by a 2005 Decree[351] Placed under the authority of a director, the Directorate of Rural Engineering and Improvement of Living Environment in Rural areas this ministry is responsible for defining and monitoring the implementation of a regulatory framework for the development and management of rural areas; carrying out, within its field of competence, programs to improve the living environment in rural areas; monitoring the implementation of programs to improve the living environment in rural areas; the design and monitoring of the implementation of programs and projects for the development of rural areas, in liaison with the administrations and organizations concerned; participation in the study and establishment of soil development and restoration plans in rural areas; the formulation of policies and strategies for the development of agricultural hydraulics; the design and monitoring of the implementation of hydro-agricultural development programs and projects; developing and monitoring the implementation of management programs for hydro-agricultural structures, in liaison with the administrations and organizations concerned; support for producers and rural communities for the development and management of their hydro-agricultural projects; the definition of water quality standards for agricultural use and the monitoring of the application of these standards, in liaison with the administrations concerned; definition and monitoring of application in terms of the use of water and agricultural machinery; approval of agricultural machinery and equipment; the development of sector performance indicators and the implementation of rural engineering programs. The implementation of these measures by this ministry further promotes the rural women economically.

5.2.8. The Ministry of Justice

An important aspect when it comes to the economic empowerment of the rural women is their ability to obtain justice from a court when their rights are being violated. The ministry of justice is out for the promotion and the protection of the rights of all its citizens, the women inclusive. This it does through its various courts available in different levels in Cameroon. In Cameroon we have the court of first instance, the high court, the court of Appeal and the Supreme Court.

---

[351] Decree No 2005/118 of 15th April 2005 organising the Ministry Agriculture and Rural Development.

Access to justice[352] refers to the substantive and procedural mechanisms existing in any particular society designed to ensure that citizens have the opportunity of seeking redress for the violation of their legal rights within the legal system[353]. It focuses on the existing rules and procedures to be used by citizens to approach the courts for the determination of their civil rights and obligations[354]. It has been said that access to justice is not limited to the procedural mechanism for the resolution of disputes but includes other variables like the physical conditions of the premises where justice is dispensed, the time it takes for the delivering of justice, the moral quality of the dispenser of justice, the observance of the general principles of the rule of law, the affordability of the cost of seeking justice in terms of time and money, the quality of the legal system. Access to justice so explained is therefore a core right essential for the protection and promotion of all other civil, cultural, economic, political and social rights. It is therefore apparent that access to justice is a charged concept that embraces the nature, mechanism and even the quality of justice obtainable in a society as well as the place of the individual within this judicial matrix. It is also important to underscore the fact that access to justice is undeniably an important barometer for assessing not only the rules of law in any society but also the quality of governance in that society. While justice itself is an elusive concept, it can loosely be said that it implies equality and fairness; and for there to be meaningful access to justice, there must be some element of fairness and equity in a system to guarantee the realization of the basic fundamental rights. Moreover, to enhance access to justice in any society, it is necessary for certain basic infrastructure to be put in place and the requisite number and quality of the personnel involved in the scheme. [355]With access to justice by all rural women, their rights are protected which will further empower them economically.

---

[352] According to John Rawls, justice is the principle that free and rational persons, concerned with furthering their own interest, would accept in an initial position of equality as defining the fundamental terms of their association. What this position supports is that while each person has different ends and goals, different background and talent, each ought to have a fair chance to develop his or her talents and to pursue those goals –fair equality for opportunity. It's not a race or contest where the talented or gifted prevails; it should be complete cooperation among all so that there may be reasonable life for all. Available at https://en.m.wikipedia.org .(Consulted on the 20/05/2024).

[353] Nzouedja Tchana Anthony (2021). Access to justice and Human Rights Protection in Cameroon: Problem and Prospects. A Bi-Monthly, Peer Reviewed International Journal.Vol.2 pp.34-35.

[354] Ibid.

[355] Ibid.

5.3. Regional Institutions for Women Economic Empowerment in Cameroon

Within the African continent, institutions such as the Economic Communities of Central African States (CEMAC), the Central African Monetary Union (UMAC), the Central African Economic Union (UEAC), the Organisation for the Harmonisation of Business Law in Africa (OHADA) and the African Union (AU), through their policies and activities are in one way or the other promote the economic empowerment of rural women.

5.3.1. CEMAC Institutions

The CEMAC treaty[356] stipulates that the main aim of the Community is to promote peace and the harmonious development of the Member States, through the institution of two Unions, an Economic Union and a Monetary Union.[357] In each of these two areas, the Member States intend to move from the existing form of cooperation between them to the creation of a Union conducive to completing the process of economic and monetary integration.

5.3.1.1. The Central African Monetary Union (UMAC)

The UMAC[358] manages all issues related to currency, finance, and banks. A central feature of the UMAC is the adoption of a common currency, the "Coopération Financière en Afrique Centrale" (CFA) franc, the issuance of which is entrusted to a common central bank known as the Bank of Central African States (BEAC).In general terms, the UMAC is responsible for the management of the rules governing currency issuance; the pooling of foreign currency reserves; a common body responsible for the supervision of insurance accounting framework, which also covers the member countries of the West African franc zone, the Organization for the Harmonization of Business Law in Africa, the free circulation of banknotes and coins and freedom of transfers among the states of the union; the preparation of measures aimed at the harmonization of monetary, banking, and financial legislation, and exchange arrangements; and multilateral surveillance, in collaboration with Central African Economic Union (UEAC), through the coordination of economic policies and the establishment of national fiscal policies consistent with the common monetary policy of the union. With this common monetary policy member countries will have a common currency and distribution that will facilitate economic growth in their various countries.

---

[356] Article 2 of the 1994 CEMAC Treaty.
[357] The texts creating and governing the Central African Monetary Union (UMAC), the Central African Economic Union (UEAC), the Community Parliament, and the Court of Justice of the Community complement the treaty establishing the CEMAC.
[358] Convention of 5 July 1996 governing the Monetary Union of Central Africa (UMAC).

Since Cameroon is a signatory to the CEMAC Treaty it will benefit from this economic development and so will the rural women in Cameroon.

The BEAC also manages the common pool of foreign currency reserves; a common authority for banking supervision and microfinance activities, the Central African Banking Commission, which has extensive powers to regulate the banking system of member states. These include administrative powers (licensing of credit institutions and their managers, and the like), and regulatory and jurisdictional powers to sanction any noncompliance observed, with all six countries being subject to a single body of banking laws; a common stock market, the Central African Stock Exchange; a common body responsible for financial market supervision, the Central African Financial Oversight Commission; a common body responsible for the management of means of payment, the Central African Electronic Banking Company; a common body responsible for the regulation of means of payment, the Central African Electronic Banking Authority; a common body responsible for combating money laundering and terrorist financing, the Task Force on Anti-Money Laundering and Combating the Financing of Terrorism in Central Africa; a common body responsible for regulation of the insurance market, which also covers the member countries of the West African franc zone, the Inter-African Conference on Insurance Markets.

The uniformity amongst member states in the management of financial transaction facilitates easy cross border business transaction for the economic development of these regions which will obviously go a long way to economically empower the rural women since their produce can be sold across the borders with ease.

5.3.1.2. The Central African Economic Union (UEAC)

The UEAC,[359] which is another institution under CEMAC is responsible for strengthening economic and financial competitiveness by harmonising the rules conducive to improving the business environment,   and regulating its functioning   promoting convergence on sustainable growth through the coordination of economic policies and ensuring the consistency of national fiscal policies with the common monetary policy; creating a common market based on the free movement of goods, services, capital, and people; and fostering the coordination of national sectoral policies, implementation of common actions and adoption of common policies, particularly in the following areas of agriculture, livestock farming, fisheries, industry, commerce, tourism, transport, community land use planning and development and major infrastructural projects,

---

[359] Convention of 5 July 1996 governing the Economic Union of Central Africa (UEAC).

telecommunications, information and communication technologies, social dialogue, gender issues, good governance and human rights, energy, the environment and natural resources, research, and education and vocational training.

Several specialised institutions of the UEAC contribute to achieving these goals: the Central African Development Bank; the Economic Commission for Livestock; Meat; and Fisheries Resources; the Court of Justice of the Community; the Regional Hotel and Tourism School; the Central African School of Telecommunications; the Development Fund of the Community; the Institute of Economics and Finance; the Sub-regional Institute of Statistics and Applied Economics; the Sub-regional Multi sectorial Institute of Ap plied Technology, Planning, and Project Evaluation; and the Organization for the Coordination and Control of Endemic Diseases in Central Africa. These are further measure which empower the Cameroonian rural woman economically since Cameroon is a signatory of CEMAC.

5.3.1.3. The Common Court of Justice and Arbitration (CCJA)

The Common Court of Justice and Arbitration (CCJA) ensures the uniform application and interpretation of the OHADA Uniform Acts across all member-states by exercising a dual role such as being the highest court of OHADA, the CCJA operates as a supreme court with respect to the OHADA uniform acts. The CCJA reviews decisions handed down by national Courts of Appeal dealing with the application of the OHADA law and ensures that any arbitration proceedings are in conformity with the uniform act on arbitration. No matter where the controversy originates, the CCJA ensures a similar outcome. As an advisory authority, the CCJA hears issues concerning the interpretation of the uniform law referred to it either by domestic courts or by the states parties themselves.[360]

5.3.1.4. The African Union (AU)

The Regional Economic Communities (RECs) are regional groupings of African states and are the pillars of the AU. All were formed prior to the launch of the AU and have developed individually and have differing roles and structures. The purpose of the RECs is to facilitate regional economic integration between members of the individual regions and through the wider African Economic Community (AEC), which was established under the Abuja Treaty (1991). This Treaty, which has been in operation since 1994, ultimately seeks to create an African Common Market using the RECs as building blocks. In so doing it will

---

[360] Article 14 (1) of the 2008 Treaty.

promote the economy of member states and in turn promote the rural economy of Cameroon of which the rural women will benefit.

5.4. International Institutions for Women Economic Empowerment in Cameroon

Apart from national and regional institutions, there are also international institutions with policies and activities which promote the economic empowerment of rural women. These institutions amongst others include the United Nation Development Program (UNDP) and the International Labour Organisation (ILO).

5.4.1. United Nation Development Program (UNDP)

UNDP Cameroon has contributed to gender equality in its area of intervention focused on transformative, inclusive and sustainable growth by relying on the country program document (CPD) 2022-2026. This document aligns with the UNDP strategic plan 2021-2025 and the gender equality strategy 2022-2025, which aim to accelerate progress towards the sustainable development goals (SDGs) and strengthen resilience to crises and shocks. UNDP Cameroon guided by its country office gender strategy has implemented initiatives to promote women's economic empowerment, to enhance their participation in inclusive governance and peacebuilding, and reduce gender inequalities and discrimination in the areas of environment, natural resources and climate change.[361] Some of achievements include: Supporting women entrepreneurs in developing innovative technologies, especially in the sectors of green energy, sustainable agriculture and circular economy, Strengthening the capacities of women leaders and women's organizations to influence public policies, prevent and resolve conflicts, and promote social cohesion in crisis-affected areas, Combating all forms of gender-based violence, including female genital mutilation, early and forced marriage, and sexual and gender-based violence, Promoting equal opportunities and access to essential services for women and girls, especially in education, health, water and sanitation and raising awareness and advocating for gender mainstreaming in natural resource management, disaster risk reduction and climate change adaptation.

UNDP Cameroon continues to work with the government, development partners, other UN agencies, civil society and local communities to achieve gender equality and women empowerment development priorities through three strategic pillars: Transformative, inclusive and sustainable growth; Inclusive

---

[361] UNDP Cameroon (2024), Gender Equality and Women Empowerment. Available at https://www.undp.org. (Consulted on the 22/05/2024).

governance and peace building; Environmental sustainability and climate disaster risk management.

5.4.2. International Labour Organisation (ILO)

International labour organisation was the first specialised agency of the United Nations Set up in 1946 and it's the only surviving organ of the league of nation established after the first war. It's functions today are to promote social Justice and ensure recognition internationally of human and labour rights[362] .Freedom of association and assembly has special relevance to employment. The need for workers to protect themselves against powerful exploitative employers was recognized both domestically through the growth of Trade Unions and through the international labour organisation, the tripartite UN agency that brings together government employers and workers of its member state in common action to promote decent work throughout the world.[363].

In Cameroon so much has been done by the ILO towards the economic empowerment of the rural women. A training of trainers on the ILO tools, Think.COOP, Start.COOP and My.COOP, was held in Bertoua, in the Eastern Region of Cameroon from 14 to 24 November 2022.This training was organised within the framework of the project "Empowering women for resilient economies and peaceful communities in the refugee-affected regions of East and Adamawa in Cameroon " funded by the Korea Cooperation Agency International (KOICA) from 2021-2024, this project aims to contribute to economic growth and social cohesion between refugee and host communities through the development of women entrepreneurship and cooperatives in agricultural value chains.

This training falls within the framework of the implementation of its 2nd objective, namely to support women refugees and host populations to establish sustainable, flourishing and ecological agro-businesses and cooperatives. As part of this objective, the project plans to strengthen the capacity of women entrepreneurs and cooperatives to create sustainable businesses and will facilitate access to relevant financial services.[364]

For the ILO, the promotion of small and sustainable enterprises is a key strategy for generating decent and productive employment for women and men. Women's entrepreneurship can make a particularly strong contribution to the

---

[362] Halstead Peter (2012), Unlocking Human Rights. Hodder Education, P.322.
[363] Ibid.
[364] ILO (2022). Training of trainers in Cameroon on ILO tools relating to the development of cooperatives. Available at https://www.ilo.org.(Consulted on 23/05/2024).

economy and society. However, since women face gender-based and systemic barriers to starting and growing their businesses, they tend to be overrepresented in micro enterprises, in low growth sectors and operate mainly in the informal economy.

In order to remove these barriers, it is important to understand the specific context and find realistic solutions to eliminating them. Therefore, the ILO and African Development Bank developed an assessment methodology that enables stakeholders to build actionable recommendations for improving the environment for women's entrepreneurship development.[365]

The ILO Women's Entrepreneurship Development and Economic Empowerment (WEDEE) Project works towards enhancing economic opportunities for women by supporting women who are starting, formalizing and growing their own enterprises and by mainstreaming gender equality into the ILO's Decent Work Agenda on enterprise development is another means by the ILO to promote the rural women economically in Cameroon. WEDEE is also being implemented in East Africa in Tanzania, Kenya and Uganda, and has been instrumental in advancing economic development and access to opportunities for women by supporting the establishment and growth of more women-led businesses, enabling them not only to sustain their families, but also to contribute to job creation and economic growth.[366]

The project strategy aims to concentrate its activities on helping micro and small women entrepreneurs access appropriate business development services (both financial and non-financial) and local and international markets, and supporting women entrepreneurs to engage further through stronger networks, notably women entrepreneurs' associations. The project also overall aims to increase the knowledge and understanding of WED of ILO constituents and implementing partners, its links to men and society at large as well as to economic empowerment of women and gender equality. Thus, economically empowering the Cameroonian rural woman.

5.5. Other Non-Governmental Organisations and Associations

There are a host of other non-governmental organisations and associations that are involved with the economic empowerment of rural women. These

---

[365] Stevenson Lois et al (2011). Assessment of the environment for the development of women's entrepreneurship in Cameroon, Mali, Nigeria, Rwanda, and Senegal. Available at https://www.ilo.org. (Consulted on the 23/05/2024).
[366] ILO (2022). Women Entrepreneurship Development and Economic empowerment. Available at https://www.ilo.org.(Consulted on the 23/05/2024).

organisations assist rural women in diverse form, be it materially or technically. Some of these NGOs or association have national competence while others are internationally recognised.

5.5.1. National NGOs and Associations

A good number of NGOs and association operating at the national level have amongst their objectives or plan of action the empowerment of women in general and rural women in particular. This is for instance the case of the Cameroon Association of Women Lawyers (ACAFEJ) this Association fights for the protection of female rights[367] thus, the rights of the rural women to become economically development.

Among other measures put in place by the Cameroon government to combat violence against women is the collaboration with several civil society organizations through the approval of a joint action platform to combat violence against women and girls. The international center for the promotion of creation, lawyer without Borders, Association to Combat Violence against women (ALVF), Cameroon Council of Imams and Muslim Dignitaries, Cameroon national Association for family and welfare, (CAMNAFAW)

Apart from financial assistance, these NGOs and Associations provide medical, psychological, social and legal assistance as well as counselling services to women to assist them resolve or overcome some difficulties such as financial instability. Most of these national NGOs and Associations work in collaboration with and receive assistance and support from international organisations.

5.5.2. International NGOs and Association

A number of NGOs and Association operation beyond the Cameroonian frontiers through their policies and actions, also contribute in the economic empowerment of rural women in Cameroon. These include amongst others: the UN Women, Association for Women's Rights in Development, Womankind Worldwide, Plan International, Equality Now, Women for Women International, Global Fund for Women, Men Engage Alliance, Gender at Work and the World Bank

5.5.2.1. The UN Women

The UN Women is the United Nations Entity for Gender Equality and the Empowerment of Women. It is dedicated to gender equality and promotes the economic empowerment of rural women. The agency was established to accelerate progress on meeting women's needs across the world. It supports the

---

[367] MINJUSTICE, Cameroon Association of female lawyers, Available at www.docstore.ohchr.org (consulted on the 12/02/2020 at 9:30am).

UN members states in achieving global standards of gender equality, and it works closely with civil society organizations and governments to design and implement policies, laws and services that benefit women. The UN women focus on four priority areas amongst which is to ensure that, women have income security, decent work and economic autonomy.

The UN Women also closely works on positioning gender equality as fundamental to the UN sustainable development goals and assists the members states to hold the UN system accountable for its own commitments on gender equality.

5.5.2.2. Association for Women's Rights in Development

The Association for Women's Rights in Development (AWID) is an international organization working to achieve gender equality and women's human rights across the word. The vision of AWID is "a world where feminist realities flourish, where resources and power are shared in ways that enable everyone, and future generations, to thrive and realize their full potential with dignity, love and respect, and where Earth nurtures life in all its diversity". The organization supports the gender justice movements to become driving forces in oppression.

The AWID closely works with activists and policy makers worldwide to influence gender policies and practice. It facilitates dialogue and strategies on key issues by connecting actors to share their knowledge, experiences and ideas on relevant issues and mobilizes gender equality movements to support collective actions with feminist causes.

5.5.2.3. Womankind Worldwide

Womankind Worldwide is an international organization for women's rights that works in solidarity and equal partnership with women's rights organizations and movements with a goal to transform the lives of women. The vision of the organization is a just world where the rights of all women are respected, realized and valued. Together with its local partners, the Womankind Worldwide helps women and girls transform their lives by providing them with shelters to escape violence and implements projects with community leaders to help women join to talk about what they want to change in their communities and how to achieve that. It also supports the women's rights movements by providing technical support, funding opportunities and advocacy platform. The organization also uses its expertise to influence policy changes and to make sure that women's rights are placed at the heart of the international agenda.

5.5.2.4. Plan International

Plan International is a global development human rights and humanitarian organization working to advance rights of children and equality for girls. It closely works with young people, children and communities to tackle the root causes of discrimination against girls, vulnerability and exclusion and enables them to respond and prepare for adversity and practice. Plan International influence policies and practices at local, national and global levels by using knowledge, experience and reach. Some of the core objectives of Plan International is achieving gender equality, promoting gender justice and fostering an inclusive society. The organization confronts, and challenges human rights violations and discrimination based on gender, as well as stereotyping and unequal power relations between women, men, boys and girls to promote rights and gender equality. Plan International fosters culture that encompasses its commitment to gender equality and adoption of good practices, positive attitudes and inclusion.

5.5.2.5. Women for Women International

Women for Women International is an international women's rights organization that supports the most marginalized women in countries affected by war and conflict. The organization conducts projects that enable women to earn and save money, influence decisions in their communities and homes, improve their well-being and health and connect to networks for support. So far, the organization has helped to more than 478.000 women across the world to rebuild their lives after the war. Women for Women International uses its voice to call for global attention to the unique role that women play in advancing peace throughout society.

Through organization's projects, women learn about their rights on key issues such as access to land, voting, divorce, domestic abuse and custody over children. In this way the organization strives to achieve gender equality and equips and empowers women to stand for themselves. The organization also advocates for a long-term change for marginalized women who survived war, by partnering up with other organizations to influence policies and practices.

5.5.2.6. Equality Now

Equality Now is an international organization founded with the mission of using legal advocacy to protect and promote the human rights of women and girls. It uses law to create equal and just world for women and girls. It attracts global attention to media on individual cases of abuse and uses international human rights law to advocate with policymakers and puts pressure on national governments to adopt and enforce good laws. Equality now partners up with other organizations to ensure that individual cases are visible on the global agenda.

Equality Now is dedicated to achieving gender equality and, thus, it cooperates with individuals, institutions, and coalitions encompassing grassroots activists, survivors, legal reformers, lawyers, service providers, corporations and national and regional women's organizations and uses their knowledge and connections to local communities to achieve change. It puts pressure on countries to adopt gender equality laws and holds governments accountable for abuses of such laws.

5.5.2.7. Men Engage Alliance

Men Engage Alliance is a global alliance consisted of many country networks that are spread across many regions, hundreds of non-governmental organizations and the UN agencies, working towards advancing gender equality and justice, human rights and social justice, with a mission to achieve a world in which all people can enjoy healthy and equitable relationships and their full potential.

The Men Engage Alliance works on engaging men and boys in gender equality and tries to build and improve the practice on engaging men in achieving gender justice. It also advocates for policy changes on key issues where gender directly affects the lives of women and men at local, national, regional and international levels. The organization works in the following areas: promoting sexual and reproductive health and rights, increasing HIV and AIDS prevention and treatment, ending violence against women and girls, combating homophobia/transphobia and advocating for LGBTI rights, reducing forms of violence between men and boys, preventing child sexual exploitation, sexual abuse and trafficking, supporting men's positive involvement in maternal and child health, as fathers or caregivers and addressing macro-level policies that perpetuate gender inequalities.

5.5.2.8. Global Fund for Women

Global Fund for Women is one of the world's leading organizations for gender equality, and human rights of girls and women. The organization was created with a mission to amplify the courageous work of women who are building social movements and challenging the status quo. The organization campaigns for zero violence, political and economic empowerment, and sexual and reproductive health and rights of women globally.

The aim of the Global Fund for Women is for every woman and girl to be able to realize their rights as set out in the Universal Declaration of Human Rights, since these are essential for women's equality. The Fund fights for and stands for woman's rights to decide when and if she wants to have child and, if so, to have a high-quality health care during pregnancy and after birth. The Fund follows and supports two critical documents about gender equality-the Convention on the Elimination of all Forms of Discrimination Against Women (CEDAW) and the Beijing Declaration and Platform for Action, both affecting women's right in all aspects of life.

5.5.2.9. Gender at Work

Gender at Work is an international feminist knowledge network working to build inclusive cultures and end discrimination against women. It partners up with researchers and activists across the world to produce new knowledge on inequality structures and embedded societal discriminatory norms and to produce innovative approaches and tools to transform them in organizations and communities.

The organization believes that the world is facing the crisis of democratic institutions, in which the actors who fight to achieve social justice have been undercut and where spaces for advocacy and action of civil society groups has been restricted. Therefore, the Gender at Work offers a wide range of consulting services to organizations to strengthen their contributions to gender equality and advance feminist leadership. It also helps activists to tell their stories and share their insights on gender inequalities with a broader public.[368]

5.5.2.10. The World Bank

The World Bank Group Entrepreneurship Snapshots, a joint effort by the World Bank Development Research Group, the international Finance Corporation (IFC) and the Kauffman Foundation is a comprehensive dataset on enterprise. It provides an indicator of business creation around the World and facilitates the investigation of the factors that foster dynamic private sector growth.

The World Development Report by the World Bank in 2012 focused on Gender Equality and Development. The report considers equality among genders as a "core development issue" as inequalities in gender can translate into inequalities in health, education economic opportunities and in the ability to make choices within households and societies; according to the World Bank focusing on gender equality is not only fair, it is smart economics[369] DUFLO explains that

---

[368] Ibid.
[369] Van O. T., (2012), World Bank Report on Gender Equality and Development Capacity, Available at <http//www.europa.eu> (consulted on the 10/02/2020 at 9:07am).

there is a direct relationship between economic development and women empowerment[370] defined by the level of access these women have to constituent variables such as health, education earning opportunities, rights and political participation. Economic development should bring together the creation and stabilisation of institutions in any country, protecting women from hunger and illnesses.[371]

5.6. Conclusion

Laws have been put in place both nationally and internationally to economically empower the rural women in Cameroon. To this effect, several national, regional and international institutions are equally in place for the implementation of these laws. We can therefore state rural women economic empowerment is very vital to the Cameroon's economy for it helps to develop the growth of the national economy.

The fight against gender-based discrimination by the government of Cameroon and those other institution both governmental and non-governmental as seen above is a great move by the government to economically empower the rural women in Cameroon. Discrimination against women is a phenomenon common in Cameroon and in the rural setting in particular where the women or girl's child is relegated to the background as will be expatiated in chapter seven of this work where we will be examining the various limitations to the economic empowerment of the rural women in Cameroon. Putting in place these institutions that educate, promote and punishes perpetrators who violate the rights of the rural women to become economically empowered only acts as a booster to rural women economic empowerment…

---

[370] Duflo E., (2012) Women Empowerment and Economic Development, Journal of Economic Literature, American Economic Association, Vol. 50, No 4, pp.1051-1079.
[371] Schuler D. (2006), The uses and misuses of gender related development index and gender empowerment measures; review of literature, Journal of Human Development. vol 7, pp. 161-181.

CHAPTER SIX

AN ASSESSMENT OF THE MECHANISMS TOWARDS THE ECONOMIC DEVELOPMENT OF THE RURAL WOMEN IN CAMEROON

6.1. Introduction

According to the theory of female Entrepreneurship coined by Babara Orser and Catherine Elliote, entrepreneurship is viewed as a mechanism to create economic self-sufficiency and equity-based outcomes for girls and women. This Chapter thus examines the various mechanisms by the government and NGOs towards the economic empowerment of the rural women in Cameroon.

The government has thus identified several policy options.[372] Among the priority options to improve business climate the government has taken into consideration the need to fight against all administrative, fiscal, custom and judicial obstacles impeding the development of economic activities, the need to improve on the incentive system for private investment to strengthen economic attractiveness and the need to alleviate the cost and procedure related to land availability among others. The economic exclusion of women is characterised by poverty and unemployment due to their limited participation in the development of the society.

It is for this reason that particular effort is made by the Cameroon government towards promoting the women especially the rural women to become economically empowered by ensuring them access to commination and technology, encouraging them pursue formal education, by fighting against discriminatory practices, by simplifying the procedure to access land and finances resources as well as promoting and protecting the rights to work.

6.2. Access to Communication and Technology

The administration in charge of telecommunications activities in Cameroon is the ministry of Posts and Telecommunications established at independence. Seeing that communications is the knot which ties both the national and international business community together and that such an activity must only be run by a structure with a business outlook, the government set up the international telecommunications corporation of Cameroon, commonly known and called by

---

[372] Kouam Jean -Cedric (2023). The Urgent Need to Improve the Business Climate in Cameroon. Available at http://onpolicy.org. (Consulted on the 15/09/2023).

its French acronym INTELCAM.[373] However in 1998 Cameroon Telecommunications Corporation (CAMTEL) succeeded INTELCAM. The law on telecommunication[374] governs telecommunications in Cameroon. It shall lay down the conditions for the installation, exploitation and balanced development of telecommunications, encourage and facilitate private sector involvement in telecommunications development within a competitive environment aim at enhancing the harmonious development of telecommunications networks and services with a view to ensuring the contribution of this sector to national economic development and satisfying the numerous needs of users and the population[375]. This law shall apply all over the territory of Cameroon to the various telecommunications services[376].This provision by the law will enable information to spread all over the national territory of Cameroon especially to the rural sector which is badly in need of information that can better her economy. The rural women in particular can be economically empowered through the information and education they get from the government and other bodies such as NGOs and civil societies from the radio or television on how they can assert their rights and become economically empowered.

However, when the law goes ahead to delimit its scope of application, excluding radio and television broadcasting enterprises in respect of all their production and programming activities as well as authorizations to use radio and television broadcasting frequencies, State installations set up for the purpose of national defence or public security, or using frequency bands directly assigned to a government service for the exclusive satisfaction of its specific needs, in accordance win the recommendations with prescriptions of the International Telecommunications Union[377], this acts as a shortcoming of the law and thus its ineffectiveness in the protection of all especially the rural population who badly need this information. It can be stated that it is due to this clause of exclusion under this law that the rural women lack information and thus the remain un empowered in every aspect of life especially in the economic domain.

Sensitisation is also another measure taken by the government to promote rural women economic development in Cameroon. The laws on sensitisation of entrepreneurship in Cameroon include the OHADA law [378] and the law of

---

[373] Law n°82-539 of 28 October 1982.
[374] Law No 98/014 of 14 July 1998.
[375] Section 1 of the 1998 telecommunication law.
[376] Section 2 of the 1998 telecommunication law.
[377] Section 2(2) of the 1998 telecommunication law.
[378] The 1997 OHADA Law as revised on the 30th of January 2014.

14th December by Cameroon authorities[379]. The First Law states that it is no longer an obligation for the registered capital of private limited companies to amount up to one million FCFA. The second Law lowers the minimum registered capital of a Limited Liability Company (LLC) in Cameroon to 100,000 FCFA. These laws help the entrepreneurs to know what it takes to create a private limited company. This will help the rural women know what it takes to create an enterprise thus becoming economically empowered.

The minister of small and medium size enterprise, Social Economy and Handicraft (MINPMEESA), Achille Bassilekin III, has urged business operators in the Northwest region to join approved management centres. He made this plea during the 8th edition of the caravan raising awareness on approved management centres of small and medium size enterprises. It was a two days event that took place in the presence of members of Parliament, regional Delegates, mayors and representatives of some businesses. The caravan had as theme" The membership of small and medium-sized enterprises from the economically depressed areas in approved canters. A Letter of competitiveness and growth". The minister called for business operators in the Northwest region to join approved centres to scale their enterprises and also to meet up with competitive markets. He continuously stated that he hoped that by disseminating the information it will help business people register and also benefit from the various facilities. He stated that they ensure that they make the right and accurate information for business men and women in the region to be part of the economic recovery and reconstruction of the region. Thus, the main aim of the caravan was to sensitize business persons on the advantages and facilities they enjoy by becoming members of the approved centres. The connection of women and family to the internet was set up as a partnership deal between MINPOSTEL and MINPROFF on July 31 2015 to connect the various centres for the promotion of women and the family in Cameroon. It aimed at facilitating access to information on economic Opportunities available throughout the nation. [380] With this, information gets to reach the rural women who will become more encouraged to carry out economic activities such as small medium size enterprises thus empowering them economically. Effective management and implementation of all these measures and strategies in the grass roots of Cameroon is still a myth. Most of the rural areas in Cameroon are still too remote with no motorable roads, no electricity not

---

[379] Law No.2016/014 of 14th December by Cameroon's authorities.
[380] Promise Mboh (2023). SMEs Minister Urges Business Persons to join Approved Management Centers. Available at https://www.the guardianpostcameroon.com. (Consulted on the 29/09/2023).

to talk of communication networks. For these reasons and more, the rural women still remain economically unempowered in Cameroon.

6.3. Access to Education

With regards to the promotion of education and vocational training for women the government of Cameroon has taken reasonable actions concerning the promotion of education and vocational training in Cameroon. To this end the government has put in place a law governing vocational training,[381] and a law laying guidelines for general education.[382] The 1998 law lays down guidelines for education in Cameroon.[383]It states that: 'The State shall guarantee the elaboration and implementation of education policy in collaboration with Regional and Local Authorities (RLAs).Families, as well as public and private institutions, in keeping with this objective, the State draws up and updates the school map".[384] The government of Cameroon has taken reasonable actions by resolving gender disparity in education and training. To this end measures such as award of prizes to the best female learners for the continuation of their studies, informing communities, non-discrimination in the education of the young girl, provision of scholarship and inducement to promote girls in scientific and technical domains, increase the technical and vocational educational schools. The creation of appropriate technological centres and the creation of women's promotion centres, all in a bid to empower these women thus the rural women included for sustainable development. Based on education and vocational training, Vision 2035 hopes that, Cameroon will have to enhance education and vocational training of human resources in many domains such as health, entrepreneurship among others.

The primary objective of the plan, "Document de Stratégie du Secteur de l'Education et de la Formation 2013-2020" is the achievement of quality universal primary education. This objective aligns with the national strategy for growth and employment goal of providing the production system with human capital capable of supporting economic growth. The country has made notable progress in recent years on some indicators, including increasing the textbook/learner ratio, recruiting and deploying new teachers and assessing learning outcomes. The current education sector plan is focused on improving access and equity, quality and relevance, as well as governance and management of the sector.[385] This

---

[381] Law No 2018/010 of 11 July 2018 governing vocational training in Cameroon.
[382] Law No.98/004 of 14 April 1998 on guidelines on general education.
[383] Ibid.
[384] Article 11 of Law No.98/004 of 14 April 1998.
[385] GPE. (2006). Transforming Education in Cameroon. Available athttps://www.globalpartnership.org. (Consulted on the 25/9/2023).

particular law will go a long way to empower the rural women educationally since the educational policies are implemented in collaboration with regional and local authorities who will be able to take into cognisance the actual situation of the women in the various local areas.

Cameroon Government is in a global partnership with PAEQUE (Equity and Quality for Improved Learning). Since 2007, the Global Partnership for Education (GPE) has been providing support to the education sector in Cameroon. The current program, PAEQUE (Equity and Quality for Improved Learning), focuses primarily on improving the quality of education and promoting equity through specific actions such as: Improving literacy and numeracy levels. This enables students to acquire a sound basis in reading and mathematics, GPE contributes to the distribution of reading and mathematics textbooks in public schools. This will encourage especially the rural women who are mostly illiterates to empower themselves through education and even be encouraged to educate their own girl children to go to school. An empowered woman will have the knowledge and even skills for her development. Thus, enabling her to develop her entrepreneurship skill. This will in the short or long run enable the rural women grow their SMEs. The program also Promotes access to education for girls. In some areas, dominant cultural practices are not very favourable to the education of girls. To increase girls' enrolment in the various regions of the country, GPE is supporting awareness campaigns that are broadcast on community radio stations in French, English and local languages (Fufulde, Baya, Bamoun and Pidgin). This effort is reinforced by the distribution of school kits for girls containing textbooks and other supplies.[386] Minorities are integrated into the Anglophone or Francophone education system. To this end, the Constitution ensures the "protection of minorities" and upholds the rights of indigenous populations in accordance with the law[387]. Since the adoption of the education framework Act, native languages have increasingly been integrated into the official curricula. This framework act aims to facilitate learners' understanding of their own and other cultures. It aims to enable students to learn to read, write and speak various languages fluently.

Lack of implementation of all these measures however still accounts for the illiteracy rates that we fine in the rural areas especially among rural women thus making them less empowered of become economically empowered.

---

[386] Signarbieux Ludovic (2017). How Cameroon is strengthening its education system with GPE Support. Available at https.//www.globalpartnership.org. (Consulted on the 29/09/2023).
[387] Education Framework Act No. 98/004 of 14 April 1998.

6.4. Fight against Discriminatory Practices

The fight against Discriminatory Practices is ensures not only by forbidding the application of some repugnant laws but also by putting in place institutions to ensure the effectiveness of the measures.

6.4.1. Non-application of Repugnant Customary Law Rules

The Southern Cameroon's High Court Law,[388] gives judicial backing to the continuous application of customary law rules as well as its applicable quantum. It provides in whole that the High Court shall observe, and enforce the observance of every native law and custom which is not repugnant to natural justice, equity and good conscience nor incompatible with any law for the time being in force, and nothing in this law shall deprive any person of the benefit of any such native law or custom. From the provisions of Section 27(1) above, it can be asserted that our customary law must be enforceable by our non-customary courts, that is, the courts of First Instance, the High Court, the Court of Appeal and the Supreme Court. The Evidence Act[389] alludes to the role of courts in enforcing customs. However, the Customary Courts Ordinance[390]shall be the native law and custom prevailing in the area of jurisdiction of the court so far as it is not repugnant to natural justice, equity and good conscience, nor incompatible either directly or by natural implication with any written law for the time being in force.

In the light of the authorities above, whenever there is a conflict between any written law and custom, the former shall prevail. In order to arrive at this, certain conditions must be met. First of all, the custom must be reasonable and must have been practised from time immemorial. Secondly, the customs must pass two tests, namely, the repugnancy and incompatibility tests. That is to say for the custom to be applicable it must not be repugnant to natural justice, equity and good conscience or incompatible either directly or by natural implication with any written law for the time being in force. However, the debate about women's rights in general and widows' particularly, has been of much concern to women, policy makers and international organisations alike. In a typical traditional African milieu, the woman virtually finds herself in an essentially male-dominated environment. The various customs that obtain in most African countries, the institutions that regulate day to day life are controlled by the men-folk. In this

---

[388] Section 27(1) of the 1955 SCHCL.
[389] Section 2 of the Evidence Act of 1995.
[390] Section 18(l)(a) of the Customary Courts Ordinance Cap. 142 of the Laws of the Federation of Nigeria 1948

way, women have very limited rights[391]. Upon the breakdown of a customary law marriage through death, the widow suddenly finds herself as an object of inheritance. Notwithstanding that this practice is contrary to the law. Cases abound which show that this practice is instead gaining ground. Indeed, upon divorce the woman has little or no rights over property.[392] Customary law is silent on women rights and our courts seem to apply and follow these practices.

Written law consists of all laws enacted by the legislative arm of our State which are binding as soon as they have been promulgated by the Executive arm of the State. And of course, mindful of the bi-jural nature of the Cameroonian State, all constitutional enactments have alluded to, and accepted foreign law: namely English and French laws. Of particular interest to us is English received law which consists of: The Common law, the doctrines of equity, and statutes of general application which were in force in England on the 1st day of January 1900[393]. Inglis, J. re-emphasised the bi-jural nature of the Cameroon[394] in the following words: 'Now there are two systems of law in this Country, in the North West and South West Provinces, it is the common law, English legislation of general application which were in force on 1st January 1900 and any particular legislation made applicable by any other law in force''.

In application of the principles above, the Cameroonian legislature expressly enacted Ordinance No. 81-02 of 29 June 1981 which deals partially amongst other matters with the question of property. This piece of legislation has failed both in its intent and spirit to give guidelines to this disturbing issue of property adjustments between husband and wife upon the breakdown of marriage. As a result, recourse is made to foreign or foreign inspired laws. The Married Women's Property Act 1882 is instructive. It provides that: ''A married woman shall [...] be capable of acquiring, holding, and disposing by will or otherwise, of any real or personal property as her separate property, in the same manner as if she were a feme sole, without the intervention of any trustee.''[395]

---

[391] Temngah Joseph N. (1996), Customary Law, Women's Right and Traditional Courts in Cameroon. Revue generale de droit.Vol 27 No 3.September 1996.

[392] In Achu v. Achu,[4] Inglis, J., held that, ' ...Customary law does not countenance the sharing of property, especially landed property, between husband and wife on divorce. The wife is still regarded as part of her husband's property ...''

[393] . S. 11 of the 1995 SCHCL guarantees the application of foreign law in Anglophone Cameroon.

[394] In the famous case of Enongenekang v. Enongene kang

[395] Section 1(1) of the Married Women's Property Act 1882.

The recent decision of Lord Denning in Midland Bank Trust Co. and Another v. Green and Another throws a lot of insight on this matter. This is what Lord Denning says:

"Nowadays, both in law and in fact, husband and wife are two persons, not one. They are partners-equal partners-in a joint enterprise, the enterprise of maintaining a home and bringing up children. Outside that joint enterprise they live their own lives and go their own ways ..."

The dictum above is reinforced by the position that English law knows no community of property[1] and the famous dictum of Romer, L.J. in the case of Cobb v. Cobb[396] when he said that:

'...I know of no power that the Court has under section 17 to vary agreed or established titles to property. It has the power to ascertain the respective rights of husband and wife to disputed property, and frequently has to do so on very little material, but whereas here, the original rights to property are established by evidence and those rights have not been varied by subsequent agreements, the court cannot in my opinion under section 17 vary those rights ...'

Section 17 would have been redundant after the divorce had been pronounced since its provisions would have ceased to apply because it refers to "husband" and "wife". To cure these maladies, the Matrimonial Proceedings and Property Act 1970 allows an application within the period of three years to be made by either party notwithstanding that their marriage has been dissolved or annulled. [397]

Cameroonian courts are content with applying the principles adumbrated above with caution. In the various local cases, effect has been given to local statutory enactments particularly the 1981[398] Ordinance. In substance, it provides that a married woman can exercise a trade different from that of her husband and can operate a separate bank account. Indeed, if the woman purchases property with her income or sums from her account, ownership and title rest in her name. Consequently, in the reasoning the High Court of Buea held in Body Lawson v. Body Lawson[399] that each spouse should continue to have ownership of property purchased in their respective names.

---

[396] Section 17 of the Married Women's Property Act 1882.

[397] section 39 of the Matrimonial Proceedings and Property Act 1970.

[398] Ordinance No. 81-02 of 29 June 1981 which deals partially amongst other matters with the question of property.

[399] Body Lawson v. Body Lawson, suit N° HCF/128Mc/86 (unreported).

With the above analysis, the rural women are empowered to stand up for their rights and acquire property especially landed property which will enable her develop her enterprise in the rural areas in Cameroon and thus become economically empowered. The only problem is effective implementation of all these measures in place and because of this we still find the rural women in the same position not able to own property in their name.

6.4.2. The Promotion and Protection of Human Rights

Cognizant that Human Rights activities are cross-cutting in nature and in a bid to ensure their seamless delivery, the Government decided to establish a National Plan of Action for the Promotion and Protection of Human Rights, which is consistent with one of the key pillars of the Growth and Employment Strategy Paper having to do with strengthening the rule of law in Cameroon. [400] The State of Cameroon has, since its independence in 1960, worked to promote and protect Human Rights. In line with that vision, it proclaimed in its successive fundamental laws the attachment of the Cameroon people to the inalienable rights of the human person, as outlined in the United Nations Charter, the Universal Declaration of Human Rights and the African Charter on Human and Peoples' Rights. To confirm its support for the international and regional system of promotion and protection of Human Rights, Cameroon also subscribed to many international legal instruments adopted under the auspices of the United Nations Organization (UNO) and the Organization of African Unity (OUA) which later became the African Union (AU).

In a bid to ensure an ongoing monitoring of Human Rights issues in Cameroon, the Government at the same time established institutions and bodies to regulate and check the actual delivery of rights enshrined in the above-mentioned international and regional conventions. This Plan of Action was designed using a broad participatory approach involving governmental and civil society stakeholders, with a significant contribution from the National Commission on Human Rights and Freedoms and the much-appreciated support of the United Nations Centre for Human Rights and Democracy in Central Africa. It will enhance the implementation of actions dedicated to the noble cause of Human Rights. The Government looks forward to the participation of all citizens and development partners in taking up the challenge of its implementation.[401] All this effort is aimed at empowering the rural women to become economically empowered. However, the implementation mechanisms are still not effective and

---

[400] Cameroon adopted its first Action Plan in 2017 for the period of 2018-2020.
[401] MINJUSTICE National Plan of Action version 2015, p.14.

for this reason the rural women still suffer from discrimination and thus are economically unempowered.

6.4.3. The fight against Gender-based Violence

Several measures both internationally ratified and national measures have been put in place by the government to fight gender-based violence. At the International level there are provisions to protect women against violence such as; Universal Declaration of Human Rights of 1948 where in it state that "No one shall be subjected to torture or to cruel, inhuman or degrading treatment or punishment"[402] ,The Convention on the Elimination of all Forms of Violence and Discrimination Against Woman adopted by the United Nations in 1979. On 14 July 2017, the Committee on the Elimination of Discrimination against Women (CEDAW Committee) adopted General Recommendation No. 35 on gender-based violence against women, updating General Recommendation No. 19. General Recommendation No. 19 from 1992 was historic as it clearly framed violence against women as a form and manifestation of gender-based discrimination, used to subordinate and oppress women. It unequivocally brought violence outside of the private sphere and into the realm of human rights. 25 years later, General Recommendation No. 35 elaborates on the gender-based nature of this form of violence, building on the work of the Committee and other international human rights mechanisms, as well as developments at national, regional and international levels.

General Recommendation No. 35 is also a milestone. It recognizes that the prohibition of gender-based violence has become a norm of international customary law. It expands the understanding of violence to include violations of sexual and reproductive health rights. It stresses the need to change social norms and stereotypes that support violence, in the context of a resurgence of narratives threatening the concept of gender equality in the name of culture, tradition or religion. It clearly defines different levels of liability of the State for acts and omissions committed by its agents or those acting under its authority - in the territory of the State or abroad- and for failing to act with due diligence to prevent violence at the hands of private individuals and companies, protect women and girls from it, and ensure access to remedies for survivors. It unequivocally calls for the repeal of all laws and policies that directly and indirectly excuse, condone and facilitate violence; and It emphasizes the need for approaches that promote and respect women's autonomy and decision-making in all spheres The Fourth World Conference on Women (Beijing, 1995) is another international instrument

---

[402] Article 5 of the 1948 Universal Declaration of Human Rights.

that fights against GBV. During this conference the governments were called upon to implement measures that will fight against GBV in their various countries. Cameroon being part of this conference and haven ratified these provisions is doing everything possible to see that they put in place, and the women especially the rural women are protected against GBV which is a dangerous weapon against her development and thus the development of the economy. The government has thus Condemn violence against women and refrain from invoking any custom, tradition or religious consideration to avoid their obligations with respect to its elimination as set out in the Declaration on the Elimination of Violence against Women; Refrain from engaging in violence against women and exercise due diligence to prevent, investigate and, in accordance with national legislation, punish acts of violence against women, whether those acts are perpetrated by the State or by private persons; enact and/or reinforce penal, civil, labour and administrative sanctions in domestic legislation to punish and redress the wrongs done to women and girls who are subjected to any form of violence, whether in the home, the workplace, the community or society; Adopt and/or implement and periodically review and analyse legislation to ensure its effectiveness in eliminating violence against women, emphasizing the prevention of violence and the prosecution of offenders; take measures to ensure the protection of women subjected to violence, access to just and effective remedies, including compensation and indemnification and healing of victims, and rehabilitation of perpetrators.

Work actively to ratify and/or implement international human rights norms and instruments as they relate to violence against women, including those contained in the Universal Declaration of Human Rights, the International Covenant on Civil and Political Rights, the International Covenant on Economic, Social and Cultural Rights, and the Convention against Torture and Other Cruel, Inhuman or Degrading Treatment or Punishment; Implement the Convention on the Elimination of All Forms of Discrimination against Women, taking into account general recommendation 19, adopted by the Committee on the Elimination of Discrimination against Women at its eleventh session; Promote an active and visible policy of mainstreaming a gender perspective in all policies and programmes related to violence against women; actively encourage, support and implement measures and programmes aimed at increasing the knowledge and understanding of the causes, consequences and mechanisms of violence against women among those responsible for implementing these policies, such as law enforcement officers, police personnel and judicial, medical and social workers, as well as those who deal with minority, migration and refugee issues, and develop strategies to ensure that the revictimization of women victims of violence does not occur because of gender-insensitive laws or judicial or enforcement practices; Provide women who are subjected to violence with access to the mechanisms of justice and, as provided for by national legislation, to just and effective remedies for the harm they have suffered and inform women of their rights in seeking redress through such mechanisms; Enact and enforce legislation against the perpetrators of practices and acts of violence against women, such as female genital mutilation, female infanticide, prenatal sex selection and dowry- related violence, and give vigorous support to the efforts of non-governmental and community organizations to eliminate such practices; Formulate and implement, at all appropriate levels, plans of action to eliminate violence against women.

Adopt all appropriate measures, especially in the field of education, to modify the social and cultural patterns of conduct of men and women, and to eliminate prejudices, customary practices and all other practices based on the idea of the inferiority or superiority of either of the sexes and on stereotyped roles for men and women; Create or strengthen institutional mechanisms so that women and girls can report acts of violence against them in a safe and confidential environment, free from the fear of penalties or retaliation, and file charges; ensure that women with disabilities have access to information and services in the field of violence against women.

Create, improve or develop as appropriate, and fund the training programmes for judicial, legal, medical, social, educational and police and immigrant personnel, in order to avoid the abuse of power leading to violence against women and sensitize such personnel to the nature of gender-based acts and threats of violence so that fair treatment of female victims can be assured; Adopt laws, where necessary, and reinforce existing laws that punish police, security forces or any other agents of the State who engage in acts of violence against women in the course of the performance of their duties; review existing legislation and take effective measures against the perpetrators of such violence.

Allocate adequate resources within the government budget and mobilize community resources for activities related to the elimination of violence against women, including resources for the implementation of plans of action at all appropriate levels; Include in reports submitted in accordance with the provisions of relevant United Nations human rights instruments, information pertaining to violence against women and measures taken to implement the Declaration on the Elimination of Violence against Women; Cooperate with and assist the Special Rapporteur of the Commission on Human Rights on violence against women in the performance of her mandate and furnish all information requested; cooperate also with other competent mechanisms, such as the Special Rapporteur of the Commission on Human Rights on torture and the Special Rapporteur of the Commission on Human Rights on summary, extra judiciary and arbitrary executions, in relation to violence against women; Recommend that the Commission on Human Rights renew the mandate of the Special Rapporteur on violence against women when her term ends in 1997 and, if warranted, to update and strengthen it.

The Governments, including local governments, community organizations, non-governmental organizations, educational institutions, the public and private sectors, particularly enterprises, and the mass media, as appropriate should equally, Provide well-funded shelters and relief support for girls and women subjected to violence, as well as medical, psychological and other counselling services and free or low-cost legal aid, where it is needed, as well as appropriate assistance to enable them to find a means of subsistence; Establish linguistically and culturally accessible services for migrant women and girls, including women migrant workers, who are victims of gender-based violence; Recognize the vulnerability to violence and other forms of abuse of women migrants, including women migrant workers, whose legal status in the host country depends on employers who may exploit their situation; Support initiatives of women's organizations and non-governmental organizations all over the world to raise awareness on the issue of violence against women and to contribute to its elimination;

Organize, support and fund community-based education and training campaigns to raise awareness about violence against women as a violation of women's enjoyment of their human rights and mobilize local communities to use appropriate gender-sensitive traditional and innovative methods of conflict resolution; Recognize, support and promote the fundamental role of intermediate institutions, such as primary health-care centres, family-planning centres, existing school health services, mother and baby protection services, centres for migrant families and so forth in the field of information and education related to abuse;

Organize and fund information campaigns and educational and training programmes in order to sensitize girls and boys and women and men to the personal and social detrimental effects of violence in the family, community and society; teach them how to communicate without violence and promote training for victims and potential victims so that they can protect themselves and others against such violence; Disseminate information on the assistance available to women and families who are victims of violence; Provide, fund and encourage counselling and rehabilitation programmes for the perpetrators of violence and promote research to further efforts concerning such counselling and rehabilitation so as to prevent the recurrence of such violence; Raise awareness of the responsibility of the media in promoting non-stereotyped images of women and men, as well as in eliminating patterns of media presentation that generate violence, and encourage those responsible for media content to establish professional guidelines and codes of conduct; also raise awareness of the important role of the media in informing and educating people about the causes and effects of violence against women and in stimulating public debate on the topic.[403]

All these the government is doing though with some shortcoming all in a bit to protect these women especially the rural women which goes a long way to promote them to become economically empowered.

The African Charter on Human and Peoples' Rights with special emphasis on the rights of women adopted in Maputo in 2003 like the Beijing conference condemned all forms of violence and discrimination against women. This African Women's protocol directs all states parties to the protocol condemns and prohibits all forms of harmful practices affecting the enjoyment of human rights by women in society through legislative and other measures necessary.[404]

At the national level, Ministry for the Protection of the Family and the Woman, created in 2004, was created in Cameroon for the implementation of these provisions. The Cameroonian Penal Code addresses issues of domestic violence. The penal code makes provision of punishment of any physical or moral violence to have sexual relations with a woman shall be punished by the imprisonment for a term of 5 to 10 years.[405]With all these the women, especially rural women will become economically empowered. This notwithstanding further implementation mechanism still needs to be put in place since GBV still persist for the rural women to become fully economically empowered.

6.4.4. The Contribution of the Ministry of Women's Empowerment and the Family

This is the main ministry in charge of gender equality and women's empowerment in Cameroon. Created in 2004[406], and born from the ashes of the former Ministry of Women's Affairs. It has as duty, the elaboration and

---

[403] The United Nations Fourth World Conference on Women, (1995). PLATFORM FOR ACTION. Available at https://www.un.org (Consulted on 04/12/2023).

[404] Article 5 of the African Women protocol. Adopted on 11 July 2003 in Maputo and entered into force on 25 November 2005.

[405] Article 296 of the 2016 Cameroon penal code.

[406] Decree No. 2004/320 of 8 December 2004

implementation of governmental measures related to the promotion and respect of women's rights and the protection of the family. As such, it has as missions to, ensure the elimination of all discrimination against women, ensure that guarantees of equality for women are increased in all areas of activity, study and submit to the Government the conditions to facilitate the employment of women in all sectors of activity, study and propose strategies and measures to strengthen the promotion and protection of the family and Study and propose measures aimed at promoting and protecting the rights of the child.

In addition, the Ministry Women's Empowerment and the Family liaises between the Government and the United Nations Entity for Gender Equality and the Empowerment of Women (UN Women), in conjunction with the Ministry of External Relations, as well as with all national and international political organisations for the advancement of women. It supervises women's training structures, excluding establishments under the responsibility of the ministries in charge of education. It comprises a central administration, territorial branches and specialized establishments, such as the women's empowerment centres and the appropriate technology centres.

I visited the women Empowerment centre in Santa sub division and had an interview with the Head of the centre. From the interview I gathered, the centre is doing its best to promote women and the girl child though facing several challenges. I was blessed to meet an on-going seminar on GBV on young girls who have been wounded in one way or the other. Madame Rose Nying head of the centre told me that it was a one-week seminar which started on the 16th to the 23rd of November 2023 to sensitise women on violence. During this seminar she said, the abused girls after making them to realise the areas where they are being abused, were directed after counselling to areas where they could be helped. Trauma healing was carried out by expert present on the raped and violated cases especially and further clinics and contacts were given to the girls to call in case of any eventualities. She said, during the seminar they were privileged to have an NGO called "Doctors for World" Present which helped in the sensitisation against GBV during the seminar.[407]

Apart from the seminar we discussed on how the centre functions. She said the centre is out to train young girls and women in the community and there is no particular age limit for intake. Registration fee is 2000frs cfa and the tuition fee for the year is 30.000 Fcfa to be a student under this centre. She says they train

---

[407] Interview with Madame Rose Nying Head of Women's Empowerment Centre Santa sub-division in the North west Region of Cameroon on the 05/12/2023 at 10:00am.

these girls and women in workshops and class rooms. In the work shop they carryout training on the creation of sandals, beats, fascinators, dress making, creation of hand fans, detergents and many other creative works of arts.

They equally have subjects taught on their rights as women such as, craft, marketing, business administration, citizenship and ICT. She said, the girls and women are trained to become entrepreneurs. When asked if these women are aware of the opportunities such as the incentives and the facilitation in creating SMEs by the government, she replied in the affirmative.[408]

The capacity building of the national mechanism, the hierarchical positioning of this ministry in the government team as well as the precise redefinition of its missions, aim to enable it to fully play its role of coordination, control and monitoring both in terms of gender equality and women's empowerment and in the planning and implementation of plans and programmes at the national level. Thus, the works of this Ministry created by the government of Cameroon actually goes a long way to economically empower the rural women though further machinery of implementation needs to be put in place to reach right down to all the grassroot sectors in Cameroon for women economic empowerment.

6.5. Access to Land Ownership

Cameroon tenure rights are characterised by the coexistence of customary law and "positive" or "modern" law. Cameroonian land tenure makes a distinction between registered and privately owned lands, and unoccupied lands that belong to the State but which are used by traditional communities.409The 1996 Constitution and 1974 Land Law apply nationally. The legal systems also recognize customary law, which, given the country's ethnic diversity, encompasses multiple and evolving traditional rules and norms. In Muslim regions, which are primarily in the north, principles of Islamic law have been incorporated into customary law, although separate Shari'a law is also recognised.410

Cameroon's 1996 Constitution provides that citizens have the right to own property individually or in association with others, and ownership includes the right to use, enjoy and transfer property. No one can be deprived of property

---

[408] Ibid.
[409] World Rainforest Movement. (2016). Women and Property in Cameroon. Laws and Reality. Available at https://www/wrm.org.(Consulted on the 17/05/2024).
[410] The 1996 Cameroon's Constitution.

unless it is taken in the public interest, in accordance with applicable law, and subject to payment of compensation as required by law[411]

Cameroon's primary land law, [412] established land tenure rules following the 1972 unification of the country. A companion law [413]addressed the governance of state land. These laws created a tenure system based on land registration: all privately-owned land must be registered and titled to retain its character as private land. All unregistered land is deemed to be either public land, which is held by the state on behalf of the public, or national land, which includes unoccupied land and land held under customary law. The laws were intended to encourage foreign investment in Cameroon as they effectively clarified private property rights and made all unregistered land available for investment. A perfect level of land consultation Board was stablished[414] and equally a decree[415] establishing prefect-level Commissions for resolving Agro-Pastoral Conflicts and Decree governing land titling and registration[416].

In the Anglophone regions of western Cameroon, formal courts will recognise and apply customary law so long as it is not inconsistent with general principles of equity and principles of formal law and the parties agree to the application of customary law.[417] In the Francophone regions, customary courts have jurisdiction to handle civil matters that have not been expressly reserved for the formal courts.

Cameroon's formal law classifies land as private, public or national. Private land can be owned by individuals and corporate entities, groups or the state. In order to be deemed private, the land must be titled and registered. Public land (e.g., highways, parks, waterways) is land held by the state for the benefit of the people of Cameroon. All other land is classified as national land, which includes most unoccupied land, land held by communities under customary law, informal settlements and grazing land. The state can allocate use rights to national land to individuals or groups or convert such land into the state's private or public property[418]

By these legal provisions guaranteeing land ownership by all in Cameroon, the rural women through the ownership of land will be economically empowered

---

[411] Preamble of the 1996 Constitution.

[412] Ordinance No. 74-1 of 6 July 1974.

[413] Ordinance No. 74-2 of 6 July 1974.

[414] Article 16 of Ordinance No. 74-1of 6 July 1974

[415]Decree No. 78/263, 1978.

[416] Decree No. 2005/481

[417] Section 27(2) of the SCHCL

[418] Article 74(1) and (2) of the 1974 land law in Cameroon.

since they can use or sell the land at their discretion. They can equally carry out gainful activities on the land. However, customary law is still hindering these rural women from owning land till date due to poor implementation mechanisms to this the country.

6.6. Measures on Access to Finance and Loan

6.6.1. Financial Inclusion of the Rural Women

The government is further intensifying its effort to fight gender inequality through economic inclusion strategies. Gender inequality is a violation of women's human right which contravenes the provisions of the Universal Declaration of Ruman rights [419], and the Constitution of Cameroon which protects the right of all its citizens on the basis of equality of all.[420] The preamble of the Cameron constitution is regarded as a national instrument or means of protection of human rights and it holds that," we the people of Cameroon declare that the human person without distinction as to race, religion ,sex or believe, possesses inalienable and sacred rights".

In order to reduce inequality in the rural sector of Cameroon, rural development needs to be engaged in. For the rural woman to be empowered, she needs to be included economically, and for this reason, the Government of Cameroon has been putting all efforts to see that she is economically included. Financial inclusion of the women especially the rural women has been recognised as it means to achieve sustainable and inclusive development. Women's financial inclusion promotes gender equality in society. Research has shown that women use their income and saving more productively than men, channelling a lot to children's nutrition, clothing, and making sure they are being educated.

Financial inclusion is defined as the ability of individuals and businesses to access, at low cost, a range of useful and appropriate financial products and services

such as transactions, payments, savings, credit, and insurance from reliable and responsible service providers, access to an account being the first step.421

On February 21st 2023 the Cameroon government published its national inclusive finance strategy (SNFI). This strategy is aimed at increasing access to all the diverse ranges of products and financial services. This strategy focuses on the most vulnerable population which is usually the rural population, women and

---

[419] Article 7 of the 1948 UDHR which is to the effect that all are equal before the law.
[420] Preamble of the 1972 constitution as amended in 2008.
[421] World Bank (2014) on financial inclusion report.

young people, the elderly and small and medium-sized businesses. 422Thus, it is a very relevant instrument, an effort by the government to promote the rural woman in the growth of the small and medium size businesses. The government has seen into it that Consumers are protected in financial inclusion, thus upholding the right to consumer protection as postulated by the consumer protection law in Cameroon[423]. Through the protection and education of financial consumers, the government has developed the use for financial services of all types including digital financial services, strengthening awareness, transparency, collection and resolution of complaints, Customer's relations in Cameroon have improved the population's confidence financial inclusion.

The CNEF, (The National Economic and Financial Committee), Play a key role in Consumer protection in Cameroon. The CNEF in its desire to promote a fair and equitable financial system has distinguished itself for many years. It was established on that sub-regional regulation 03/2019 in all CEMAC countries. Its mission is to regulate the relationship between customers and credit payment and micro finance institution, insurance company's brokerage and management of company's portfolio and as such to develop and propose action plan to the minister of finance to improve access to financial services[424]. CNEF also Cooperate with the Central African banking commission (COBAC), regulator and a supervisor of the protection of financial consumers in the CEMAC zone to organize the mediation process concerning financial consumers.[425]

The Central African Banking committee (COBAC) housed in the BEAC's office in Yaounde regulate the banking sector in the CEMAC zone. It is out to promote the integration of persons with disabilities within the communities in which they reside, enabling them to become viable and contributing neighbours, employees and citizens of the community. Utilizing the strengths and resources of the business community, persons with disabilities will achieve self-determination and independence. COBAC has as mission to, assist Community Options staff in networking with the business community, help individuals with disabilities integrate into their communities, ensure utmost quality in Community Options services educate local business owners and the corporate sector about persons with disabilities and the role that the business community can play in their lives, attain a societal understanding and acceptance of a person with a disability

---

[422] UNCDF (2014). Analysis: The National Economic and financial committee (CNEF) is an essential actor for financial inclusion in Cameroon. Available at https://eujournal.org. (consulted on 20/09/2023).

[423] Law no. 2011/012 of 06 May 2011 on consumer protection in Cameroon.

[424] UNDAF (footnote 2 p.2).

[425] Ibid.

as a productive member of the community.[426]It has as action plan, the development of a program to foster cooperation between Community Options, and the corporate community which can be replicated nationally, the development of a network which ensures successful community involvement and job placement for individuals supported by Community Options, ensuring quality assurance in all local services, the establishment of an educational and outreach program which assists the business community in understanding and welcoming people with disabilities into the community, the development of a mentoring program with a network of business mentors to assist candidates in improving their self-presentation for employment, and to provide advocacy on their behalf with a network of employers. This program will also develop a network of resources in the business community which could offer programs for employment of people with disabilities, the development of a guide for interview preparation, including handling information about a disability, to communicate information to business organizations and trade associations about the employment of people with disabilities and about using Community Options as a resource, to request production companies to donate videos and literature developed for ADA purposes, and to establish a library which is accessible for presentations at business conventions and to develop a network within the business community to assist Community Options with fundraising events and corporate funding efforts.[427]

COBAC regulates the Micro financial institutions (MFIs) in Cameroon. MFIs are small financial institutions which are usually easily accessible by the rural population unlike the big banks. MFIs in Cameroon are regulated by the national law, the economic and monetary community of central Africa (CEMAC) Laws which are instituted by COBAC and the pan African Organisation of Harmonisation of Business Law in Africa (OHADA).[428] Approving, and ratifying these Conventions by the Cameroon Government is a great step to empower the women especially the rural women economically since their provision facilitates entrepreneurship for all. Encouraging the growth of these micro financial institution will enable the rural women to have easy access to finance which will help them to engage in economic activities such as the growth of SMEs especially

---

[426] Community Options Inc. (1989). Supporting people with disabilities. COBAC. Community Options. Business advisory council. Available at https.//www.comop.org. (Consulted on the 20/09/20230).

[427] Ibid.

[428] Article 45 of the 1996 Cameroon Constitution is to the effect that all ratified International Agreements and Convention shall override National laws from the date of entry into force.

as there is a law governing micro finance activities in place in Cameroon[429] to regulate their financial transactions.

The history of microfinance is closely linked with poverty reduction. Microfinance was originally conceived as an alternative to banks, which in most developing countries serve only 5 to 20% of the population, and informal moneylenders. With the passage of time, the microfinance sector has evolved. Microfinance institutions now have more than 100 million clients and achieve remarkable repayment rates on loans. The rapid growth of microfinance has brought increasing calls for regulation, but complying with prudential regulations and the associated supervision can be especially costly for microfinance institutions. Since regulation remains a precondition for deposit taking in many countries, more MFIs seek to transform into regulated entities to access cheap and local currency deposits. Regulation also opens the door to a variety of funding opportunities and helps to reduce the overreliance on subsidies. Donors and microfinance practitioners are well aware that micro lenders need to prepare for the day when subsidies disappear. Just like many other African countries, the microfinance sector's springboard in Cameroon was the banking system restructuring engaged by the Ministry of Finance (MINFI) and the Banking Commission for Central Africa (COBAC). The expansion of MFIs in Cameroon during the 1980s can highly be explained by the gap left by the restructuring of the banking sector in most developing countries, which was characterized by the restraining or rationing of credit opportunities. Cameroon was not an exception.[430]

In Cameroon, the history of microfinance dates back to more than one century in its traditional form popularly known as "Njangi or Tontine". The introduction of "modern" microfinance in Cameroon started in 1963 by a Catholic priest Father Alfred Jansen, in Njinikom in the North-West Region of Cameroon. This idea of Credit Unionism spread all over the North-West and South-West regions of Cameroon and by 1968, 34 credit unions that were already in existence joined together to form the Cameroon Cooperative Credit Union League (CamCCUL) Limited. CamCCUL is therefore the umbrella organisation of

---

[429] Law No 2019/021 of 24 December 2019 to lay down some rules governing credit activities in the banking and micro-finance sector in Cameroon.

[430] Akume Daniel A. et al., (2017), The performance of microfinance Institutions in Cameroon: Does financial regulation really matter? Research Journal of Financial and Accounting, Vol. 8. No. 2, p.

cooperative credit unions and the largest MFI in Cameroon and the 'Communauté Économique des États de l'Afrique Centrale' (CEMAC) sub-region[431]

Microfinance has been defined therefore as "a credit methodology that employs effective collateral substitutes to deliver and recover short-term, working capital loans to micro entrepreneurs".[432] The roots of microfinance lie in a social mission of enhancing outreach to alleviate poverty. More recently there has been a major shift in emphasis from the social objective of poverty alleviation towards the economic objective of sustainable and market based financial services the difference between microfinance and commercial lending lies within the concepts of joint liability or group lending, dynamic incentives that allow for an increase in size of loans over time, regular repayments schedules and alternative collateral through forced savings.

On a global note, the microfinance industry has realised important growth rate and as the number of microfinance institutions and customers continue to grow, regulation of the industry becomes a question of interest since the sustainability of these institutions is highly debated. [433]A more efficient micro financial sector may eventually translate into higher rates of economic growth and thus the ability of governments to alleviate poverty.

There are several ways in which the industry might gain from financial regulation It might enhance competition and the overall efficiency of the industry; increase consumer welfare and encourage a better management of financial risks by the supervisees. Providing access to finance to the poor has been considered as one of the tools for poverty reduction and economic development. lack of collateral explains, at least partially why the poor lack access to financial services. Irrespective of the approaches to microfinance, millions of poor people are in need of financial services and this calls for regulation in order to protect both the depositors and the lenders, and in a long run, to prevent the systemic risk.

Before 1998, MFIs activities in Cameroon were placed under the tutorship of the Ministries of Agriculture and the Ministries of Finance because microfinance was initially seen as essentially suited for the promotion of rural and agricultural activities. As a result of many irregularities in the field and due to little or no supervision and control expertise at the level of personnel working in the Ministry of Agriculture, there was an urgent need to protect the public and guard depositors' funds. This led to a Prime Ministerial decree that puts the

---

[431] ibid

[432] Kakan Julia (2024). Microfinance Definition: Benefits, History, and How it Works. Available https://www.investopedia.com. (Consulted on 27/08/2024)

[433] Akume Daniel A. et al., (2017), (note 510).

granting of licenses, supervision, and control of all MFIs under the Ministry of Finance and the Central Africa Banking Commission (COBAC).[434]

Several national laws govern MFIs activities in Cameroon. We have the budget law for the 1998/1999[435] fiscal year in Cameroon, the law aims at improving administrative and legislative environment for business through the elimination of obstacles to investment, production and commerce. The prime ministerial Decree setting the modalities for the exercise of the activities of savings and credit cooperatives[436] as amended and supplemented by the PM decree in 2001.[437] The 2019 law[438] equally lays down some rules governing credit activities in the banking and micro finance sectors. Regulating these activities help open access to all and thus the rural women can benefit from the credits without fear of being duped since it is regulated by the law.

The OHADA Business law in Cameroon also regulates the Cameroons' business climate The UA on General Commercial Law, introduced the entrepreneur's status, a simplified legal regime for microenterprises, and formalised the OHADA wide effort to computerise the Trade and Personal Property Credit Registry [439].The UA on Secured Transactions[440] broadened the range of assets that can be used as collaterals and introduced out-of-court, autonomous collateral realization. The UA on Company Law[441]introduced a new legal form for businesses known as the SAS and simplified the creation of the SARL and the UA on Insolvency [442] simplified and safeguarded liquidation procedures, facilitating recovery after business discontinuation. All these have the potentials to promote the rural women since the procedures are simplified to grow and develop her SME in the rural areas in Cameroon. However, lack of information and implementation mechanisms still hinders these women from obtaining loans and taking off economic activities to become economically empowered.

6.6.2. Finance Agricultural Projects

Lack of employment, poor access to water, electricity and roads, lack of healthcare and education facilities, corruption and mismanagement of public

---

[434] Ibid.
[435] Law No. 98/009 of 1st July 1998.
[436] Decree No 98/300/PM of September 9,1998.
[437] Decree No 2001/023 of January 29 2001.
[438] Law No 2019/021 of 24th December 2019.
[439] UA on General Commercial Law 2010
[440] UA on General commercial law 2010
[441] UA on General commercial law 2014
[442] UA on General commercial law 2015

funds all contribute to poverty. Women in rural areas are among the most vulnerable. The family smallholdings which dominate farming often rely upon manual effort and casual labour and use few or no external inputs. Because commercial farming is underdeveloped, Cameroon imports large quantities of food. Yet it has great potential to meet its food demand and improve the living conditions of the rural population.

For this reason, the government has taken some measure such as sponsoring agricultural projects to improve in agricultural production especially in the rural areas. Most if not all the activities of the rural women are focused on agriculture and the sale of agricultural produce. Thus, promoting agriculture is another means of promoting these rural women to become economically empowered since there will be availability of agricultural produce at all time for marketing. The Cameroonian government, through its National Strategy for Inclusive Finance (SNFI), announced the disbursement of CFA10.5 billion to boost agricultural financing in the country over the next five years. The government plans to rely on its existing partnerships with the Agency for the SME Promotion Agency (APME) to reach the target. The plan also includes training and support sessions for stakeholders on agriculture financing and the establishment of permanent consultation frameworks between financial institutions and producer organizations[443].A decree[444] has also been ratified by the Cameroon Government to ratify loan agreement to finance the agricultural production enhancement support programme in Cameroon (PARPAC).To this effect, a loan agreement No 2000200005512 for an amount of EUR 62.993 million or approximately CFAF 41.408 billion signed on 29 September 2022 between Republic of Cameroon and the African development Bank (AfDB),to finance agricultural production enhancement to support programme in Cameroon (PARPAC) is ratified.[445]However, due to the situation of the rural women in Cameroon, who are mostly illiterates, they are hardly informed about these governmental funding and even if they are, they will not know how to go about it, thus remaining less economically empowered

6.6.3. Legal Aid

Another effort by our government to promote rural women entrepreneurship is the provision of legal Aid. These rural women lack money to take care of themselves and their families. This hinders them to even think of

---

[443] Aizan Firimine (2023), Cameroon, government to boost agricultural financing over the next 5 years. Available at https://www.businessin Cameroon.com (Consulted on the 1/10/2023).
[444] Decree No 2022/523 of 28th November 2022.
[445] Article 1 of decree No 2022/523 of 28 November 2022.

taking matters such as violation of their rights to own property by customary law court. This makes the rural women remain in the state of poverty without even thinking of one day coming out of it. With the provision of legal Aid in Cameroon these women can easily access justice to claim their rights. The Cameroonian legislation has made provision of legal Aid[446]to vulnerable group of persons in Cameroon. According to the law, legal aid shall be granted on application to the categories of persons whose resources are inadequate to have their rights enforced by a court or to follow up the enforcement of any writ or process of execution; previously obtained without such legal aid. In assessing the ability or inability to pay the costs, account shall be taken of a procedure of the external elements of lifestyle, ownership of movable and immovable property whether or not income-generating, however, excluding those that may be sold or pawned without affecting the economic situation of the proprietor.

The law [447]equally states that "cases where judicial proceedings are free, legal aid shall be granted as of right to the following persons: work accident victim seeking compensation from his/her employer; an unemployed person without resources, deserted by their spouse and seeking to be granted alimony and child support by court order and a person under death sentence making an appeal. "The rural women are mostly unemployed and lack resources. This provision will actually be of benefit to them.

6.6.4. Develop Public- Private Partnership (PPP)

By definition, a PPP is a public contract in which a public body and one or more private partners agree to carry out all or part of the design, construction, financing, operation, and maintenance of public infrastructure and associated services.[448] The Cameroonian government is taking action to strengthen the country's business climate, improve its competitiveness, and boost economic growth. Cameroon needs significant investment in all infrastructure sectors at national and regional levels, and it needs the financial and managerial resources of the private sector to make that happen. Launched in 2003, the Vision Cameroon 2035 development plan, aims to chiefly bring about economic 'prosperity' and 'universal access to quality social services. In a climate of limited public capital, multi-stakeholder partnerships form an increasingly important factor in this economic vision, whether private actors, civil society organisation or donor organisations. Infrastructural development is sought by Cameroon through a

---

[446] Law No. 2009/004 of 14 April 2009 to Organize Legal Aid in Cameroon.
[447] Ibid Section 6 (1).
[448] Department of Economic (2022). What is PPP? Available at https://www.pppinindia.gov.in.(Consulted on27/08/2024).

'planned liberalism 'approach. Vision 2035 articulated major infrastructure works requiring construction including dams, bridges, roads and housing. In 2005 to 2009, Cameroon established its policy framework for public-private partnerships. Subsequently, in 2013, the government released details of 21 projects to be financed and executed via PPPs, in the areas of transport, urban development, energy and the agro-food industry. Six of these have currently been awarded contracts, with private partners all drawn from expatriate nations France, South Korea and South Africa.[449]

Cameroon faces many infrastructure challenges that are typical of poorer countries. The World Economic Forum's 2019 Global Competitiveness Report ranks Cameroon at 132 out of 141 countries in transport infrastructure, 114 in access to electricity, and 128 in the reliability of water supply. Inequalities between north and south persist, as do inefficiencies in public resource allocation.[450]The World Bank Country Partnership Framework with Cameroon recommended a step-by-step approach to infrastructure development through private-public partnerships, or PPPs. Major milestones include strengthening private-sector regulatory frameworks, engaging stakeholders, improving project development, deploying advisory services for PPPs and project finance, and providing appropriate financing.[451]Cameroon has taken steps in the right direction[452].

In Cameroon, the preferences of decision-makers for PPPs are most often directed towards foreign investors. The reason generally given is that foreign investors have a certain financial capacity that would allow them to effectively participate in the improvement of public investments through a PPP. However, the country also has a large number of small and medium-sized enterprises (SMEs) that can effectively contribute to the improvement of a number of public infrastructures in different sectors. By going into partnership with SMEs especially those in the rural areas and those owned by the rural women will go a long way to pave the way for other rural women to be encouraged to grow their own enterprises and thus economically empowered since these rural women will fast develop and even give birth to other SMEs that will help boost both the private and public sector of the Cameroonian economy. The participation of national

---

[449] PPIAF (2021). Cameroon. Building a workable PPP Framework. Available at https://www.ppiaf.org.(Consulted on 30/09/2023).
[450] Ibid.
[451] Ibid.
[452] Cameroon has taken measures such as such as enacting its PPP law in 2006 and establishing a PPP unit, Le Conseil d'Appui à la Réalisation des Contratsde Partenariat (CARPA).

private companies in this type of partnership with the public sector has many advantages.[453]Some of which are:

PPPs are an effective and timely financing model when both parties involved from the public and private sectors strictly adhere to the terms of the contract governing their partnership agreement.[454] By negotiating such agreements with domestic private companies, the government can ultimately improve the quality of its investments and rationalize the operation of public services. In addition, PPPs are an excellent way to stimulate the domestic private sector, which has the expertise and a strong capacity to innovate. They offer the State the possibility of mobilizing the necessary and sufficient resources to finance its development projects without having to resort to debt or oppressive taxation. PPPs depend on a fully improved business climate, which can stimulate the performance of local companies. PPPs can be achieved through good planning, careful analysis by the relevant actors, and a smooth, objective, and transparent process.

Also, a strong and resilient private sector naturally offers many opportunities for public decision-makers to contribute to the improvement of infrastructure in several sectors, including telecommunications, communication, energy, and real estate, as well as the realization of major public works. Indeed, within the framework of PPPs, the costs are generally pre-financed by private funds such as, shareholder companies' own funds, bank debts, bonds to which can be added public aid in the form of subsidies or guarantees.[455]

To reap the full benefits of the African Continental Free Trade Area (AfCFTA), Cameroon must strengthen its industrial system. This implies not only strengthening the competitiveness of national enterprises but also developing basic public infrastructure: energy, water, transport, housing, telecommunications, and communications. Given the importance of the projects and the financial needs required to implement them, the government of Cameroon, has generally resorted to two main sources of financing: debt/borrowing and increased taxation.[456] However, these methods are no longer effective in achieving the development objectives set by the government. In order to explore new

---

[453] Commonwealth governance (2023) public-private partnerships of Cameroon. Available at https://www.commonwealthgovernance.org. (Consulted on 30/09/2023).

[454] Bernath Matthew, (2019). Public Private Partnership-Leveraging private Sector investment and capital to deliver public infrastructure. Available at https://financialmodellingpodcast.com. (Consulted on 27/08/2024).

[455]Ibid.

[456]Kouam Jean-Cedric (2023, Focus on public- private partnership in Cameroon. Available at https://onpolicy.org.(Consulted on the 30/09/2023).

sources of financing, the government of Cameroon has set up a legal framework that provides incentives, stability, and guarantees to the government's private partners free access, equality, transparency, objectivity, and equity in public procurement. In addition to the general code of decentralized territorial collectivises[457] which provides for various public-private partnership mechanisms at the level of the regions and municipalities, these include the general regime for partnership contracts.[458],Decree on the organization and functioning of the Council for the Support of Partnership Contracts[459],Decree on the general regime for partnership contract[460],the law setting the fiscal, financial and accounting regime applicable to partnership contracts[461].The order setting rates and modalities of collection of fees payable under partnership contracts[462]and the decree setting the organisation and operation of the partnership contracts support council.[463]

To facilitate the application of these legal texts, public authorities in Cameroon, decided in 2006 to create the Council for the Support of Partnership Contracts (CARPA). The vision that justifies the creation of this public body is to accelerate the realization of major public service infrastructures through public-private partnerships (PPP).[464]Thus empowering the women especially the rural women to become economically empowered.

6.7. Measures on the Promotion and Protection of the Right to Work

The right to work is a fundamental right to be enjoyed by all irrespective of sex. To this effect, some institutions carry out activities which are aimed to ensure the enjoyment of these right.

---

[457] Law No. 2019/024 of 24 December2019 on Decentralised territorial collectivities.
[458] Law n° 2006/012 of 29 December 2006.
[459] Decree n° 2008/035 of 23 January 2008 on the organization and functioning of the Council for the Support of Partnership Contracts.
[460] Decree n° 2008/0115/PM of 24 January 2008 specifying the modalities for the application of law n° 2006/012 of 29 December 2006 laying down the general regime for partnership contracts.
[461] Law n° 2008/009 of 16 July 2008 setting the fiscal, financial, and accounting regime applicable to partnership contracts.
[462] Order No. 186 CAB/PM of 15 November 2011 setting the rates and modalities of collection of fees payable under partnership contracts.
[463] Decree No. 2012/148 of 21 March 2012 amending and supplementing certain provisions of Decree No. 2008/035 of 23 January 2008 on the organization and operation of the Partnership Contracts Support Council.
[464] Ibid.

6.7.1. The National Employment Fund (NEF) Promotes Rural Women Entrepreneurship

The National Employment Fund was created by a presidential decree in 1990 [465] .Its overall mission is to promote employment. It is a tool used by the Ministry of Employment and Vocational Training[466].It is out to offer self-employment and micro-enterprise Programs (PAME). In this domain it supports project promoter technically in Project feasibility analysis and financially by funding small projects. Its objective here is to promote safe employment through entrepreneurship. Facilitates transformation of actors of the informal sector into the formal sector. This upholds the right to employment advocated by the Universal Declaration of Human Rights,[467] the preamble of the Cameroon's constitution [468] , the labour code,[469]as examined in the previous chapter.

The rural women benefit from the National Employment Fund. The Government knows that the women constitute a strong force in the rural community and to attain its 2035 emergency goal it has to go down to the roots and encourage these women, doing feasibility studies, and sponsoring these women in a bit to remove them from informal to formal sector of the economy through the creation of Small Medium-Sized Enterprises by these rural women The National Employment Fund has 10 regional branches and 6 local branches all over Cameroon, thus extending to every sector of the national economy.[470]

6.7.2. The Decentralisation of Centres for Business Creation Formalities (CFCE)

This is another governmental effort put in place to promote entrepreneurs in Cameroon which goes a long way to benefit the rural women to be economically empowered through the creation of SMEs. For ten years, now, Cameroon has under its framework of the Cameroon Business Forum (CBF), undertaken several reforms to improve its business environment. The country aims to attract the local and foreign   direct investment necessary for its economic growth, job creation, and living conditions

---

[465] Decree No 90/805/PR of 27 April 1990.

[466] Cynthia Wanchia (2023). NW Regional Assembly, National Employment fund, orientate youths on careers. Available at https://the guardianpostcameroon.com. (Consulted on the 15/09/2923).

[467] Article 23 of the 1948 UDHR.

[468] The constitution of 2 June 1972 as amended by the law of 18th January 1996.

[469] Act No.92/07 of 14 August1992 on the Labour code provides in its preamble Article 2(1).'The right to work is recognised as a fundamental right of all citizens.

[470] Haman Jibirila (2015): Case of Cameroon. National Employment Fund (NEF). Available at https://www.fnecm.org.(Consulted on 15/09/2023).

of its populations.[471] In Cameroon, there is the Business Creation Formality Centres (CFCE) which is a public organ existing in Cameroon, there is a representation in each region. The CFCE are generally housed in the same premises as the Regional Delegation of the Ministry of Small and Medium-Sized enterprises, Social Economy and Handicrafts, their ministerial department of supervision. Its primary role is to lead the administrative process of creating news business. This helps the entrepreneur who wants to create an establishment his business, (Sole proprietorship). The correct address will be the CFCE located in the region in which he wishes to set up his business.[472]

The minimum share capital and the conditions for resorting to the services of notary during the creation of a Limited Liability Company is fixed by the 2016 law [473]The Cameroonian legislator reduced the minimum share capital of LLCs to one hundred thousand (100,000) francs and made optional the use of notarial deed for the creation of LLCs where it is owned by one person or where its capital does not exceed one million (1,000,000) francs.

The Decree specifies how the articles of association are to be authenticated when the LLC is created by private deed: within 24 hours of the filing of application, the head of the business formalities centre authenticates the articles of association by signing at the bottom and by affixing, on each page, the following information. The articles of association by private deed are drawn up and authenticated in as many originals as is necessary, an original copy is given to each shareholder and a copy is kept at their disposal at the registered office. The Decree also lists companies that are targeted by these provisions. They include, limited liability companies with a share capital of less than one million francs and LLCs with sole proprietor regardless of the amount of share capital, being understood that the minimum capital for any form of LLC is fixed at one hundred thousand (100,000) francs.[474]

The government has been cultivating small-business growth in recent years through initiatives, such as one-stop business registration centres. Now, entrepreneurs can apply for business licenses, taxpayers' cards and two-year tax exemptions in one place, saving time and money. In the past, applicants had to

---

[471] Denis &Lenora. starting a business in Cameroon, A critical analysis. Available at https://nkafu.org(Consulted on the 21/09/2023).

[472] CFCE in brief (2022): Business creation space in the republic of Cameroon. Available at https://minfi.gov.cm.(consulted on the 21/09/2023).

[473] Article 3 of Law No. 2016/014 of 14 December 2016.

[474] Article 5 of Decree No. 2017/0877 / PM of February 28, 2017, the Republic of Cameroon lays down the modalities for authenticating, in Business Formalities Centres (BFC), the articles of association of Limited Liability Companies (LLCs) drawn up as private deeds.

obtain these documents from different offices, making the procedure long and scary for these rural women. The putting together in one place of all administrative services concerned equally reduces the loss of time and transport money to different locations charged with the formalisation.

The creation of the Cameroon SMEs Bank (BC-PME) was announced by the President of the Republic of Cameroon, His Excellency Paul Biya, during the Ebolowa Agro-Pastoral Show in 2011, as well as the creation of the Agriculture Bank (CARFIC)[475]. These two public banking institutions are each endowed with a share capital of 10 billion CFA francs.The Cameroon SMEs Bank aims at providing financial support to business promoters, through the granting of short, medium and long-term loans to SMEs in order to finance their operating activities. This bank was created because, in Cameroon, SMEs represent nearly 95%[476] of the country's economic fabric. But most SMEs promoters find it very difficult to access bank credit from traditional banks, which generally require guarantees that are difficult to access for local entrepreneurs who do not own fixed,assets such as land and buildings and have few resources. This situation is highly faced by the rural women who most often than not are hindered by customary law practices to own property and so land and other asset really stands as a barrier for these women to use as collateral to borrow money from banks to grow their businesses and become economically empowered. The creation of this bank by the government is actually a great move towards the promotion of these women the grow their SMEs in the rural sectors of Cameroon and become economically independent. Upon application loans from this bank is granted within three months. Even if your business is still on papers, you can still apply provided you have a person at the BCPME who has promised to get it settled since the bank works with SME promotion Agency in setting up, creation and financing of companies. The policy interest rate is 11% which is advantageous compared to other financial institutions. The rates are equally negotiable when the amount of credit is very high.[477]

Another step by the government to economically empower the rural women is the partnership agreement with Cameroonian bank CCA on June 29 2023. The agreement allows the Cameroonian bank to grant loans to MSMEs, with a particular emphasis on women-led or owned businesses, thanks to a 10 billion

---

[475] MINPMEESA (2019). The SMESs Bank (BC-PME). Available
  <https://www.minpmeesa.cm.(Consulted on the 22/09/2023)
[476]Ibid.
[477] ibid

CFA Francs ($16.6 million) credit line opened by the IFC.[478] "Understanding the important role women play in the economy, CCA-Bank, through its women-specific banking program and in collaboration with IFC, will position itself as the choice bank for women currently unserved or underserved by the formal financial system. The initiative thus aims to finance and strengthen Cameroon's female entrepreneurs, to stimulate development and economic growth. As for MSMEs, which form the backbone of the Cameroonian economy, the need to support their expansion cannot be overstated."[479] However, because of illiteracy, information lags and implementation lags, these women cannot access these grants for their development.

6.7.3: Decentralised Authorities and the promotion of rural women Economic Empowerment.

Under the 2004 law on decentralisation, many powers were devolved to regions and councils in the economic, health, social, educational, sport and cultural domains.[480]

The local authorities have exclusive exercise of the powers devolved to them by the state.[481]

Regions have been given a general duty to promote economic development and social progress such as the promotion of the growth of SMEs for the harmonious, balanced, supportive and sustainable territorial development.[482]

With these powers conferred on the regions and in a bit to promote entrepreneurship, they organise trade fairs promoting handicraft creation in the region. This brings together groups of economic operators supporting income generating and job creation, promoting micro finance projects and promoting tourism in the regions.

---

[478] Business in Cameroon. (2023). MSME, financing, CCA Bank secures fcaf 10bln credit line to improve credit access. Available at
<https;//www.businessincameroon.com.(Consulted on 22/09/2023).
[479] By Marguerite Fonkwen Atanga, the new managing director of CCA Bank.
[480] MINDDEVEL(2025)."Les Regions Vues du code General des CTDEN" .Available at https://www.minddevel.gov.cm.(Consulted on the 22/04/2025).
[481] Section 18 of the 2019 Decentralisation Code.
[482] Section 259(2) of the 2019 Decentralisation Code.

The Regions are equally endowed with powers to promote regional tourism, creation and operation of regional amusement parks; and the organisation of regional leisure, socio-cultural events.[483]

The code equally gives powers to the councils to ensure local development and the improvement of the living environment and condition of its inhabitants.[484]

These councils have the powers to promote council agriculture, pastoral, artisanal and fish farming, develop and manage council tourist sites; construction, equipment, management and maintenance of markets, motor parks and slaughterhouses. Organise local trade fairs, supporting income generating and jobs. Creating micro-projects and exploiting mineral substances that can be given out as concessions.[485]

In addition, a law was passed in 2007[486].This law defines Craft as all activities of extraction, production, transformation, maintenance, repairs, essentially manual services and exercised as a main activity.

These notwithstanding, lack of political will by some competent authorities to implement these provisions right down to the grassroot level without discrimination acts as a serious hindrance for the economic empowerment of these rural women. Communication gaps, implementation gaps are equally some hindrances to this government's laudable initiative to promote its Country's economy especially the rural communities. Illiteracy and fear equally hinder these women to move forward to showcase their economic prowess thus keeping the in the same economically backward position.

6.7.4. The investment Charter and the Economic Empowerment of the rural women.

The Charter states that, the state shall oversee and promote the SMEs and industries by establishing a financial service system that supports SME operators through appropriate regulations and supervisions; establish financing mechanism for SMEs and industries that addresses specific and sectorial needs through appropriate regulations and supervision.[487]

---

[483][483] Article 2 of Decree No 2021/746 of 28 December 2021 to lay down the conditions governing the exercise of some powers devolved by the state upon the regions in the areas of tourism and leisure.
[484] Section 147 of the 2019 Decentralisation Code.
[485] Section 156 of the 2019 Decentralisation Code.
[486] Law No 2007/004 of July 3 2007 governing Craft in Cameroon.
[487] Article 38 of Cameroon's 2010 Investment Charter.

It should be noted here that this powerful portion of the law promotes only SMEs and industries that are already operating. It provides financial services, regulate and supervise only SMEs and industries in existence. This is one of the reasons why the rural women are still where they are in Cameroon. These women are unable to create enterprises mostly due to financial difficulties. If this law had also made provision for start-ups capital especially for rural women in Cameroon before proceeding to grant financial assistance for them with serious supervision on provision and implementation, then these women would have greatly emerged for the economic development of our nation.

6.8. Measures on the Promotion and Protection of The Right to Social Benefits

The economic empowerment of women cannot be achieved without ensuring their rights to social benefits such as electricity, water and transportation.

6.8.1. Improve Access to Electricity Facilities

The law governing electricity sector in Cameroon[488] focuses on ensuring its modernisation and development. Part IV of the law sets out general goals for promoting renewable energy and energy efficiency, and for the use of renewables within the context of expanding rural electrification. The law states that the government shall ensure the promotion and development of rural electrification nationwide, through connection to an interconnected network or through distributed generation. Within the general framework for increased electrification, priority is to be given to distributed generation from renewable sources. The law allows for surplus electricity generated from renewable energy sources to be purchased by the transmission system operator or by local distributors. This provision of the law by the government will go a long way to promote these rural women since the lack of electricity in the rural areas actually acts as a hinderance to these rural women. Most of these women still use bush lambs as a source of energy for their homes. With this provision of this law, we realise that most of the rural areas are being electrified thus easing the stress of these rural women. This will go a long way to encourages these rural women to create SMEs since electricity will be available which is highly needed to run any business. The law says that the State will ensure the promotion and development of renewable energy through establishing regulation for conditions and mechanisms for research, development, production of equipment and project financing. The government may also establish an agency to promote and develop renewable energy as and when necessary. The law also requires any electricity utility operate

---

[488] Law No 2011/022 Governing the Electricity Sector in Cameroon.

to connect renewable energy sources to networks (with connect fees borne by the applicant), with the conditions, volume and price for purchase of energy by utilities to be fixed by decree.

The law[489] calls for the implementation of energy efficiency measures in the industry, transport, commercial and residential sectors, and allows for the government to establish regulation for the obligations, conditions and resources necessary to implement such measures. The government of Cameroon correctly identifies an increase in reliable electricity supply and the realization of Cameroon's significant hydropower potential as key to achieving non-oil growth and improving the investment climate. Unreliable and costly electricity supply is cited among the top five constraints to doing business in Cameroon. Electricity access rates are low and unequal (48 percent for the whole of Cameroon, but only 14 percent for rural areas, with significant regional differences),[490] and Cameroon's current installed generation capacity is not sufficient to meet an electricity demand growing at 6 percent annually on average. Investments in the Kribi gas to power plant and the Lom Pangar hydropower project are government investments in the sector. In particular, the realization of the Lom Pangar hydropower project, creating a regulating dam for the Sanaga River, will provide access to substantial future hydropower capacity from existing and future downstream investments, thus reducing power costs. Electrifying the rural area will enable these rural women to invest in gainful economic activities such as creation of small businesses which needs electricity to run, making the economically empowered. However, till date most rural areas still lack electricity supply and even where they have electricity cuts remains the order of the day.

6.8.2. Improvement of Transportation network

The country's road network, which accounts for 85% of transport in the country, suffers among other problems from lack of signalling and markings, cracks, potholes, poor drainage, lack of sidewalk and cycle path, and disorderly parking.[491]A large number of people live in the rural areas in Cameroon, so road transport occupies and important role from farm to market role and for linking villages and towns. The government has realised that better road accesses increase the number of activities carried out by the users. Access to roads will probably lead to access to local market, the developing of good roads and multiple activity

---

[489] Ibid.

[490] Ezekwesili Obiageli et al. (2010). Cameroon. Poverty Reduction Strategy Paper-joint staff advisory note. IMF country Report No.10/258.

[491] UNECE (2018). Road safety: Cameroon must redouble its efforts and strengthen coordination. Available at https://unece .org. (Consulted on the 30/09/2023).

and of course to the income diversification to the rural sector of the economy. If the rural roads are good, it will induce market-led-local development through agricultural marketing and increases income from farming activities rural roads equally increases revenue from non-farming activities by spurring shift from subsistence agriculture to commercial agriculture or known farm activity such as creation of small and medium-sized enterprises by the rural women. This is so because better road access led to a diversification of the economic activities.[492] Subject to the Power transferred to regional and local authorities regarding public Highway management, the construction on a private or public basis of any structure leading to the road of way shall require prior authorization from the Minister in charge of road[493]The principal legal instrument which regulates road transport is the Economic and Monetary Community of Central Africa (CEMAC) Highway Code of 2001, the Cameroon Highway Code of 1979 as amended in 1986, the OHADA Uniform Act on the Carriage of Goods by Road of 2004 which regulates the contractual aspects of domestic and international carriage of goods by road. It applies on all contracts of carriage of goods by road once the place of collection of goods as well as the place of delivery of the goods, as specified in the contract, are situated within the territory of an OHADA member state or within the territory of two different states, of which at least one is a member state of OHADA, without regard to the residence or nationality of the parties to the contract of carriage of goods by road.

All these legal provisions ensure the provision of good roads and regulates activities carried out on the road which goes a long way to economically empower the rural women since they will be able to easily transport their raw materials from farm to their business site and equally transportation of material for the development of their enterprises in the rural areas. However, roads in Cameroon especially in the rural areas are still in a deplorable state. Roads in the rural sectors are mostly not motorable roads.

6.8.3. Provision of Portable Water

Access to water especially portable water is a great challenge to the rural women which acts as a hinderance to her development for she has to move to far distance just to fetch water for her household. She has no time for herself to even sit and reflect on what she can do to better her tomorrow. Even if she does, she

---

[492] Gachassin Marie et al (2015). Road and diversification of activities in rural areas. A Cameroon case study. Available at https:www.researchgate.net.(Consulted on the 29/09/2023).

[493] Section 5 of law No.2022 / 004 of 27 April 2022 relating to the protection of the National Road assets.

cannot realise it since water is needed for any developmental project which include the growth of SMEs by these women. For this important role played by water to human life and to the women at large, the government has realised that to promote the growth of the rural communities and the nation as a whole, it has to provide pipe borne water. These rural women who are most affected by lack of water will be encouraged in their entrepreneurship ventures and thus become economically empowered.

Water features as the most indispensable of all the natural resources in the world. It's for this reason why the right to water is increasingly recognised universally as a fundamental and inalienable right of the human person and states are called upon to recognise and enforce in their internal legal order with the cooperation of the international community. Forming part of economic and social rights, the right to water means that everyone without discrimination, must have access to water in quality and quantity sufficient to meet his/her basic needs. The right to water consists in the provision of sufficient, physically accessible and at an affordable cost, clean and quality water acceptable for personal and domestic use of everyone.[494] The right to water has also been defined as the right of everyone regardless of his economic standard, to possess a minimum quantity of water of good quality which is sufficient for his life and health.[495]

The right to water is also of capital importance in the ongoing battle against poverty.[496] In this regard, it relates more to the social categories of poor or vulnerable people in the rural areas and those in the urban setting as well. Indeed, the poor are those most affected or essentially deprived of the right to portable water basically as a result of their economic and physical inaccessibility. The Universal Declaration of Human Rights[497] recognises a wide range of social, economic and civil rights such as right to life, right to health, right to housing which are today inextricably linked to the right to water.

The Millennium Declaration adopted by the General Assembly of the United Nations[498] after the Millennium Summit in New York which brought

---

[494] Tamasang C. F. (2007), Paper prepared for the workshop entitled 'Legal Aspects of Water Sector Reforms to be organised in Geneva from 20 to 21 April 2007 by the International Environmental Law Research Centre (IELRC) in the context of the Research partnership 2006-2009 on water law sponsored by the Swiss National Science Foundation (SNF).

[495] UN Committee on Economic, Social and Cultural Rights, The Right to Water, General Comment N° 15; UN DOC.E/C.12/11,29th Session, (2002).

[496] Ibid.

[497] The Universal Declaration of Human Rights was adapted by the General Assembly of the United Nations on 10 December 1948.

[498] Resolution 55/22 of August 2002 Millenium Development goals.

together Heads of States and Governments. Their objectives are expressed in a number of chapters. The following commitment was taken "to reduce to half by 2005 the proportion of the world's population whose income is less than a dollar per day and that of people suffering from hunger, and to reduce to half within the same period, the proportion of people who have no access to portable water or who lack the means to procure it".

It was also firmly promised in the same Declaration, to put an end to the irrational exploitation of water resources by formulating strategies at the regional, national and local levels to enable the guarantee of equitable access and adequate provision.[499] Cameroon has participated in most, if not all of the above international meetings and has appended its signatures to the legal instruments translating the intentions of the government to ensure a quiet enjoyment of the right to water.

Another legal instrument ratified by Cameroon Government is the Convention on the Elimination of All Forms of Discrimination against Women (CEDAW).[500] States that "State parties…shall ensure to women the right…. to enjoy adequate living conditions, particularly in relation to housing, sanitation, electricity and water supply."[501]

The Geneva Convention of 1949[502] and its Additional Protocols II of 1977[503] on the treatment of prisoners of war, and on the protection of victims of non-international armed conflict, respectively, have clearly imposed on states the obligation to implement the right to water even during war situations. The right to water is an integral part of these rights universally recognised or which could be considered as an indispensable component to the enjoyment of existing social and economic rights. Within the framework of implementation of the Covenant, the UN Committee on Economic, Social and Cultural Rights recognises that water is a fundamental right [504]. In the African Charter on the Rights and Welfare of the Child.[505]The Charter recognises that "State parties to the present Charter… shall ensure the provision of adequate nutrition and safe drinking water…" The fact

---

[499] Ibid.
[500] The Convention on the Elimination of all Forms of Discrimination against Women was adopted by the General Assembly Resolution 34/180 of 8 December 1979.
[501] Art 14 (2) (h) of the 1979 CEDAW.
[502] Arts 20, 26, 29 and 46 of the 1949 Geneva Convention.
[503] Arts 5 and 14 of the 1997 Additional Protocol II.
[504] Article 11 the ICESCR.
[505] Art 14 (1) (2) (c) of the 1966 Economic, Social and Cultural Rights

that Cameroon has also signed and ratified[506] this charter implies that the rights to water of the Cameroonian child are recognised under Cameroonian law.

The constitution of the Republic of Cameroon[507] does not explicitly provide for the right to water. However, it has a number of preambular provisions relating to economic and social rights. Since it is admitted that the right to water is an integral part of economic and social rights, it could, therefore, be submitted that the constitution makes implicit reference to the right to water through its provisions for economic and social rights.[508] As an integral part of environmental law, the right to water has a comfortable foundation in the constitutional provisions. It is provided in the preamble [509]that every person has a right to a healthy environment, that the protection of the environment shall be the duty of every Cameroonian, and that the state shall ensure the protection and improvement of the environment. Therefore, in this light, there is an implicit commitment to protect and improve on the right to water.

Cameroonian legislator has also passed the Water Code [510]within the respect of environmental and management principles and public health protection. In it, it is expressly provided that water is a public good or utility which the state ensures its protection and management and facilitates access to all.[511] The measures of protection are clearly spelled out in the Code[512] and violators come under heavy criminal sanctions [513] without prejudice to civil claims. To ensure conservation, protection and sustainable utilisation, the Code institutes a National Water Committee, an institution placed under the Ministry in charge of water resources.

With all these provisions both international and national put in place by the Government the right to access portable water is guaranteed all over the national territory with the rural sector in focus thus promoting the rural women especially economically since water facilitates production activities and equally gives enough time for the rural women to be creative since they will no longer go long distances to fetch water. Today however, because of poor implementation mechanisms, portable water still remains a scarce resource in Cameroon as a whole but particularly in the rural sector of the economy.

---

[506] Cameroon ratified the Charter on December 17, 2004.
[507] Law N° 96/06 of 18 January 1996 of the Cameroon Constitution.
[508]Paragraph 17, 24 and 27 of the 1966 Economic, Social and Cultural Rights
[509] Preamble of the 1996 Cameroon Constitution.
[510] Law N° 98/005 of 14 April1998 to lay down the Water Code and its Enabling Statutes.
[511] Ibid Art 4-7.
[512] Ibid Art. 19-20.
[513] Ibid Art. 26 (1).

6.9. Conclusion

The Vision 2035, which served as the anchor for these governmental and non-governmental efforts, spells out the government's ambition to position Cameroon as an "emerging nation, democratic and united in its diversity" by 2035. Its principal objectives include, reducing poverty to less than 10 percent, becoming a middle-income country, being an industrialized nation; and consolidating democracy and national unity. Since the women constitute a strong force in this developmental process envisaged by the government, the government is leaving no stone unturned to economically empower these rural women who constitute the backbone of the economy. In this light, the government has ratified so many international treaties that promotes women's rights and is making efforts towards their implementation as has been examined above. National laws to this regard are equally being passed and efforts towards enforcement are being made. NGOs, on their part are playing a primordial role in the economic empowerment of the rural women. As has been seen above, these NGOs offer legal aid to the rural communities, they promote women rights, foster an inclusive culture in the rural areas in Cameroon, promote rural women development, promote sustainable development in the rural communities. They fight rural poverty, and promote rural women's right to infrastructure. All these are effective means in promoting the rural women to become entrepreneurs thus becoming economically viable both for her development and the development of the national economy as a whole. The Problem here is that these measures remain mostly at the level of paper work. Most have not been implemented thus leaving these rural women less economically empowered.

After assessing these governmental and non-governmental efforts put in place to economically empower the rural women in Cameroon, it is but imperative to look at the limitations to the economic empowerment of the rural women since these women still remain less economically empowered as compared to her male counterpart.

156

CHAPTER SEVEN

LIMITATIONS TO THE ECONOMIC EMPOWERMENT OF THE RURAL WOMEN IN CAMEROON

7.1. Introduction

Grounded under the Natural law theory by Aristotle who postulates that "there is a social injustice when equals are treated unequally and conversely----", cities, towns, and all local entities in a global economy have the challenge of crafting their own economic destinies.[514] The rural women in spite of the plethora of legal provisions in place for her development still finds it so difficult to become economically developed as her male counterpart. This chapter has as objective to examine the various challenges faced by the rural women in Cameroon which renders them less economically empowered. It seeks to explain why in spite of the efforts of the government of Cameroon and many non-governmental organisations to improve on the socio-economic conditions of women in Cameroon, disparities continue to exist in areas of education, health and land ownership and other economic domains for the rural women in Cameroon making her less economically empowered.

Some of these difficulties are institutional related while others are due to weak implementation of mechanisms. Illiteracy, lack of commercial network, gender-based violence, multiple responsibilities and non-enforcement of regulations equally constitute some of limitations faced in economic empowerment of rural women.

7.2. Limitations within Institutional Settings.

7.2.1. The Cameroon's Growth Performance relies mostly on Public Investment

The Cameroon growth performance policy which is a tool put in place by the government to target all sectors of the economy is out to achieve and overall development in the country. This agenda for development was set in 2003 by poverty reduction strategy paper and has a vision that, Cameroonian being a united nation enjoys peace and security, democracy, decentralized administration prosperity and universal access to quality and social service[515]. Under this growth

---

[514] Blakey Edward J. and Leigh Nancy Green (2010). Planning local Economic Development: Theory and, Practice. SAGE Publications inc.4th edition, p.1.

[515] Common wealth governance, Cameroon Available at https://www.commonwealthgovernance.org (consulted on the 6/06/2023 at 5:25 am).

performance policy however economic growth has not succeeded in carrying out equitable poverty reduction, reasons being, special and social iniquities, and unfavourable business climate such as infrastructures lags and weak governance. Wide's spread regional disparity exist with the rural areas carrying the bulk of the country's poor.

7.2.2. Insufficient Infrastructure as challenge to Female Entrepreneurs

Looking at Africa as a whole under the structural adjustment, in comparison with other regions of the world, African economic performance indicator evinces a continental "drag effect". Output measures like GNP, export earnings and capital endowments such as infrastructure and skills are on average the world's lowest.[516]Cameroon which is an African country suffer from infrastructure lag. The development of sustainable, affordable, safe and reliable infrastructure has huge potential for reducing the barriers to entry and growth that prevent rural women from growing and striving in it. These are essential factors that hinder these women. They include among others.

7.2.2.1. Water and electricity

There are laws put in place in Cameroon for the provision of water and electricity to be provided all over the National territory. For instance, the law on water resources is to the effect that, "…. water shall be a common national resource protected and managed by the state which facilitate access to by all its citizens…."[517]

The law on electricity on its part states that, State government shall ensure the promotion and development of rural electrification, nationwide, through connection to an interconnected network or through distribution generator[518].However, the growth performance policy of Cameroon has up till this date not realized the provisions of portable water and constant electricity in Cameroon as a whole and especially in the rural areas in particular. The majority of the rural poor in the North west Region of Cameroon for instance depend on natural resources for their sustenance and wellbeing. It has been argued that the population growth, water scarcities, and incidence of poverty are exerting pressure on the already scarce natural resources in this region.[519] These rural women still go into the stream to fetch water and equally use bush lamps most at

---

[516] Eade Deborah (2004). Development and Rights. Oxfam GB.Vol.3. P.54.

[517] Article 2(1) of Law no 98/005 of 14 April 1998 on the law on water resources.

[518] Law No 2011/022 governing electricity supply in Cameroon.

[519] Bikwibili T.H. (2017), Sustainable Community Based Natural Resources Management in Sub-Sahara Africa: Perspectives on portable Water Supply in then North West Cameroon. Ph.D. Theis, University of Witwatesrand, Johannesburg, P.18.

times as a source of light. In the first place, the lack of water and light hinders these women's ability to carry further activities thus rendering them economically powerless. They spend up the whole day fetching water for household chores. The availability of which could have given them the time to ponder over further activities in life. Equally, water and light are essential before any enterprise can be put in placed successfully. These hinder the women to develop economic activities such as the creation of SMEs. In the workplace, a lack of water and electricity connection is a barrier for creation of new businesses and the expansions for old ones. Better infrastructures include reliable electricity or owning a generator improves the performance of businesses. Clean water, cooking fuel, heating and cooling equipment's and lighting are critical for many businesses to function properly. These women mostly engage in the food sector thus may face personal security when its dark. When forced to turn to other non-public sources of power, firms must bear the cost such as purchasing a generator or operating it. Purchasing energy privately instead of through public grid is extremely expensive and can be a barrier for women to become economically empowered and thus develop her SMEs. This is so because female entrepreneurs more often self-select low revenue sectors such as food, retail and services, they may be less able to overcome these barriers as a cost for a generator for instance represent a far larger percentage of their revenue.

7.2.2.2. Transportation Difficulties

For more than three decades investment in the transport sector has been a priority for the developing Country's governments. With a few exceptions, roads have accounted for a major part of these investments. The explicit and often articulated assumption upon which the decision to allocate such huge sums of money to road transport has been made that road transportation and development are inextricably linked. If roads do not actually produce economic development, they certainly play a major[520]

The Cameroon's growth performance strategy has as one of its developmental goals, the provision of good roads and improve means of transportation. Till date, most of our towns are characterized with very bad roads. The worst of it is that there are hardly farm to market roads in the rural areas. This makes it so difficult for agricultural produce to leave the farm to the market. As stated earlier this woman focus low-cost items such as food crops and agricultural product for the small enterprises. With these food crops not available in great

---

[520] Barwell T. J et al., (1985), Rural Transport in developing Countries. Intermediate Technology Publication, Vol.1. P.2.

quantities because of the nature of the roads or coming in bad because of bad roads can actually scare women from creating this small enterprise and become economically empowered. Take for instance, a small enterprise for the sale of tomatoes to retailers, if because of bad roads the tomatoes don't come on time or are delivered semi-perished, the business woman can lose half or even all of her capital thus hindering most women from venturing into the creation of small and enterprises. The prevalence of bad roads and public transit system have significant implication for the success of the rural women in any economic activity they are carrying out. Transportation determines the level of interaction between economy actors including partners input providers and consumers. Where transport linkages are weak and unavailable business interactions are constrained. Same like electricity and water.

Transportation shortage affect women and male business owners differently and men may have more freedom to adjust to missing transit links. While men may be content to wait for unreliable or infrequent buses or trains to deliver or to travel long distances on foot, women household activities will not allow them to spend as much time in transit. In addition, informal or poorly designed transportations system may present unique danger to women. Long and unpredictable wait time increases the risk of sexual and sexual based violence. This threat can be a measure factor that scares women from creating small businesses.

Legal provisions have been made in Cameroon to regulate road transport. We have the CEMAC Highway code,[521]the Cameroon highway code[522]the OHADA Uniform Act on the Carriage of Goods by Road[523]which regulates the contractual aspect of domestic and international carriage of goods by road. These provisions are put in place for the regulation of safety by all in the course of business transactions and especially when it comes to transportation of goods from one destination to the other. The highway code on its part obliges drivers to have mastery of their vehicles, have first Aid kids amongst others all in a bid to ensure the safety of its passengers. The Uniform Act on carriage of Goods regulates all aspects of transportation. This Acts states that, a contract for the carriage of goods exists as soon as the sender and the carrier reach an agreement concerning carriage of goods and consideration of an agreed price.[524]The Uniform

---

[521] The 2001 CEMAC highway code.
[522] The 1976 highway code as amended in 1986.
[523]The 2004 OHADA Uniform Act on the Carriage of Goods by Road.
[524] Article 3 of the 2004 OHADA Uniform Act on the Carriage of Goods by Road

Act equally states that, in case of any dispute arising from a contract, it shall be settled by way of arbitration.[525]

In case of any legal proceedings arising out of the inter-state carriage under this Uniform Act where the parties did not designate an arbitral tribunal or national court, the plaintiff may bring an action in the courts or tribunal of a country within which the defendant is ordinarily resident[526]or to where the goods were taken over by the carrier or the place designated for delivery is situated[527].

All these provisions are present for all to benefit from but for the fact most of these women are illiterates and are not even aware of the laws in place to recover their lost or damaged goods by legal means makes most of these women afraid and scares them from venturing into entrepreneurship thus unlike their male counterparts they remain less economically empowered.

7.2.2.3. Internet and Communication Network

The growth performance policy program has not made provision for strong reliable communication infrastructures. The primary law which regulates electronic communications[528] takes care of all issues concerning internet and communication in Cameroon. However, we have very poor communication system in Cameroon talk least of the rural areas in Cameroon. Where the networks are even available the women are the least likely to have access to. Fewer women than men in the rural setting have telephone than their male counterparts. These women in the context where social norms or household responsibility restricts their mobility, this communication tools could have given them access to opportunities for e businesses allowing them overcome the restrictions. However, the situation they find themselves in the rural settings such as no network connection, no electricity and even where these are available illiteracy of these women on how to manipulate these communication tools is a serious setback for these women making them to remain in their backward economic situation.

7.3. Weak Implementation Mechanisms

7.3.1. Predominance of the Informal Sector in the Economy

Looking at weak governance, Cameroon has failed to stimulate private sectors led growth to a reasonable extent to promote a better business climate. The overdevelopment of the informal sector in Cameroon is mainly due to the lack of

---

[525] Ibid   Article 27.
[526] ibid Article 27(a).
[527] ibid Article 27(b).
[528] Law no 2010/013 of December 21, 2010 as amended and supplemented by law no 2015/006 of April 20, 2015.

productivity and deficiencies in terms of economic governance. This has led to poor business environment and low-cost input, since the government is much more fucus on the public sector growth. The term informal sector is characterised by no administrative registration, little or no regulation of activities, relatively small scale of activities and capital, no fixed business premises that is developing out of organized circuits, such as markets. Family labour is mainly used. Finally, there is no security and social protection system.[529]

The informal sector in Cameroon occupies a predominant position in its economy. The Cameroon's informal sector officially occupies 90% of the active population in the country, and accounts for between 20 and 65% of the country's GDP.[530] Payment for an hour's work in the informal section in Cameroon stands at 463 CFAF, this can be increased to a maximum of up to 1,037 FCFA for informal production units, reasons being the level of education and the level of information explains to some extent the scale of the informal sector. In 2010, 27.4% of informal production unit promoters said that they did not know that an administrative registration was necessary and 45% thought it was not mandatory.[531]

Excessive development of this sector also stems from deficiencies related to economic governance. Indeed, the economic regulation system still carries the stigma of its colonial origins, where it was designed to regulate the subsidiaries of international groups. The indigenous economy, a refuge sector, which existed at the time outside regulations, gradually developed towards the current informal sector. Unfortunately, it is still not taken into account when designing regulation policies, whose requirements continue to be designed with reference to large companies. The informal sector, regarded as a refuge sector for many people finding it hard to integrate the formal fabric, benefits from an "administrative tolerance". In addition, the laxity, lack of transparency and deficiencies of the public service foster the maintenance of a significant segment of production units in the informal sector.

The rural women mostly if not all operate informal businesses and because of these government laxed policies, these women are not even aware of the fact that they can transform their businesses into a formal business by registering them

---

[529] Kuete Vincent (2020): Cameroon:90% of labour force trapped in the informal sector. Available at https://blog.private-sector and-development.com/2020/01/23/Cameroon-90-of the labour-force-trapped-in-the-informal-sector (consulted on the18/06/2023 at 2:50pm)

[530] Business in Cameroon: In Cameroon, the informal sector weighs as much GDP as in South Africa and Mauritius but less than in Nigeria. Available at https://www.businessincameroon.com.(Consulted on the 18/06/2023 at 2:20pm)

[531] ibid

and benefiting from the advantages of being a registered company. Thus, not effectively empowering these women economically.

The informal sector is characterised by numerous negative effects. Socially, it sustains poverty due to the very low wage levels of the jobs on offer which, in addition, they are very precarious, non-compliance with standards and hygiene rules results in high health risks, due to the dubious quality and origin of products (food products and drugs, in particular). Economically, for the State, the informal sector represents a shortfall in taxes. Many parts of the economy are tax-free, reducing the tax base and obliging the State to constantly increase levies on the structured and visible sector. The tax injustice resulting from the low level of taxation of the informal sector discourages the formal investors already in place and drives them to concealment and sometimes to tax evasion. The informal sector sows the seeds of illicit trade practices such as smuggling, counterfeiting, and fraud· Generally speaking, the informal sector maintains the overall lack of competitiveness of the economy, thus keeping the rural women stagnant in their economic growth.

7.3.2. The Predominance of Customary Law Rules

Customary law is equally referred to as "the generally accepted usage in any given group" and as "the body of law deriving from established local customs and usage of a tribe or community". It is equally referred to "as native laws and customs, traditional laws or autochthonous laws" and varies according to various communities.[532]

The rural setup which is our point of fucus depicts a typical traditional setting where customary law rules obtain. So many international conventions have been ratified by our Cameroon government for the protection of women's' right especially the rural woman. The convention on the Elimination of All Forms of Discrimination which was adopted in 1979 by the UN General Assembly is described as an international Bill of Rights for women. This convention sets the basis for the realization of equality between women and men through ensuring women's equal access to and equal opportunities in politics and public life including amongst others, the right to education, health and employment.[533]The International Labour Organisation (ILO) equally has as goal to promote equal opportunities for women and men to obtain decent work. The ILO's mandate to promote gender equality in the world of work is enshrined in its constitution and

---

[532] Mbetiji M. M. (2021), Integrating indigenous communities in the management of environmental resources in Cameroon: A legal appraisal. GALDA VERLAG. P. 32.

[533] UN Women: Convention on the Elimination of ALL Forms of Discrimination against women. Available at https://www.Un.org.(Consulted on 01/06/2023 at 12:00 noon)

is reflected in the relevant international labour standard .ILO considers gender equality as a critical element in effort to promote and realise standards and fundamental principles and rights at work and create greater opportunities for men and women to secure decent employment and income[534].Another International instrument which promotes gender equality is the Universal declaration of Human rights. This Declaration makes women's right, Human Rights. Gender equality was made part of international human rights law by the UDHR adopted on the 10th of December 1948,These Rights applies to all rights and freedom equally to end and women and prohibits discrimination on the basis of sex .These freedoms and rights include, equal pay for equal work, the right to health and the right to and the right to education for all[535].The UDHR equally states that, everyone has the right to freely participate in the cultural life of the community, to share scientific advances and its benefit and to get credit for their own work [536]The Economic, social and cultural rights are indispensable for human dignity and development of the human personality [537]Cameroon being a signatory to all these conventions thus implies that these provisions are supposed to be applicable in throughout our national territory. Even the Cameroon's constitution states that" ... all persons shall have equal rights and obligation. The state shall provide all its citizens with the conditions necessary for their development "[538]

The non-contentious probate rules of 1987 are to the effect that in case a deceased died on or after 1st January 1926 wholly intestate, the person or persons having beneficial interest in the estate are, the surviving husband or wife[539] The administration of Estates Acts 1925 holds that if the intestate leaves no issue, the residuary estate shall be held in trust for the surviving spouse or civil partner absolutely[540].

These legal provisions notwithstanding, the rural women are still unable to benefit from these rights because of weak implementation mechanisms and thus are not economically empowered as their male counterparts. Customary law rules in the rural sectors have succeeded to keep these rural women in the kitchen and farm only, causing them not to go to school thus remaining illiterates and thus cannot be economically developed.

---

[534] ILO: ILO and gender equality. Available at https://www.ilo.org (consulted 01/06/2023 at 1:23pm)
[535] Article 2 of the 1948 UDHR
[536] Ibid Article 27.
[537] Ibid Article 22.
[538] Article 1 of 1972 Constitution as amended in 2008
[539] Section 1(a) of the 1987 non-contentious probate rules.
[540] Section 46(1) of the 1925 Administration of Estate Acts.

7.3.2.1. Violation of Women's Rights to Inheritance

The men folk controls the various customs that operate in Cameroon as well as the institutions that regulates the day-to-day life. This hampers women's rights. When a customary law marriage falls apart, due to death, the widow finds herself as a beneficiary of an inheritance. Despite the fact that this is illegal, it keeps gaining popularity. Customary law does not allow for the sharing of property especially landed property between husband and wife on divorce. This position was taken by Inglis J where he held that, the wife continues to be part of the husband's property.[541]

The entrenchment of patriarchy in customs, traditions, attitudes have led to an intensification of discrimination against women in all forms. More brutal forms of violence and deprivation of rights confront women. Levirate marriage is normal practice in the rural settings where a widow is being inherited by the late husband's brother.[542] Cultures are being reinvented with a male face rather than from the perspective of gender justice.

The economy, civil society and the family are a powerful source of discrimination against rural women in Cameroon, and can limit their access to and control over resources that are crucial to starting and consolidating a sustainable enterprise. Rural women entrepreneurs in Cameroon are often thwarted by discriminatory property, family and inheritance laws and practices. Even when those laws and practices are equitable, women are often unaware of their rights to land and other productive resources or fear a backlash within the family or community if they claim them. This limits rural women's economic development.

7.3.2.2. Lack of Finance resources

The need for collateral is a major problem since women are denied or limited in their right to own property, buy or inherit assets; many women around the world are not legally entitled to own any asset that could serve as collateral when applying for a loan. A Hallward-Driemeier report from 2011, explains that if women and men were granted enough funds to start a business, women would open new establishments and invest in more machinery in both the formal and informal sectors. However, even in the event of having more starting income, women would not contemplate changing their line of business or locating the company in a different place. This indicates that most women have their idea and business plan clear and ready to go, and external limitations are as the reasons they do not advance. The types of businesses women run affect their ability to

---

[541] The case of Achu v.Achu Appeal No.BCA/62/86 supra
[542]See the Estate of Agboruja, (1949) 19 N.L.R.38

access finance, as they are concentrated in less profitable industries consumer-oriented activities and services in higher income countries where fewer assets are required.[543]

The fact that most women are underrepresented in traditional sectors makes it more difficult for them to access traditional loans due to the lack of assets as well as the fact that sources of funding such as venture capital are historically more interested in financing more innovative sectors such as biomedical engineering or technology companies, cooperatives or microfinance institution. Limited capital may affect women's ability to make optimal business choices. Still, the gender differences in mere access to finance having or not a loan or a bank account appear to be modest. The fact that the microfinance industry has focused largely on making services available to women may have limited the extent of gender disparities in credit.

Low rates of female land ownership can hinder access to financial assets that are necessary to set up a business. Available information suggests that less than 20% of agricultural land holdings in developing countries are operated by women (10% in Western and Central Africa and in the Near East and North Africa).[544]

Limited access to financial and business services affects the growth of rural women's businesses. Few banks operate in rural areas. Although financial institutions have increased access to micro finance in many countries, loans are seldom large enough to enable significant growth of enterprises. Women entrepreneurs, particularly in rural areas, often experience difficulties accessing relevant financial products and services due to a lack of appropriate products, information, understanding of their needs and collateral.

Business Development Services are not readily available in many rural areas where there is low population density. Where they do exist, women may rely on informal sector, failing to meet the decent work requirements.

Women-led businesses often concentrate in low paying, feminized markets (handicrafts, agricultural, fish and livestock products for local markets, food processing, sales of goods and services). In the informal economy with no legal registration, no regular workforce with rights and freedom of association, and no adequate operating capital to cover employees' social protection and health

---

[543] Makena P. et al., (2014) Challenges facing Women Entrepreneurs in Accessing Business Finance in Kenya, IOSR-JBM vol.16. PP 83-91.
[544] Reardon T. et al., (1998) Rural Non-farm Income in Developing Countries, FAO, Agriculture series, No.31. p.

benefits. Legal capacity and Property rights, Gender-based discrimination permeates through society, and it is sometimes reflected in laws, policies, and practices of institutions. According to the Women, Business and the Law Report by the World Bank, almost 90 out of the 143 economies in 2014 have at least one legal difference between men and women, in all cases restricting women's economic opportunities.

As expected, informal enterprises usually avoid using formal financial instruments and the finance their operations through alternative sources (internal funds, moneylenders, family and friends, etc.). Between formal and informal small-sized firms, the former shows a higher use of bank accounts and loans. Savings and reinvestment patterns, women reinvest a smaller portion of their profits compared to men, which limits their opportunities to expand. The reason is that most income is reinvested in their children or in family expenses, which trades off with opportunities to grow the enterprise. In many cases, as women face biased access to health, education or public services, they are forced to cover themselves and instead use the earnings from their businesses.

Marital property policies can compromise female savings from their businesses, as in full and partial community regimes, assets are initially legally considered as jointly owned. Not only is this lack of safety one of the reasons for women's lower savings rates, but it also puts women in a difficult situation by removing the option of using those grants as collateral. Lack of human capital, Limited knowledge of financial documentation and government legislation makes women an easy target for manipulation by financial institutions in certain countries. Low levels of literacy and low professional and management skills make female business-owners more vulnerable to signing disadvantaged loan documents.

Women entrepreneurs have greater difficulties accessing finance than men. Women are less likely than men to indicate that they can access the financing female-dominated sectors, gender-biased credit scoring and gender stereotyping in the lending process. Consequently, women entrepreneurs typically start their businesses with less money and are more reliant on self-financing. A consequence of the difficulties in accessing finance is that self-employed women are more likely than self-employed men to be discouraged borrowers, i.e., people who do not apply for loans because they believe that the loans will not be appropriate or that they will not be successful.

In Cameroon, women, especially the rural woman those who have taken up the challenge to start up a business more often than not finds it more difficult to raise capital to start up this business. Taking into consideration the societal norms and the position in which these women are kept in the society, individuals and even some institutions find it extremely difficult to grant loans to these women to start up their business, they prefer to grant loans to the male counterpart since they believe they are capable to handle businesses and thus pay back the loan. Even in the case where these loans are available, women who have access to it most often discovers that these loans have very high interest rates which discourages her to get the loan. This notwithstanding the presence of the National economic and financial Committee (CNEF), COBAC, OHADA and the creation of MFI particularly in the rural sectors as governmental efforts to promote the creation of businesses in Cameroon as examined the previous chapter. Thus, still keeping most of these rural women in a less economically empowered position.

7.3.2.3. Discriminatory Laws against women in Cameroon

Inheritance has been addressed as part of a large problem of discriminatory property rights regime against women.[545]Many victims of succession-based violence abstain on their own volition from going to court. Women would not want to take their husbands' relatives or brothers to court, as they think that they will need their support in rainy days.

There is also illiteracy and ignorance among the rural populations which make them oblivious of the fact that law at least provides some measure of protection for their interests. The conception here is that the successor of the deceased, who manages the property on behalf of the family, is already known and what is needed is for the new "father" and "husband" to continue providing for their subsistence. The fear and threat of witchcraft has also been identified as deterring many a meritorious beneficiary from seeking legal redress in a court of law. Witchcraft as defined by the Penguin English Dictionary consists in "the use of sorcery or magic" and the practitioner of witchcraft is said to be "a person who is credited with supernatural powers."[546]

Furthermore, the High Courts with the competence to administer the laws are inaccessible to many who would have sought legal redress. These courts are said to be located at divisional levels, but the divisions are generally large and most of the countryside is without motorable roads, and this makes access to them

---

[545] The protection of women inheritance Right in Cameroon. Available at
https://www..research key.net (Consulted on the 02/12/2023).
[546] Nzalie Joseph (2008): The structure of succession law in Cameroon: Finding A balance Between the needs and interests of different family members. A Thesis submitted to the University of Birmingham for the Degree of Doctor of Philosophy. School of law University of Birmingham October 2008

difficult, if not impossible. Thus, the provisions 2009 of offering legal aid in Cameroon has no impact on these rural women since they are not even aware that their rights are being violated. The rural populations which constitute the majority are therefore governed mostly by customary law. It is not uncommon also for matters arising in the urban areas where the courts are located to be governed by customary law because of the cost involved in suing in the modern jurisdiction.[547]Although Ordinance 74-1 of 6 July 1974 guarantees without discrimination, to any natural or legal person having landed property the right to freely enjoy and dispose of it, in practice, the situation does seem to hardly favour women. Most Customs recognizes only women's Usufruct rights over land, not ownership rights even if the woman purchases the land by herself. In patrilineal and matrilineal societies, women's rights to land are derived from men as wives, daughters, sisters or in laws.[548]

The Cameroon's French civil code states that, the husband alone administers the common property. He can sell, dispose of and mortgage the property without the consent of the wife. The husband under the French civil code equally has the sole right of Administration over all his wife's property. He alone exercises all property rights and possessory actions belonging to him.

According to the civil code women are not fully entitled to use, enjoy or sell their property, although this right is stipulated in the Constitution. In this context, the civil code grants the husband the right to administer communal property, thereby giving him the right to sell or mortgage the couple's property without the wife's consent.[549]

For a marriage to be effective, both parties must have the capacity to understand the meaning of marriage. Age, consent and illness should be taken into consideration to ascertain the full capacity of both parties to a marriage as was in the British case of Sheffield city Council v. E[550].However, the minimum age for marriage in Cameroon is 15 years for girls and 18 years for boys[551].Girls under 18 are not required to consent to marriage, parental consent is sufficient[552] The man can choose which matrimonial regime applies (monogamy or polygamy). If no choice is made, the couple is married under common law, which allows

---

[547] Ibid.
[548] See note 25 supra
[549] According to articles 1421 and 1428 of the 1981 Cameroon Civil Code
[550] Munby J.in Sheffield city council v. E (2005) 2 WLR 953.
[551] See article 52 of the Cameroon civil code.
[552] Ibid article 49.

polygamy and community of marital property. The payment of dowries is authorized.[553]

The husband is considered to be the head of the family[554] He also has the sole right to determine the family domicile[555] and, in the interest of the household and the children, may prevent his wife from taking employment

There are no laws prohibiting traditional harmful practices, and female genital mutilation (FGM) and the practice of breast ironing persist in parts of the North and the South-West of the country. These provisions are contrary to the Constitution which provides for equality of all irrespective of sex. Thus, this goes a long way to hinder female in the entrepreneurial ventures making her less developed.

Lack of legal definition of discrimination exists. Customary law, another source of law in Cameroon, which is far more discriminatory against women is applicable especially in the rural sectors in the Anglophone regions of Cameroon. The broad persistence of customary law infringes the human rights of women, particularly in the areas of marriage and inheritance. However, due to the importance attached to traditions and customs, international commitments are not respected. Laws, cultures, religion, and politics are built upon a patriarchal foundation. Women must work their way up in the masculine world while facing stigma and discrimination. Although laws and policies have attempted to create a favourable business environment for everyone, the actual changes have not yet been implemented.

Empowering a woman with knowledge is just the beginning of a long journey to business success. Life is a daily learning process where each day comes with new information. Unfortunately, women's access to this information and emerging knowledge is limited. Although it could be a result of the competitive environment, women take the extra step and seek relevant and practical information.

In agriculture women do the bulk of the work and produce, but are not taken into consideration when it comes to decision making. Given the recent strides made in removing regulatory discrimination, business law may not be strongly binding for female entrepreneurs in Africa. While rigorous measures of the impact of legal reforms promoting gender equality in business outcomes are still lacking, African economies have adopted these reforms at a fast pace. In 2012, Mali

---

[553] Ibid article 70.
[554] Ibid article 213.
[555] Ibid articles 108 and 215.

removed legal restrictions which prevented married women from registering a business. Zimbabwe's 2013 constitutional reform ensures that customary law is no longer exempt from protection against gender discrimination. However, even when business law is gender neutral, family law may introduce constraints to married women and their ability to manage their businesses.

For instance, in Cameroon, Côte d'Ivoire, Chad, the Democratic Republic of Congo (DRC), and the Republic of Congo, customary law gives husbands sole control over marital property. Such provisions restrict women's ability to buy, own, sell and use property. This makes it more difficult for married women to obtain loans to finance their businesses, as these loans usually require collateral in the form of property. On the other hand, work in Ethiopia indicates that joint ownership of land in marriage increases the position of women. In the context, marital property issues are examples of the interaction of different constraints. Legal discrimination interacts with differences in assets endowment, and these constraints jointly limit women's opportunities. Even when statutory law provides for gender equality, such as with a non-discrimination clause in the constitution, women may face important restrictions if customary law takes precedence over statutory law.

In addition, these women especially the rural women have to take care of the home and the children and any woman most often who struggles to succeed in business gets sabotage and even faces violence at home by the husband. Women are underrepresented in entrepreneurship in nearly all developed nations not to talk of less developed countries.

Women entrepreneur typically take longer than their male colleagues to achieve public trust and recognition after starting a business because there are women with specific roles attached to them by society. These women have to strive to succeed in a male dominate world which is not an easy task.

Men and women have different motivations for starting their businesses. The primary motivation for women to start businesses is principally the need for autonomy and freedom. Take off capital is usually small as compared to men. These women take off businesses basically because of their Families. Since they don't want to depend on the men to care of their children.

7.3.2.4. Constraints to Women Land Right

Land is very important asset for indigenous women's development. For the rural women to grow businesses such as small and medium size enterprises they need land. Unfortunately, there is insecurity of land tenure for the indigenous

171

women in Cameroon, to access control over and ownership of this resource remains a male privilege.[556]

This situation in the rural area in Cameroon has negatively affected indigenous women's ability to contribute to the development of the communities. Barriers which often hinders these women to own land and other productive resources often include inadequate legal standards and /or ineffective implementation at the national and local levels as well as discriminatory cultural attitudes and practices at the institutional and community levels.

7.3.2.4.1. Lack of Appropriate Recognition of the Rural Women

The government of Cameroon has not taken a kin interest in providing constitutional recognition to its indigenous population even though mention is made in the preamble of the Constitution. This lack of proper recognition has seriously limited indigenous women's ability to own and control land even though their existence depends on it. Ownership of land will enable the rural women to be economically productive. Land is a human right that encompasses all facets of life at all levels of human society.[557] The notion of land as human's survivor and livelihood is to the effect that those who own and control land indirectly controls the lives of others. The inability to own land by these rural women renders them underdeveloped and relegates them to a destitute situation. Some scholars hold and rightly so that women's access to and right to land will greatly improve their economic power as they could use land as security to secure loans that will help them to improve their lifestyles. This situation has hindered the rural women greatly in creating small and medium sized enterprises in the rural sector of the economy of Cameroon thus rendering her economically inviable.

7.3.2.4.2. Poverty and Ignorance hinders Rural Women to enjoy their right to land

The economic and socio-cultural hindrances to women's access to land are due to poverty and ignorance. The global rate of education is very low in the rural area in Cameroon. The provisions of the modern land law enacted the provisions of titling and land titling[558] as a measurement of acquiring land in both the rural

---

[556] Yenkong E. S (2020), Land law and post-colonial constraints to women's land rights in Cameroon. International journal of resource and environmental Management, vol.5, No.1, pp.140-142.

[557] Fombe L. F et al (2013), "Securing tenure for sustainable livelihoods: a case of women land ownership in anglophone Cameroon". Ethics and economics pp. 73 – 86.

[558] A land certificate is provided by Decree No. 76/165 of 27th April 1976 which sets out the conditions for obtaining land tittle in Cameroon, amended and supplemented by Decree No.2005/481 of 16th December 2005 is defined as the official certificate of ownership.

and urban areas. However, the complexity of procedures, the rigidity of the conditions demanded and all the bureaucratic slow procedures constitute serious obstacles for the ignorant women. Obtaining a land title for instance requires several formalities that ignorant peasants cannot fulfil. The high cost of obtaining land titles discourage and disable these rural women keeping them in an undeveloped situation.

7.3.2.4.3. Institutional hindrances

These institutional hindrances include the void and muteness of positive law on some important points relative to the women's land status. As well as the fear of banalisation of justice, most women are incapable of defending their rights in court. Very few choose judicial solution because they lack confidence in the institution of the ever-present corruption. These women equally fear the retaliation that are likely to be subjected to their families or villages following judicial actions. So, they adopt attitude of resignation or compromise.

7.3.2.4.4. Variability and Instability of Traditional Land Practices

The changing nature of traditional land system in Cameroon characterise the custom in the land situation. Land practices vary from one region to the other. Almost all the customs however, exclude women from land ownership, though some customs are more rigid than others. For instance, according to the Bety custom, the land is patrilineal that is to say land is transferred from father to son. If the man has only daughters, the land generally will go back to the diseased man's family member.

These indigenous women remain marginalized and this situation exposes them to gross human rights violations such as rape and prostitution. Lack of inheritance right which is attributed to high level of illiteracy, ignorance of their civic and political rights and extreme poverty hinders the rural women from owning and controlling land which acts as a great challenge to the rural women economic empowerment.

7.4. Lack of Education

Obstacles to access education have been a major constraint. The literacy rate for adult male population is 81.15% (6,818,208) persons, 1,583,463 are illiterates while, Literacy rate for adult female population is 68.88% (5.784,044persons).2,613,111 are illiterates[559] This disparity can be explained in part by families' decisions to favours boys' education if financial resources do not

---

[559] Cameroon population (2023). Literacy of population. Available at https://countrymeters.infos.(Consulted on the 03/12/2023).

permit sending all children to school. Although some efforts have been made by the government to promote girls' access to education, there remain fewer girls than boys in secondary and higher education. Only a handful of girls have been able to benefit from the scholarship policy. In rural areas, the quality of education is far lower than in urban areas.

Except among the very younger generation, the degree of scholarisation among the female population is still very low. Most of those who are encouraged to go to school because of the government's policy of compulsory education for all, are often forced out of school because of different social factors. Some of them are unemployed, vulnerable and powerless and are living in abject poverty.

Despite the fact that most African countries have achieved gender parity with respect to access to primary education, the educational gender gap in previous cohorts still affects older generations of entrepreneurs. In addition, younger cohorts still face a gender gap in accessing higher levels of education. A number of factors may have contributed to current and past gender differences in access to education, including greater parental investment in sons' education and girls' early marriage. Women whose access to education has remained limited are likely to have lower levels of literacy and numeracy, which may adversely affect both the scope and the productivity of their business activities. Beyond greater access to formal education, opportunities for developing entrepreneurial skills may be higher for men than for women There is equally the issue of lack of education thus lack of knowledge. The rural woman lacks the knowledge of transforming her agricultural produce to other product for better development. For instance, she lacks the knowledge that some the corn she produces can be transform into animal feed diversifying her production and making more money. From the production of feed, she can equally do animal or poultry farming to make her enterprise grow but she lacks the knowledge and so is limited and focuses only on her corn farming which is mainly for home consumption and left over for sale so as to buy other food items in the house. With this she cannot expand and develop her enterprise.

The high illiteracy rate of the rural woman is a big challenge because they cannot access available necessary information easily. It is also a big problem because the women find it difficult to understand some of the critical issues of gender and development.

7.5. Lack of Commercial networks

The lack of commercial networks by the rural women should be noted contravenes the provisions of right to association postulated by the legislator .Further provisions are even made every day to enhance this right.[560] Freedom of association encompasses both an individual's right to join or leave groups voluntarily, the right of the group to take collective action to pursue the interests of its members, and the right of an association to accept or decline membership based on certain criteria. It can be described as the right of a person coming together with other individuals to collectively express, promote, pursue and/or defend common interests.[561] Freedom of association is both an individual right and a collective right, guaranteed by all modern and democratic legal systems.

Freedom of association is manifested through the right to join a trade union, to engage in free speech or to participate in debating societies, political parties, or any other club or association, including religious denominations and organizations, fraternities, and sport clubs and not to be compelled to belong to an association.

The general freedom to associate with groups according to the choice of the individual, and for the groups to take action to promote their interests, has been a necessary feature of every democratic society.

The fact that most of these women are illiterates and semi-illiterates, they lack skills which permit them to have effective commercial networks. Most women are producers, processors, marketers etc. Without division of labour the women are overloaded and will hardly succeed in their endeavours. There are hardly any available services like information services, market services. Help services that can effectively help women and advance in their economy level·

Women, especially from the working classes (agricultural labourers, sharecroppers, those from poor peasant and landless households) face tremendous barriers to effective participation in organisations which represent their own interests. These obstacles include ideological, cultural and institutional factors, some of which are general to both men and women. At the same time, women even more than men, face a variety of specific problems in their attempt to

---

[560] See Law No.2021/022 of 16 December 2021 to amend some provision of law No.90 0f 19 December 1990 relating to freedom of Association in Cameroon.

[561] Articles 20 and 23 of the 1948 Universal Declaration of Human Rights and article 22 of International Covenant on Civil and Political Rights. The Declaration on Fundamental Principles and Rights at Work by the International Labour Organization also ensures these rights.

organise. Very few women actively participate in public bodies, whether they are of an economic or political nature. Their representation is strongest in social/religious traditional networks, which seldom influence policies and programme at the national or even local level. Clearly the fact that women often occupy a dependency status visa-vis man and the community generally, makes it more difficult for them to organise to defend their interests. Moreover, the discrimination they face in their world of work (lower wages, job insecurity, dependence on home-based production at pieces rates dictated by private contractors, a heavy workload, resulting from their dual role at home and on the work sites, in the productive and reproductive process) creates serious barriers to their getting together to organise. In most situations, they have little time to attend meetings. [562]

Aside even from the heavy workload which precludes women from participating, in many cultures' seclusion is practiced and women have little freedom of choice in participating in organisational activities of a public nature. Often, they do not control their own movements, even their decision as to where to work being controlled by other household members - father, husband, mother-in-law. Moreover, in most traditional cultures, women seldom dare to speak in meetings when men are present, so that their views are frequently not taken into account in arriving at decisions. This is re-enforced, by women's perception of themselves, conditioned by their cultural and social environment, as being inferior to that of men. All of this means that women are heavily exploited. Whilst being badly in need of group solidarity, they face serious obstacles to organisation. They lack commercial networks because of all these which hinders them to become economically empowered.

Moreover, women appear to have greater difficulty acquiring entrepreneurship skills. This is because of the low level of education or the fact that most women in rural areas are illiterates or semi-illiterates making it difficult for the acquisition of the required entrepreneurship skill. Thus, impossibility of becoming economically developed.

7.6. Gender Based violence

According to the Universal Declaration of Human Rights which holds that "No one shall be subjected to torture or to cruel, inhuman or degrading treatment or punishment"[563] and many other international and national instruments that fight

---

[562] Ahmed Zubeida (2023), Rural women, their conditions of work and struggle to organize. Available at https://horizon.documentation.ird.fr.(Consulted on the 03/12/2023).
[563] Article 5 of the 1948 Universal Declaration of Human Rights.

against GBV have been put in place by the Cameroon Government. There is no available case law in Cameroon regarding domestic violence, however, the Ministry for the Protection of the Family and the Woman ensure that "all acts of violence and discrimination against women are reported and that the police force receives support in caring for and assisting in the reintegration of women victims of violence into society and their families." The reality is that domestic violence in Cameroon is still considered a private matter and the law enforcement officers do not consider it a serious issue; therefore, victims are reluctant to report abuse. Furthermore, the Cameroonian judicial system usually applies customary rules that discriminate against women. it is considered that a man has "disciplinary rights" over his wife[564]as demonstrated in the discriminatory provisions in the civil status registration ordinance in Cameroon. Judges in Cameroon are usually reluctant to apply international legal instruments ratified by Cameroon, making these beautiful provisions remain only on papers thus making these women especially the rural women remain under constant GBV, hindering them from excelling in their full potentials and in becoming economically empowered.

Victims of domestic abuse have little recourse for protection in Cameroon since there is no domestic violence law providing women with an order for protection against abusers. Women in Cameroon experience high levels of discrimination, despite Constitutional provisions against such violence[565] recognizing the human rights of all.

As noted, isolation, emotional, physical, and economic can be a factor why some victims stay in abusive relationships; the geographical circumstances of rural living can exacerbate this factor. There are numerous behaviours employed by abusers to create isolation for their victims, such as limiting a victim's access to family vehicles or preventing her from obtaining a driver's license, ridiculing her in front of others, or accusing her of flirting, thus making her even less likely to invite others to the home or go out herself and even removing the telephone when leaving the house so that she has no means to communicate with others. For rural victims, these abuser behaviours may be compounded by the realities of rural living, including: lack of phone service (landline or cell access), limited or no public transportation, limited access to routine health care, long response times for police and medical emergency teams, weather and road conditions, weapons and dangerous tools more commonly available, Seasonality of work that may leave the woman "trapped" with her abuser for long periods of time. Economic conditions of farm life, single income, value tied to land, need for all to work to

---

[564] Ordinance No 81-02 of 29th June 1981.
[565] See the preamble of the 1996 Cameroon Constitution.

stay solvent. If a farm is only source of income, a restraining order can't be used to keep the abuser away. Emotional conditions of farm life, strong ties to animals and land. Rural citizens tend to have fewer insurance resources, and tight-knit communities may discourage people from reporting abuse. Locating shelters in rural areas is also more difficult because they are harder to hide.[566]

7.7. Multiple Responsibilities

Women's entrepreneurships are also affected by the extent to which women are able to reconcile family obligations with work outside the family, and there are particular barriers in those countries where traditional gender roles go hand in hand with a lack of public or private childcare and eldercare services. Furthermore, maternity leave provisions have a confirmed impact on the general rate of female entrepreneurship.

This is probably the first thing most people think about not only when it comes to women entrepreneurs, but also in the context of women who do any job. The thing is even those women who have perfectly organized all their work, will pay dues to tiredness and too many obligations. Not to mention those who agree to play under full equipment on two grounds: a housewife and a businesswoman. One thing certainly doesn't rule out another, but it requires serious planning, quick adjustment and compromises. If the man is the head of the house, then the woman is his spinal column, and this is precisely what society is likely to fear when looking at the female entrepreneurial spirit. However, instead of waging war on the role of garbage disposal, wouldn't it be more constructive to make a plan – and then adheres to it?

Cultural practices Custom and habits are dangerous routines for women who continue being the main providers of household duties and childcare, which results in their having less time available for other tasks. These restrictions may disincentives businesses growth and thus women's abilities to access financial services. There is no formal evidence, but anecdotal evidence suggests that women «have been socialized into bearing the highest share of the workload». Social norms define the activities women can engage in, imposing restrictions on mobility. Family and tax policies can discourage female labour market participation, including entrepreneurship by women.

---

[566] Glinski Stefanie (2020). What is gender-based violence and how do we prevent it. Available at https://www.rescue.org. (Consulted on the 04/12/2023).

7.8. Non-Enforcement of Internationally Ratified Instruments

The greatest challenge to the implementation of the BPFA (Beijing Platform for Action) is the lack of a proper evaluation of the different cultures regarding women at the local levels to see how comprehensive engagement can be carried out to end the different forms of violence against women in the many cultures that exist. The absence of monitoring mechanisms in the state and non-state sector and a clearly articulated agenda in support to women's social, economic, political and cultural rights are the main constraints to implementation measures. With the non-implementation of these measures, the rural women are doomed to remain where they are. They remain marginalised and thus cannot step up in their line of activities. Thus, making economically underdeveloped.

7.9. General Challenges Faced by Female Entrepreneurs

7.9.1. Launching a new business especially for women can be scary

Bringing their hard work in to the world by these female entrepreneurs is actually nerve-racking especially when you have to take much time to build and refine a company from the scratch. It is quite challenging to conduct simple market research. In addition, you have to put in many hours in to building a brand, finding a product, packaging, finessing the looks of a store to make sure everything is perfect. Even the process of registering these companies to make them formal scares most if not all of these rural women which is one of the reasons for the prevalence of the informal business sector in the economy. Most of these women are illiterates or semi-illiterates and so do not even know how to go about these formalities. The challenging nature of launching a business is the reason that 72% of entrepreneurs are directly or indirectly affected by mental health Issues compared to 40% of non-entrepreneurship[567] These rural women have much to do, from taking care of the home, giving birth to children, working in the farm and then thinking about a new venture such as creating a small enterprise is no easy task to achieve. The too many activities become most at times too overwhelming for these rural women.

7.9.2. Entrepreneurship is Fraught with uncertainties

Entrepreneurship comes with so many ups and downs logistics, you need to think about the man power financing, that is where to get money to take off the business and equally the type of goods to offer to the public. You can never tell what problem may arise the same day or the next day in the business and you need

---

[567] Benz Alexander (2022): Entrepreneurs are struggling with mental challenges. Available at https://www.entrepreneur.com.(consulted on 08/06/2023 at 8:47 am).

to always proffer solution to all these problems. This can be so challenging for Female entrepreneurs who in addition to that need to take care of the family's own needs and problems. Entrepreneurs wear many hats. From marketing, that is going to social media, packaging and fulfilment this in addition with the fact that you have to access your business 24hours a day.[568] Self-doubt, lack of respect, Getting unsolicited advice, Making authoritative first impression, expanding business, collaborative partners, battling unrealistic expectations, finding capital ,no support system, deciding what to sell ,hiring talents, delegating authority ,managing time, managing employees, maintaining a budget-sustaining revenue and staffing the organization are further challenges and uncertainties faced by female entrepreneurs especially the rural women making them economically underdeveloped.

7.9.3. Stress

Stress is definitely not reserved for women entrepreneurs. It affects all people who care what they do in order to meet the set criteria. However, if we recall that women, besides business, have to bear with everything described above – it is clear that this stress is even more complex. Therefore, it's necessary to deal with everyday challenges. What more, with things that make the position of a female entrepreneur different in relation to the male. There isn't an almighty recipe that will take away all these problems. But the awareness of them, as well as the way we choose to deal with such challenges, is what can make this game more equitable.

7.9.4. Fear of Failure

Women are more likely than men to report that a fear of failure prevents them from starting a business. Entrepreneurship or running a business is risky and entails unforeseen circumstances. Never fear failure; you will never try if you fear failure. No one goes into business with a guarantee of success. Fear of the known and the unknown is a major issue for women. They dread failing, especially if the people surrounding them were sceptical of their capability in business. This fear is toxic and perilous, because women may end up operating from a place of fear instead of confidence. As a result, they will fail in business even when they were meant to succeed.

---

[568] Ibid.

7.9.5. Negative Business Environment

Although we are living in the 21st century, the number of people who still believe that men are more adequate for business is not negligible. However, we are still inclined to believe in certain stereotypes about what are "masculine" and what "feminine" jobs are.

You have probably happened to see a woman driving a bus, maintaining call Centre software, or being a mechanic, and think: "Why does a woman do this job"? The truth is that behind, stands a deep culturally and socially conditioned view that some jobs are simply not for women. The fact is that many would rather choose to work with a man than with a woman. This particular point of view makes problems for many women entrepreneurs.

More developed and liberal societies also face these challenges. This battle is taking place on a huge number of fronts, every day. Therefore, it is important to know that such stereotypes and prejudices can be found anywhere and at any time.

Social norms and attitudes influence women's and men's choices and opportunities. Women's entrepreneurship is not broadly accepted in many societies and women face attitudinal obstacles in their starting, consolidating and developing a sustainable business. Women often enter a business when they are older, divorced or become household heads. Few young women see business development as an appropriate or viable livelihood option.

Social norms and attitudes affect the implementation of laws, policies and programs. Even though relevant laws and regulations may not be discriminatory on paper, discrimination often takes place during their implementation (or lack of implementation).

Women's obstacles in accessing domestic and export markets (small scale of operation, lack of transportation and information, and time constraints) limit their capacity to achieve growth, create decent working conditions and build sustainable livelihoods.

Women engaging in rural businesses with their spouses often invest considerable time, but do not always share decision-making power and may not identify themselves as business owners. This may limit their opportunities to grow professionally, be innovative or demonstrate entrepreneurial attitudes that could lead to business growth.

Most micro and small businesses, especially those led by women, are underrepresented in employers' associations. Therefore, they lack voice and representation to raise awareness and A lack of effective social and political reforms has kept women in a secondary position, and customary interpretation of the law also makes political reforms and legislation an ineffective tool to begin within certain regions and countries. In other cases, female enterprises remain small because women do not want their businesses to grow bigger.

Furthermore, norms about how different genders should behave may restrict women in access to important resources such as human, financial and social capital. The small number of successful women entrepreneurs who can act as role models is highly detrimental in encouraging women to consider entrepreneurship as a career, especially in science and technology related fields.

The bottom of the gender equality pyramid lies in environments where basic rights are not respected. As we have seen before, disadvantages such as land ownership being constrained by the application of customary law prohibit women from acquiring land without their husbands' authorization. Unfortunately, the answer to the question has to be no, not all women have access to financial products, as they are limited by legal and business environments as well as social, cultural, educational and financial constraints. Policymakers, researchers and both the private and public sectors need to work together to support women's empowerment in financial and non-financial institution.

Cameroon has high levels of discrimination against women in social institutions and the society as a whole. The notion that women are to be in the kitchen while the men are the ones to confront the business world still operate in Cameroon today. Women have fixed duties to perform such as bearing children, farming for home consumption and carrying out household chores. Women in Cameroon especially those in the rural areas are limited to these stereotype activities, and any woman who wants to change the traditional practice is being looked upon as being in submissive to the husband if married or being arrogant or rude if single and the society will look at that lady as wanting to defile social norms. This situation is however improving in Cameroon today but much still needs to be done. But the crucial is that we accept them just as they are prejudices and stereotypes. We cannot change what the environment thinks, but we can influence what we will do with our own capabilities.

Government action is not coherent because initiatives are put in place aimed at reducing poverty, but at the same time high taxes are levied on individual initiatives aimed at raising income level of women, for example rural women are given tax in the market to pay as an income generating activity for the councils[569]

Women's participation in the chambers of agriculture and commerce. These structures are not gender sensitive and women's concerns are hardly taken into consideration. Those who benefit from these chambers are those who are rich, meaning that women, who form the greater portion of the poor, can hardly benefit from their services. The registration cost for these chambers is usually so high making it even more difficult for women to be members and be able to participate in the decision-making process and management of the structure[570].

At the level of the government, the government of Cameroon has not taken measures to eliminate domestic violence against women which is still regarded as culturally accepted by certain sectors of the economy. Women in Cameroon experience high level of discrimination despite constitutional provisions recognizing the constitutional rights of all without discrimination.

The most important limitations negatively affecting the ability of women to become entrepreneurs in the first place or to grow their existing enterprises, besides the pure access to capital, are very much related to institutional, cultural and infrastructural issues. Investment climate, environments with informal businesses, limited transportation infrastructure, weak governance, crime or corruption affect the way women are able to do business. Women deal worse with corruption and red tape, but also, they are more vulnerable to abuses while in the informal sector.

7.9.6. Access to Networks and Information

Women may struggle more than men to grow their businesses if they have more limited social networks and information. Gender differences in access to networks may stem from norms limiting women's ability to venture away from their home or to interact with strangers working in female-dominated sectors are not aware that women (and men) in male-dominated sectors tend to make much higher profits. Hence, women's limited access to information contributes to gender segregation across sectors.

There is long-standing evidence that women entrepreneurs tend to have entrepreneurial networks that are smaller and less diverse than male entrepreneurs. Furthermore, women's entrepreneurship networks appear to have a different composition than the networks of men entrepreneurs, being more likely

---

[569] Kumichii T. N., Assessing the Implementation of the Beijing platform of Action in Cameroon. Available at< https://www.library.fes.de> (consulted on the 5/23/2020).
[570] Ibid.

to include family, friends and educators rather than business services providers or other entrepreneurs

7.9.7. Access to Loans

7.9.7.1. Access to Financial Institution

Limited capital may affect women's ability to make optimal business choices. Still, the gender differences in mere access to finance – having or not a loan or a bank account - appear to be modest. The fact that the microfinance industry has focused largely on making services available to women may have limited the extent of gender disparities in credit,

Low rates of female land ownership can hinder access to financial assets that are necessary to set up a business. Available information suggests that less than 20% of agricultural land holdings in developing countries are operated by women (10% in Western and Central Africa and in the Near East and North Africa).[571]

Limited access to financial and business services affects the growth of rural women's businesses. Few banks operate in rural areas. Although financial institutions have increased access to micro finance in many countries, loans are seldom large enough to enable significant growth of enterprises. Women entrepreneurs, particularly in rural areas, often experience difficulties accessing relevant financial products and services due to a lack of appropriate products, information, understanding of their needs and collateral.

Women-led businesses often concentrate in low paying, feminised markets (handicrafts, agricultural, fish and livestock products for local markets, food processing, sales of goods and services)1 in the informal economy with no legal registration, no regular workforce with rights and freedom of association, and no adequate operating capital to cover employees' social protection and health benefits. Legal capacity and Property rights, Gender-based discrimination permeates through society, and it is sometimes reflected in laws, policies, and practices of institutions. According to the Women, Business and the Law Report by the World Bank, almost 90 out of the 143 economies in 2014 have at least one legal difference between men and women, in all cases restricting women's economic opportunities. For instance, to mention some of the most extreme situations, women are forbidden from opening a bank account in the Democratic Republic of Congo and in Niger, and the Democratic Republic of Congo and

---

[571] Reardon T. et al., (1998) Rural Non-farm Income in Developing Countries, FAO, Agriculture series, No.31.

Pakistan do not allow women to register their own businesses. Further, women's usage and control of property remains limited, especially for married women. Property rights and land ownership and access provide and reinforce income and female empowerment.[572]

As expected, informal enterprises usually avoid using formal financial instruments and the finance their operations through alternative sources (internal funds, moneylenders, family and friends, etc.). Between formal and informal small-sized firms, the former shows a higher use of bank accounts and loans. Savings and reinvestment patterns Women reinvest a smaller portion of their profits compared to men, which limits their opportunities to expand. The reason is that most income is reinvested in their children or in family expenses, which trades off with opportunities to grow the enterprise. In many cases, as women face biased access to health, education or public services, they are forced to cover themselves and instead use the earnings from their businesses. Provided grants and in-kind grants to male and female entrepreneurs. These grants had a small but positive impact on male-owned enterprises but didn't seem to have any impact on female-owned companies. Male owners invested the whole grant, while females only invested large grants and on average didn't have any return on these grants. Tried to encourage men and women to apply for a microcredit by providing a brochure to men and women borrowing groups

Marital property policies can compromise female savings from their businesses, as in full and partial community regimes, assets are initially legally considered as jointly owned. Not only is this lack of safety one of the reasons for women's lower savings rates, but it also puts women in a difficult situation by removing the option of using those grants as collateral. Lack of human capital, Limited knowledge of financial documentation and government legislation makes women an easy target for manipulation by financial institutions in certain countries. Low levels of literacy and low professional and management skills make female business-owners more vulnerable to signing disadvantaged loan documents.

Women entrepreneurs have greater difficulties accessing finance than men. Women are less likely than men to indicate that they can access the financing female-dominated sectors, gender-biased credit scoring and gender stereotyping in the lending process. Consequently, women entrepreneurs typically start their businesses with less money and are more reliant on self-financing. A consequence

---

[572] Ford L., (2014) Women's Right and Gender Equality, Available at <https://www.theguardian.com> (consulted on the 19/02/2020 at 3:45pm).

of the difficulties in accessing finance is that self-employed women are more likely than self-employed men to be discouraged borrowers, i.e. people who do not apply for loans because they believe that the loans will not be appropriate or that they will not be successful.

In Cameroon, women, especially the rural woman those who have taken up the challenge to start up a business more often than not finds it more difficult to raise capital to start up this business. Taking into consideration the societal norms and the position in which these women are kept in the society, individuals and even some institutions find it extremely difficult to grant loans to these women to start up their business, they prefer to grant loans to the male counterpart since they believe they are capable to handle businesses and thus pay back the loan. Even in the case where these loans are available, women who have access to it most often discovers that these loans have very high interest rates which discourages her to get the loan.

7.9.7.2. Lack of Investor Confidence

This is a challenge that arises when you need to raise money to start your own business. Investors, in general, are more inclined to believe men, but this is not something that could be pronounced just like that. Behind this, stands the fact that women generally need much more time and effort to prove their value. In any case, women will certainly need more patience and persistence to present their business story to parties interested in financing it. All in order to find the sustainability of the idea rather than the gender of the presenter male counterpart since they believe they are capable to handle businesses and thus pay back the loan. Even in the case where these loans are available, women who have access to it most often discovers that these loans have very high interest rates which discourages her to get the loan.

7.9.7.3: Management of Finances

Women face financial and non-financial constraints, both being highly interconnected in many cases, and traditionally these constraints disproportionately affect women entrepreneurs rather than men. It is finance that is essential to create an environment that increases the share of women in small but also larger and growing businesses, and also in more profitable sectors, in order to fully leverage the economic power of women for growth. Having basic rights such as the right to travel freely within and out of the country, have a passport, open a bank account or sign financial documents without the presence of a male is key to empowering women. Corruption, lack of information of the process to start a business, weak property rights, lack of access to technology, low education, less control over earnings, low intra-household power, limited access to business networks, lack of access to childcare and limited skills and experience are a few of the limitations that women around the globe have to face today.

7.10. Climate Challenges

The global food economy is vast and technologically advanced but none the less prone to substantial negative outcomes in poor weather years. The economic gains or losses associated with climate change will depend on the pace of climate change, the response of cropping system including the vast number of growers, researchers, extension agents and other who determine how cropland are managed.[573]

Climate change is a phenomenon that affects the world globally. It affects the world in general and sub-Saharan Africa in particular. Subsistence farming is one of the key sectors which are vulnerable to such changes. This climate change affects the ecosystem making it unstable which in turns affects plant growth, depression and soil degradation.[574]

The rural woman is most often affected by this climate change than her male counterpart. This climate change affects the livelihood and food security of the rural sector. This makes the women so vulnerable because of their limited means of diversifying their resources that is lack of finances as opposed to their male counterparts who can simply diversify their activities or move to the urban areas in search of different jobs. These women cannot move for lack of finances and for the fact that they have to take care of family back home. So, they stay behind managing by planning crops that can mature fast and using pest-resistant seeds in order to survive during such periods when the climate turns to be unfavourable for food crop production.

7.11. Conclusion

Women have a great role to play in achieving sustainable development goals. Women and young girls, especially those in rural settings face a lot of challenges. Customary law in rural communities presents unique challenges in that sense. Women farm workers feed the country but their production labour is uncounted. Patriarchal societal structures only increase their troubles[575]in villages. Women work the land but customary laws reserve exclusive land

---

[573] Reynolds Matthew P. (2014), Climate Change and Crop Production: Economic impacts of climate change on agriculture till 2030, CABI Climate change series, P.38.

[574] Mckulka Tim (2009), Women, Gender Equality and Climate Change. Available at UN Women Watch: www.un.org.(Consulted on the 17/05/2024).

[575] Ibid.

ownership to male family members. Widows are not entitled to any right and are at times driven away from their homes or abused after their husbands' deaths.

Due to poverty and the lack of financial means to educate children, young girls are often marginalized, sent to early marriages in rural areas of Cameroon. For most parents, early marriages are a solution for the girls and education is not so important for girls because they have to marry and be under the responsibility of a man in future. The non-enforcement of laws both national and ratified international laws continue to put these rural women in a marginalized position in Cameroon. As seen above. Infrastructure   lags as examined is equally a serious hindrance to these rural women. Equally some general challenges such as stress, negative business environment etc. as examined above pose serious challenges to entrepreneurs as a whole and rural female entrepreneur in particular thus making these women to be economically less developed.

CHAPTER EIGHT

GENERAL CONCLUSION

8.1. Synopsis of the Work

This study examined the economic empowerment of rural women in in Cameroon. The research gap that this research seeks to fill relates to the fact that in spite of the several legal provisions put in place by the legislator in Cameroon for the economic empowerment of women especially the rural women, they still find it so challenging to become economically empowered. In an attempt to provide answers to this worry, this research work was divided into 8 chapters with the general introduction and general conclusion constituting chapter one and eight respectively.

For better understanding of the topic under consideration, chapter one presented the problem, the research questions, hypothesis, objectives, methodology and the like. The general background of the study was also presented highlighting the fact that, the economic empowerment of rural women is not only a national but an international issue.

The rationale for the economic empowerment of rural women was studied with a bias on the human rights and economic perspectives. Everyone has the right to work and earn a gainful employment. Work is a national right for every adult and valid citizen[576] Respecting human rights and implementing gender balance policies as advocated for by the 1995 Beijing platform for action, the CEDAW[577] in every sphere of life will promote the economic empowerment of rural women and consequently their rights of subsistence right[578], that is their rights to a standard of living adequate for their wellbeing and families. Economic stability will enable the rural women to uphold their human rights in the community which will beneficial not only to them as persons but also to the community and the national economy as a whole. If these women are empowered, they will foster economic development for women economic empowerment is a prerequisite for sustainable development and for achieving the Millennium Development Goals. Economically empowering them will improve a standard of living, will promote community development and will create social change. It will

---

[576] Article 2(2) of the 1992 Labour code.
[577] Article 14(2) of 1981 CEDAW.
[578] Encyclopaedia of Global Justice.PP.1042-1045.

equally promote the growth of entrepreneurship initiative, combat poverty, improve national income, and promote the growth of national economy.

The economic empowerment of rural women as a concept is well grounded under guiding principles to the right development. These guiding principles are postulated by the UN Sustainable Development Goals for 2030, which brought out 17 principles for development, the Universal Declaration of Human Right which advocated that development is a human right that belongs to everyone individually and collectively. Everyone is" entitled to participate in, contribute to, and enjoy economic, social, culture and political development, in which all human rights and fundamental freedoms can be fully realized[579]. To ensure the economic empowerment of women based the guiding principles, development should be people centered, non-discriminatory, it should have a Human Right based approach, it should be participatory, accountable, and equal it should be based on empowerment, it should be collaborative, be of equal partnership, it should be supportive, sustainable and should be representative and it should be self-determined.

The respect of the above principles in development agendas as provided for in both international and national legislations United Nations Declaration on the Rights of Indigenous People in 2007, the Rio Declaration on Environment.[580] the Sustainable Development Goals of Agenda 21. The UN Millennium Declaration, African charter on Human and People's Right which holds that all people shall have the right to their economic, social and cultural development[581], the principles and guidelines on the right to fair trial and legal assistance in Africa 2003, the Declaration of Principles of freedom of Expression in Africa 2002, guidelines and measures for the prohibition and prevention of torture, cruel, inhumane and degrading treatment or punishment in Africa since 2002. The Cameron constitution equally put in place guiding principle which promotes women's right to development[582] will to a long way to enhance the economic empowerment of rural women.

The various policy standards for the economic development of rural women in Cameron were examined in chapter four with a clear distinction between the standards established by the national, regional and global legal instruments.

---

[579] 1986 UN Declaration on the Right to Development.

[580] Principle 3 of the 1992 Rio Convention.

[581] Article 22(1) and (2) of the African Charter on Human and People's Rights 1981.

[582] Law No 96/06 of 18th January 1996 on the revision on the constitution of June 1972. It postulated the principle of non-discrimination, the principle of liberty and security, the principle of inviolability of correspondence, the principle of non-retroactivity of the law.

At the national level, a difference was made between the general policy standards for economic development that benefits all thus the rural women inclusive and specific policy standards that focused directly on women. The general policy standards include the Cameroon's social economy law [583] and its provisions on economic empowerment, law governing SMEs in Cameroon investment law[584], Cameron's industrial policy and highlighted how these policies promote the economic empowerment of rural women in Cameroon. Specific policies deduced from the general code on regional and local authorities[585] (CGCTD) that transferred some competence to the regions including economic development. This decentralisation policy is beneficial to rural communities including rural women thus promoting their economic development. The National Gender Policy where in the Government's Growth and Employment Strategy[586] recognises the promotion of gender equality as the key to achieving inclusive growth and meeting with Sustainable Development Goals. The same spirit was deduced from some provisions of the labour code[587] which accord special protection to female workers thus promoting their economic empowerment.

At the regional level, the harmonisation of business law brought forth by OHADA does not only provides Judicial insecurities and simplifies business procedures but equally facilitate trade between countries and develop a vibrant private sector which goes a long way to better the economic condition of the rural women in Cameroon since all economic interest groups which are common in rural sector of the country are subjected to the provisions of the Uniform Acts.

The coverage of agricultural risk by the introduction of agricultural insurance through the CIMA Code, could be argued, is another regional policy for the economic empowerment of women y of these women is agriculture. The Economic Community of Central African States (CEMAC) on its part promote women economically when it makes provision for economic empowerment by strengthening competitiveness of economic and financial activities and by harmonizing regulations that governs member States.

At the international level, the 1948 Universal Declaration of Human Rights clearly states that "everyone has the right to work...." [588] This provision is

---

[583] Law No 2019/004 of 25th April 2019.
[584] Law No 2002/004 of 19th April 2002.
[585] Law No 2019/024 of 24th December 2019.
[586] 2010/2020 Growth and Employment strategy Paper.
[587] Law No 92/007 of 14th August 1992.
[588] Article 23 UDHR 1948.

buttressed by the United Nations Charter which advocates for higher living standards, full employment and economic and social progress and development.[589] This cannot be achieved without promoting the economic aon that empowerment rural women. It is certainly for this reason that the Convention on the Elimination of all Forms of Discrimination against Women, clearly states that "parties shall take into account the particular problems faced by rural women and the significant role which rural women play in the economy survival of their families including their work in the non-monetised sector of the economy...."[590] To economically empower the rural women, they must not be subjected to violence as condemned by the International Covenant on Civil and Political Rights, for violence constitute a cause and consequence of women's unequal enjoyment of their human rights when compared to men.[591] Violence which certainly does not promote the economic development of rural women is contrary to the preaching of the International Covenant on Economic, Social and Cultural Rights[592] and the spirit of the International Convention against Torture and other Cruel Inhumane and Degrading Treatment. With the application of these instruments rural women will be economically empowered and not relegated to the background as is often the case.

The institutional frameworks for the economic empowerment of the rural women are classified at the national, regional and international, highlighting the role of NGOs and associations with either national or global competence. Within the national sphere the roles of various ministerial departments and other national structures in the promotion of women economic empowerment of rural women were detailly studied. These included amongst others the ministry of Women Empowerment and the Family which is responsible for women's affair, the Ministry of Decentralization and Local Development (MINDDEVEL), which promotes local development, the Ministry of Small and Medium Size Enterprises which support the creation and development of small and medium size enterprise, the Ministry of Economy Planning and Regional Development in Cameroon (MINEPAT), which coordinates industrial, commercial and trade matters amongst others, the Ministry of Post and Telecommunication which ensures the development of information and communication technologies (ICTs) as well as electronic communication in all forms, the Ministry of Justice which promotion and protection of the rights of all its citizen the women inclusive, the Ministry of

---

[589] Article 55 of the 1945 UN Charter.
[590] Article 14 of the 1981 CEDAW.
[591] Article 2 of the 1976 ICCPR.
[592] Article 7 makes it clear that the right of everyone to enjoyment of just and favourable conditions of work must be recognized

Mines, Industry and Technological Development (MINMIDT) which among its several duties include local transformation of mining, agriculture and forest products in conjunction with the Ministry of Agriculture and Rural Development which is responsible for defining and monitoring the implementation of regulatory framework for the development and management of rural areas thus the development of the rural women.

Institutions at the regional level CEMAC, OHADA UNDP ILO, all have programmes and activities that in one way or the other promotes the economic empowerment of rural women. The same holds with some other NGOs and Association operating at both the national and global level that equally have programmes that enhance the promotion of women economic empowerment. Some of these NGOs and Associations include: ACAFEJ ALVFAMNAFAW, RENATA, UN Women and the World Bank,

The measures used by state and other non-governmental organizations for the economic empowerment of the rural women in Cameroon were assessed. Governmental measures included access to communication and technology, access to education, non-discriminatory practices, and the promotion and protection of human rights. The government equally took has equally taken measures to fight gender-based violence which is a common phenomenon in the rural sector in Cameroon.

The creation of institutions with either general or specific competence in the promotion of economic empowerment of women also constitute government measures to enhance the economic development of rural women. These institutions include amongst others the various ministerial departments. Assistance in diverse forms given to various NGOs well as the measure to provide social amenities also constitutes government efforts in ensuring the economic empowerment of the rural women.

Despite the above measures, challenges of varied nature are still faced in the economic empowerment of rural women. These are institutional limitations such as Cameroon's Growth Performance which rely basically on public investment. There is equally infrastructure challenges lack or insufficient social amenities like water, electricity, transportation, and communication facilities. The weak implementation legal mechanism coupled with the predominance of bias customary law rules and practices relation to land ownership, inheritance rights, illiteracy all constitute some of the challenges face in promoting the economic empowerment of rural women. Based on these challenges, some recommendations have been made to promote the economic empowerment of rural women.

8.2. Findings of the Work

Our findings shows that the regulations put in place by the government do not effectively promote the economic empowerment of the rural women in Cameroon. We realised that in as much as there are regulations put in place for the development of the economy as a whole, there is weak implementation of these provisions in the rural settings in Cameroon, thus the continuation of discriminatory practices.

With regards to assistance from the State or NGOs and other Association to enable rural women be economically empowered, it was discovered most of the women do not receive any form of assistance. Statistics from the field reveal that 77.42% of the rural women did not receive any assistance from NGOs[593] while 41.93% received financial assistance which was still very negligeable to enable be financially independent.[594]

The study equally found out that the rural women face several challenges to be economic empowerment. For instance, 42% of the those struggling to develop small businesses complained of inadequate finance as a major challenge[595] for their economic empowerment. Land ownership is equally a major challenge faced by rural women. 86.66% of these rural women have no land tittles[596]. This acts as a hindrance to rural women economic development since role of land as a factor of production, as a collateral for loans and economic empowerment cannot be gainsaid.

Due to illiteracy, we discovered that these women do not know the importance of Economic groupings such as CIG. Only 16% of the rural women belong to these CIG. However, 61% of these women belong to Njangi which is not financially viable enough to provide fund for these women for their economic empowerment[597].

In as much as the 2009 law makes provision for legal Aid in Cameroon which targets particularly the local communities, we realised that these rural women due to ignorance, and fear do not carry any of the violations against them to court. They prefer to settle amicable. 61% of these women prefer amicable

---

[593] Figure 1. Source (field work 2024).
[594] See figure 3. Source (field work 2024).
[595] See figure 2. Source (fieldwork,2024).
[596] See figure 10. Source (field work 2024).
[597] See figure 6. Source (field work 2024)

settlement as opposed to court settlement[598]. This continuously keep them in a disadvantaged position in the community.

8.3. Recommendations

On the basis of the challenges faced by the rural women which acts as setbacks for rural women economic development through the creation of economic activities such as the creation of SMEs, and taking into consideration the important role played by the rural women in the development of the local community and the national economy as a whole, it is quite imperative for serious measures to be taken to remedy the situation. The plights of the rural women need to be handled from all angles by all stakeholders concerned. To this effect some institutional or legal reforms are indispensable.

8.3.1. Institutional Reforms

The institutional framework for gender related matters should be completed by setting up a gender equality observatory. The Observatory will thus have a role of consultation, observation, evaluation, dialogue, regulation and coordination in the promotion of gender equality and women's empowerment in Cameroon. The government should institute gender units at the cabinet level of the ministries in all technical and small structures, in the police and gendarmerie stations, draw up new terms of reference and strengthen the capacities of members and equally ensure a gender audit of sectorial ministries with a gender analysis of existing sectorial policies, strategies and action plans.

The National Gender Policy[599] should be revised including its multi-sectorial plan, ensure its appropriation and implementation through targeted actions in sectorial plans and programmes; institutionalise gender reports to be presented by sectorial bodies to Parliament. This could start with some pilot ministries and scale up. To this end, a gender sub-committee could be set up in parliament to better examine these issues

Another measure which the government can take is to conduct a study on women's entrepreneurship in the formal and informal sectors, focusing on the specific needs and constraints of women entrepreneurs, including analysis of gender norms in production, including time budgeting, access to productive resources (including access to finance), barriers to accessing markets and information as well as factors that could affect their productivity, and barriers and

---

[598] See figure 7. Source (fieldwork 2024)
[599] The 2005 Gender and Development Policy Act.

opportunities for women agricultural entrepreneurs to move from agriculture to agro-industry that adds value to the entire value chain.

The UN should continue its programmes in governance, economic empowerment, the fight against gender-based violence, humanitarian action, women, peace and security. Second Chance Education, Monitoring International Commitments and Gender Responsive Planning and Budgeting should be priority programmatic areas for the country. Support the Government in the implementation and monitoring of the NGP, and CEDAW national plans, contextualized SDGs and other international commitments.

UN Women should strengthen its gender coordination activities, by mentoring CSO gender platforms. To this end, support the annual organisation of a national forum on women in collaboration with MINPROF.

- Develop with the Government and other partners a flagship programme on economic empowerment.

- Support the revision of the national strategy to combat GBV and ensure better coordination of interventions to combat violence against women.

- To support the inclusion of gender in local development plans and to strengthen the capacities of officials and populations on this issue. Promote women's participation in peace processes.

- Develop a coordinated strategy on gender issues and protection of the girl child.

- The Civil Society and Women's NGOs should ensure adequate ownership of the NGP and that actions taken are consistent with the implementation of this framework.

- Become more involved in information, awareness-raising and training activities for the general public and for women, on the knowledge and exercise of women's rights, including the right to participate in public life;

- Focus their efforts on educational actions for women to acquire the appropriate know-how for their development and emancipation, and for communities to appropriate socio-cultural values that are egalitarian for women and men.

- Carry out reflection on the ways and means to play their role of encouraging and controlling government action and the implementation of the National Gender Policy.

The private sector should review its national Corporate Social Responsibility (CSR) policy by putting in place tools such as the gender marker for those companies that respect the commitment to gender issues. Provide financial support to gender projects that have an impact on its activities.

8.3.2. Legal Reforms

In addition to sensitisation of the rural women on their rights and the power of education, a specific law should be made that takes care of the specific needs of the rural women in Cameroon for them to emerge. These women should be highly communicated to these women using all mechanism possible for her to be aware.

- Set up legal mechanisms for a better integration of gender into public policies, notably through the preparation and adoption of a framework law for an effective gender equality in Cameroon.

- Ensure that laws, policies and programs should prohibit discrimination against women in relation to access, use, and control over land and other productive resources.

- National laws, Policies and programs should be harmonized especially those related to access, use and control of land and other productive resources. When there is a consistent and coherent legal and policy framework protecting women's rights to land and other productive resources the rural women will be highly empowered to emerge.

Another measure that can be taken by the government is to strengthen the capacities of judicial personnel making them have a greater mastery of the legal arsenal. That is the international, regional and national instruments on women's rights, the revision and reformulation of certain legal provisions that are contradictory to these rights or to fill certain legal gaps on this subject and the reference to and application of the provisions of positive law in pre-eminence over customary rules.

- Ensure that International Human Rights instruments such as the Convention on the Elimination of All Forms of Discrimination Against Women are incorporated in national laws as applicable and reservations are removed.[600]

---

[600] Articles,13,14(2),15(2) and16(1) of the convention of the Elimination of All Forms of Discrimination Against Women and article 11 of the International covenant on e Economic Social and Cultural Rights.

- Capacity building of members of the legislature on women's rights is also needed. Strengthen the role of parliament in gender monitoring in public policies, programmes and budgets.

- Review the 1325 National Action Plan on Women, Peace and Security and ensure its effective implementation through secretariats in the 10 regions.[601]

- Generate political will for gender mainstreaming at the local level: taking gender into account in the decentralisation process calls for the primary responsibility of the governing bodies, that is the municipal council and the executives. To date, there is still a lack of interest on the part of some mayors and their municipal councils in the promotion of women. Gender issues should be seen as obligatory and not optional.

---

[601] Cameroon (2018-2020). 1325 National Action Plan. Available at http://1325naps.peacewomen.org.(Consultrd on 12/01/2024).

SELECTED BIBLOGRAPHY

A. TEXT BOOKS

Blakey E. J., and Leigh N. G., (2010), *Planning Local Economic Development: Theory and Practice,* 4th Ed, Sage Publications.

Halstead P., (2012), *Unlocking Human Rights, Hodder Education.*

Hoare J., and Gell F., (2009), *Women's Leadership and Participation: Case Studies on Learning for Action,* Practical Action Publishing Ltd.in association with Oxfam GB, p.1.

Lauterburg D., (2010), *Core Statutes on Employment Law,* London, Palgrave Macmillan.P.192.

Mbetiji M. M., (2021), *Integrating Indigenous Communities in the Management of Environmental Resources in Cameroon*: A Legal Appraisal, Germany, Galda Verlag.

Smith J. R., (2016), *Property Law, Cases and Materials,* 5th Ed, Longman Law Series.p.28.

Turner C., (2012), *Key Facts: Employment Law,* 3rd Ed, Hodder Education.3rd edition.p.58.

B. ARTICLES

Agu E. O., (2015), *"An Assessment of the Contribution of Women Entrepreneur Toward Entrepreneurship Development in Nigeria"*, International Journal of Current Research and Academic Review, Vol. 3.

Akume D and Badjo, M.A., (2017), *"The Performance of Micro-Finance Institutions in Cameroon Does financial regulation really matter?"*, Journal of Financial and Accounting, Vol. 8. No 2.

Ascher J., (2012), *"Female Entrepreneurship-An Appropriate Response to Gender Discrimination"*, Journal of Entrepreneurship Management and Innovation, Vol. 8, No. 4.pgs 79,81,97,114.

Atanga L., (2021), *"Gender Ideologies, Leadership, and Development in Cameroon"*, Washington D.C, Georgetown Journal of International Affairs.

Ayuk P. N., (2021), *"The protection of Cameroon Female Workers under the Labour code"*, International journal of social sciences and Humanities Research, Vol.9, No. 3.

Barwell, G. A., Edmonds, Howe and J. Veen, (1985), *"Rural Transport in Developing Countries"*, Intermediate Technology Publication, Vol.1.

Boohene R., and Agyapong D., (2017), *"Rural Entrepreneurship in African Countries: A Synthesis of Related Literature"*, Journal of Small Business and Entrepreneurship Development, Vol. 5, No. 1.pps.43,44,54.

Bouab A.H., (2004), *"Financing for Development, the Monterrey Consensus: Achievements and Prospects"*, USA, Michigan Journal of International Law, Vol. 26, No. 1.

Dam Van, Valk, Cummings (2000), *"Institutionalising Gender Equality: Commitment, Policy and Practice"*, KIT Publishers, Vol.1 p.13.

Daniel M. T., and Sophie N. N., (2018), *"Entrepreneurial-ship Venture and Economic Development in Cameroon"*, Journal of Global Economy, Vol. 6 No. 2.

Duflo E., (2012*), "Women Empowerment and Economic Development"*, Journal of Economic Literature, American Economic Association, Vol. 50, No. 4.

Eade D., (2004), *"Development and Rights"*, Oxfam GB, Vol.3.

Fombe Laurence, Sama Lang, Irene F, (2013), *"Securing Tenure for Sustainable Livelihoods: A Case of Women Land Ownership in Anglophone Cameroon"*, Journal of Ethics and economics.

Fonjong L, (2001), *"Fostering Women's Participation in Development through Non -governmental Efforts in Cameroon"*, The Geographical Journal, Vol. 167, No. 3.

Makena P. Thiaine Kubai Simon, Ibuathis, Njati., (2014), *"Challenges Facing Women Entrepreneurs in Accessing Business Finance in Kenya"*, IOSR-JBM, Vol. 16.

Narayan Madhusudan, Adera Manisti (Dr)., (2018), *"Rural Entrepreneurship in India: An Overview"*, International Entrepreneurship and Management Journal, Vol. 8, p.280-284.

Ndangle K. W., (2019), *"Aspects of Poverty and Inequality in Cameroon"*, Peter Lang. Internationaler Verlag der Disenchanted, Vol. 28.

Nguindip N. C. and Samuel Akama P., (2021*), "Ensuring the Right to Liberty and Security of Person: An Application or Nightmare in Respecting Human Right Standard in Cameroon"*, International Journal of law Management and Humanities, Vol. 4, No.2.

Nzouedja T. A., (2021), *"Access to Justice and Human Rights Protection in Cameroon: Problem and Prospects"*, Peer Reviewed International Journal, Vol. 2.

Posner R. A., (1998), *"Creating a Legal Framework for Economic Development"*, The world Bank Research Observer, Vol. 13, No 1.

Schuler D., (2006), *"The Uses and Misuses of Gender Related Development Index and Gender Empowerment Measures*; Review of Literature"*, Journal of Human Development, Vol. 7.

Temngah J. N., (1996), *"Customary Law, Women's Right and Traditional Courts in Cameroon"*, Revue Generale de droit, Vol. 27, No. 3.

Yarik K., and Shaun M., (2021), *"Non-Retroactivity as a General Principle of Law"*, Vol, 17 No. 1.

Yenkong E. S., (2020), *"Land law and Post-colonial Constraints to Women's Land Rights in Cameroon*, International Journal of Resource and Environmental Management, Vol. 5, No.1.

C. THESIS AND DISSERTATIONS

Agbor D. A., (2018), *"The Right to Self-Determination in Southern Cameroon"*, Public International Law and Human Rights. Bachelor Degree, (Unpublished), P.1.

D. SEMINARS AND PAPERS

Guloba M., Ssewanyana S. Birabwa E., (2017), *"Rural Women Entrepreneurship in Uganda: A synthesis Report on Policies, Evidence and Stakeholders,* Research series No. 134, p.6.

Henry T. B., (2017), *"Sustainable Community Based Natural Resources Management in Sub-Sahara Africa: Perspectives On portable Water Supply in then North West Cameroon"* (Unpublished).

Reynolds M., (2014), *"Climate Change and Crop Production: Economic Impacts of climate change on Agriculture till 2030.*CABI Climate change Series.

Tamasang C. F., (2007), *"Paper Prepared for the Workshop Entitled Legal Aspects of Water Sector Reforms' to be organised in Geneva from 20 to 21 April 2007 by the International Environmental Law Research Centre (IELRC) in the context of the Research partnership 2006-2009 on water law sponsored by the Swiss National Science Foundation (SNF).*

F. INTERNET SOURCES

Advocacy (2012) The voice of Small Business in Government, Frequently Asked Questions, Available at <https://www.sba.gov> (consulted on the 18/02/2020).

African Development Bank Group, (2012), African Economic Outlook Available at <https://www.afdb.org> (consulted on the 7/02/2020).

Ahmad Z. (1980) The plight of the rural women: alternatives for action. Available at https://pubmed.ncbi.nlm.nih.gov.(Consulted on the 10/03 2024)

Ahmed Zubeida (2023). Rural women, their conditions of work and struggle to organize. Available at https://horizon.documentation.ird.fr.(Consulted on the 03/12/2023).

Aizan Firimine (2023). Cameroon: government to boost agricultural financing over the next 5 years. Available at https://www.businessin Cameroon.com (Consulted on the 1/10/2023)

Amnesty International (2006). A guide to the African charter on Human and people's Rights. International secretarial Peter Benenson House Eastern street London. Available at www.amnesty.org

Article 3 of the 1993 OHADA Uniform Act on Commercial Companies and Economic interest groups.

Asghar A. J. and Nawaser N., (2010) Issues and Challenges for Women Entrepreneurs in Global Scene, with special reference to India. Available at < http://researgate.net/publication> (consulted on the 9/02/2023 at 9:54 am).

Battybot (2024). Rural women. Available at https://en.m.wikipedia.org.(Consulted on 25/04/2

Behera Bansanta, Prasad R.M and Behera Shyambhavee. (2022). Rural women's health disparities. Available at https://www.sciencedirect.com.(Consulted on 25/04/2024).

Benz Alexander (2022): Entrepreneurs are struggling with mental challenges. Available at https://www.entrepreneur.com.(consulted on 08/06/2023 at 8:47 am).

Boris Andzanga. N and Kouam Jean. C (2023): Cameroon, promoting Rural Development to reduce gender Inequalities. Available at https://on policy.org. (Consulted on the 27/07/2023)

Business in Cameroon. (2023). MSME, financing, CCA Bank secures cfaf 10bln credit line to improve credit access. Available at <https;//www.businessin cameroon.com. (Consulted on 22/09/2023)

Business in Cameroon: In Cameroon, the informal sector weighs as much GDP as in South Africa and Mauritius but less than in Nigeria.

Business News (2014) Company Formation in Cameroon now possible in 72 hours, Available at <https://www.camerounweb.com> (consulted on the 7/02/2020 at 2:16pm).

Cameroon (2023). The Convention on the Right to Development on the right track. Available at https;//www.cetim.(Consulted on 18/01/2024)

Cameroon country, climate and Development Report. Available at https://www.reliefweb.int. (consulted on the 27/07/2023).

Cameroon population (2023). Literacy of population. Available at https://countrymeters.infos.(Consulted on the 03/12/2023).

Cameroon:(2016) Creating Opportunities for inclusive growth and poverty reduction. Available at www.worldbank .org (Consulted on the 28/02/2023).

Care International (2023). Women Economic Justice. Available at https//www.care-internation.org. (Consulted on the 14/09/2023)

CFCE in brief (2022): Business creation space in the republic of Cameroon. Available at https://minfi.gov.cm.(consulted on the 21/09/2023)

ChildHope (2022). Function of NGOs: its integral contributions to building a better society. Available at https://childhope.org.(Consulted on 26/10/2023).

CIA World Fact Book, (2020) Economy of Cameroon. Available at <, https://en.wikipedia.org> (consulted on the7/20/2020).

Climate change laws. (2019) National strategy 2020-2030 for structural transformation and inclusive development. Available at https://climate-laws.org.(Consulted on the 26/01/2024).

Common Wealth Governance (2015). Economy of Cameroon. Available at https://www.commonwealthgovernance.org.(Consulted on 01/05/204).

Common Wealth Governance (2015). Economy of Cameroon. Available at https://www. commonwealth governance.org. (Consulted on 01/05/204).

Common wealth governance, Cameroon Available at, https://www.commonwealth governance.org(consulted on the 6/06/2023 at 5:25 am)

Commonwealth governance (2023) public-private partnerships of Cameroon. Available at https://www.commonwealthgovernance.org.(Consulted on 30/09/2023).

Community Options Inc. (1989). Supporting people with disabilities. COBAC. Community Options. Business advisory council. Available at https.//www.comop.org. (Consulted on the 20/09/2023).

Connecticut (2023). Connecticut Self Determination Initiative. Available at https://portal.ct.gov.(Consulted on 18/09/2023).

Corolin Petterson (2019) "The Biggest Challenges in Women" Entrepreneurship, Available at <https://thriveglobal.com> (consulted on the 18/02/2020 at 12:10pm).

Council of Europe (1993). The evolution of human rights. Available at https://www.coe.int (Consulted on 18/01/2024).

Cromartie John (2019): Economic Research Service. Available at https://www.ers.usda.gov.(Consulted on 02/07/23)

Cultural Rights (2010). Rio Declaration on Environment and Development 1992.Available at https://culturalrights.net.(Consulted on 22/01/2024)

Denis & Lenora Foretia Foundation (2022). Promoting Women's Access to information and Economic Opportunities in Cameroon. (OWG). Available at https://www.foretiafoundatio.org.(Consulted on the 22/11/2023).

Denis & Lenora. starting a business in Cameroon, A critical analysis. Available at https://nkafu.org(Consulted on the 21/09/2023)

Dr Kouam Jean-Cedric (2023): Focus on public- private partnership in Cameroon. Available at https://onpolicy.org.(Consulted on the 30/09/2023).

Dr. Sultan Ahmad Taraki :(2019)" The Role of SMEs in Capital Formation, Equitable Growth and Income Distribution in Developing Countries'' Volume 8. Available at <www.ijsr.net> ((Consulted on the 25/03/2023)

Efroymson D. Biswas B., and Ruma S. (2010), Women, Work and Money: Studying the Economic value of Women's unpaid work and using the results for advocacy, Available at<https//healthbridge.ca> (consulted on the 28/02/2020).

EFSAS (2019). The Organisation for Poverty Alleviation and Development (OPAD). Available at https://www.efsas.org.(Consulted on the 12/11/2023).

Egoh Modi and Louis Marie (Dr) (2020). Examining Business Creation in Cameroon from the perspective of women. Available at https://nkafu.org.(Consulted on 24/04/2024).

Encyclopaedic Entry: Rural Area. Available at https://national

Entrepreneurial feminism. Available at https://en.m.wikipdia.org. (consulted on 12/06/2023)

ESCR-Net (1966) Introduction to Economic, Social and Cultural Rights. Available at https://www.escr-net.(Consulted on the 0/05/2024)

Espinoza Carlos Rios. (2022). Everyone deserves the right to make decisions about their lives. Available at https://www.h.w.org (Consulted on the 18/09/2023).

Estevez Eric and Schmitt Kirsten R. (2023). Natural law in ethics. Available at Available at https://www.investopedia.com.(Consulted on 24/04/2024)

Federick Meunier, Krylova Yulia and Ramalho Rita. (2017): Women's Entrepreneurship: How to measure the gap between new female and male entrepreneur. Available at https://www,researchgate.net (Consulted on the 18/03/2024)

Finkelstein Darren (2022). What are the 4 core components of Accountability? Available at https:/tickhoseboxes.com.9consulted on the 20/01/2024)

Ford L., (2014) Women's Right and Gender Equality, Available at <https://www.theguardian.com> (consulted on the 19/02/2020 at 3:45pm)

Francoise O. E and Gaelle T. T., (2015), Female Entrepreneurship and Growth in Cameroon. Available at <https://ideasrespec.org> (consulted on the 14/02/2022).

Freeman V. (2021) History of Women Entrepreneurs. Available at https://www.linkeden .com/pulse/history -women-entrepreneurs-Valerie-freeman (Consulted on the 1/12/2022)

Fund for NGOs (2023). Functions of an NGO. Available at https://www2fundsforngos.org.(Consulted on the 26/10/2023)

Gachassin Marie, Najman Boris and Raballand Gael. (2015). Road and diversification of activities in rural areas. A Cameroon case study. Available at https:www.researchgate.net.(Consulted on the 29/09/2023).

Gender and Development Policy Act. (2005). Available at https://en. Unesco.org (Consulted on 11/01/2024).

GICAM: Business in Cameroon (2018). Available at http://www.businessin cameroon.com.(Consulted on 12/03/2023)

Glinski Stefanie (2020). What is gender-based violence and how do we prevent it. Available at https://www.rescue.org.(Consulted on the 04/12/2023).

GPE. (2006). Transforming Education in Cameroon. Available athttps://www.globalpartnership.org.

Gurria Angel (2020): SMEs are key for more inclusive growth. Available at<https://www.oecd-ilibrary.org> (consulted on 11/03/2023)

Haman Jibirila (2015): Case of Cameroon. National Employment Fund (NEF). Available at https://www.fnecm.org.(Consulted on 15/09/2023).

Hans Kelsen. (2005). The Pure Theory of Law. Available at https://blog.ipleaders.in. (Consulted on 24/04/2024)

Hasanagic Ada (2024). Human Rights Careers. Available at https://www.humanrightscareer.com.(Consulted on the 23/05/2024)

Human is Right (2018). About Human is Right Cameroon. Available at htts://www.hisrcameroon.org (Consulted on 16/11/2023).

Ibrahim Ali Badawi E. Preliminary Remarks on the Right to a Fair Trial Under the African Charter on Human and Peoples' Rights. Available at http://hrlibrary.umn.edu/fairtrial/wrft-bad.htm

ILO (1996), ''Women Swell Ranks of Working Poor'', Available at <www.ilo.org> (consulted on 14/02/2022).

ILO (1996-2023). Millennium Development Goals. Available at https://www.ilo.org. (Consulted on the 14/08/2023)

ILO (2022). Training of trainers in Cameroon on ILO tools relating to the development of cooperatives. Available at https://www.ilo.org.(Consulted on 23/05/2024)

ILO (2022). Women Entrepreneurship Development and Economic empowerment. Available at https://www.ilo.org.(Consulted on the 23/05/2024).

ILO: ILO and gender equality. Available at https://www.ilo.org (consulted 01/06/2023 at 1:23pm).

IMF (2003). Cameroon. Poverty Reduction Strategy Paper. Available at https://www.imf.org.(Consulted on 13/11/2023).

IMF elibrary (2024). Industrial policy in Cameroon. Available at https://www.elibrary.imf.org. (Consulted on the 01/05/2024)

Inf scipedia: world's largest database of information science and technology. Terms and definitions. Available at https://www.igi.global.com.(Consulted on 25/04/2024)

International Labour Organization (1996-2024). Rural Women at work: Bridging the gaps. Available at https://www.Ilo.org.(Consulted on (22/02/2024).

International Labour Organization (1996-2024). Rural Women at work: Bridging the gaps. Available at https://www.Ilo.org.(Consulted on (22/02/2024).

International Monetary Fund (1999) Cameroon enhanced structural adjustment facility. Medium-term economic and financial policy framework paper. (1999/2000-2001/02). Available at https://ww.inf .org. (Consulted on 01/05/2024).

Jeane halladay coughin et al in "The Rise of Women Entrepreneur, People, Processes and Global Trend' Greenwood, publishing group Available at https://www.amazon.fr (consulted on 30/06/2023).

Kengne Fodouop (2003). Developpement rural dans la province du Centre au Cameroun.Available at https://www.researchgate.net.(Consulted on the (31/05/2024).

Kindzeka Moki E. (2019): Cameroon's Second largest employer crippled by separatist conflict. Available at <httpps://www.voanews.com> (consulted on the 17/03/2023

Kouam Jean -Cedric (2023). The Urgent Need to Improve the Business Climate in Cameroon. Available at http://onpolicy.org.(Consulted on the 15/09/2023).

Kuete Vincent (2020): Cameroon:90% of labour force trapped in the informal sector. Available at https://blog.private-sector and-development.com/2020/01/23/ Cameroon-90-of the labour-force-trapped-in-the-informal-sector (consulted on the18/06/2023 at 2:50pm)

Kumichii T. N., Assessing the Implementation of the Beijing platform of Action in Cameroon. Available at< https://library.fes.de> (consulted on the 5/23/2020).

Laurent Brice (2023). Entrepreneurship, Youths and Women Economic Inclusion in Cameroon. Available at https://nkafu.org.(Consulted on 15/09/2023)

Lawrence Murugu Mute (2019). Declaration of Principles on Freedom of Expression and Access to Information in Africa 2019.Available at https://achpr.au.int/(Consulted on the 25/01/2024)

Lois S. and Annette S., (2011) Assessment of the Environment of Women's Entrepreneurship in Cameroon, Mali, Nigeria, Rwanda and Senegal Employment, Report No. 15, Available at <https://www.africabib.org> (consulted on the 18/02/2020)

Maria F. Cesaroni in, "Strategies Adopted by Male and Female Entrepreneurs in Italy to face the Economy Crisis". Available at htts://papers.ssrn.com (consulted on the 30/06/2023).

Maria Minniti, (2010). "Female Entrepreneurship and Economic Activities". Available at https://www.researchgate.net.(Consulted on the 18/03/2024

Marta R.V., and Lisa R. P., CEDAW and Rural Development: Empowering Women with Law from the top-down, activism from the bottom-up. Available at www.law.ubalt.edu (consulted on the 7/02/2020 at 8:45am).

Mckulka Tim (2009). Women, Gender Equality and Climate Change. Available at UN Women Watch: www.un.org.(Consulted on the 17/05/2024).

Mefo Mimi (2019) Cameroon: Women Entrepreneurs on the rise-Top five to watch in 2019.Available at mimimefoinfos.com. (Consulted on 12/08/2023).

MINJUSTICE, Cameroon Association of female lawyers, Available at www.docstore.ohchr.org (consulted on the 12/02/2020 at 9:30am).

MINPMEESA (2019). Sound Normative Framework for Small and Medium-Sized Enterprises in Cameroon. Available at https://www.minpmeesa.cm.(Consulted on 01/05/2024)

MINPMEESA (2019). The SMESs Bank (BC-PME). Available <https://www.minpmeesa.cm.(Consulted on the 22/09/2023)

Mission 21 (2023). Help for particularly vulnerable people in Cameroon. Available at https://www.mission 21.org. (Consulted on 26/04/2024)

Monterrey Consensus. Available at https://en.m.wikipedia.org. (Consulted on the 22/01/2024)

Ngo Tong Chantal Marie (Pr) (2023). Regions and Economic Development in Cameroon. Available at https://nkafu.org/regions-and -economic-development-in -Cameroon. (Consulted on 02/05/2024)

Okafor Chinedu Obiora. A regional perspective: Article 22 of the African Charter on Human and People's Rights. Available at https://www.ohchr.org.(Consulted on 25/01/2024)

Olomo Daniels B (2023). Women in science, two Cameroonians win prize. Available at https://africanews.com.(Consulted on (23/04/2024).

Oyono P. R and L. Temple (2003). Metamorphose des organisations rurales au Cameroun. Available at https://www.erudit.org.(Consulted on 09/06/2024).

Patricia G. Q., (2016). Female Entrepreneurs, adding a New Perspective to Economic Growth, Available at <https://espacioinvestiga.org> (consulted on the 18/02/2020).

Patrick P. (2018) Cameroon Business Forum: Government and Private Sector Talk Business, Available at <www.crtv.cm> (consulted on the 7/02/2020 at 2:37pm).

PPIAF (2021). Cameroon. Building a workable PPP Framework. Available at https://www.ppiaf.org.(Consulted on 30/09/2023).

Promise Mboh (2023). SMEs Minister Urges Business Persons to join Approved Management Centers. Available at https;//the guardianpostcameroon.com. (Consulted on the 29/09/2023).

Republic of Cameroon (2024). Economic Emergence Action. Available at https://www.prc.cm.(Consulted on the 27/05/2024)

Roland M., (2017) Small and Medium Sized Enterprises from 95 percent of the country's economic landscape, but its co. Cameroon business. Available at < https://www.cameroonbusinesstoday.cm>.(consulted on 18/02/2020 at 6:57am)

Signarbieux Ludovic (2017). How Cameroon is strengthening its education system with GPE Support. Available at https.//www.globalpartnership.org. (Consulted on the 29/09/2023)

Sirri A. Terjesen in "Conditions for High Potential Female Entrepreneurship''. Norwegian school of economics. Norway, and America University. Available at https://wol.iza.org(consulted on the 30/06/2023)

Ssewanyana S. (2017), Rural Women Entrepreneurship in Uganda. A synthesis report on policies, evidence and stakeholder. Available at https://includeplatform.net. (consulted on the 30/06/23)

Stevenson Lois and St-Onge A. (2011). Assessment of the environment for the development of women's entrepreneurship in Cameroon, Mali, Nigeria, Rwanda, and Senegal. Available at https://www.ilo.org.(Consulted on the 23/05/2024).

Subedi Surya P. (2021). Declaration on the Right to Development. Available at https://legal.un.org.(Consulted on the 18/01/2024)

Sujay M. K., (2015) Problems and prospects of women entrepreneurs, Scholarly Research Journal for Interdisciplinary studies. Available at <wwwoaji.net> (consulted on the 6/02/2020). Freeman V. (2021) History of Women Entrepreneurs. Available at https://www.linkeden .com/pulse/history -women-entrepreneurs-valerie-freeman (Consulted on the 1/12/2022)

Sustainable Development Goals. Available at https://www.Unodo.org (consulted on the11/03/2023)

Tardi Carla et al (2023). Utilitarianism: what it is, founders, and main principles. Available at https://www.investopedia.com.(Consulted on 24/04/2024)

Team S. and Doss C., (2011), The Role of Women in Agriculture, Available at <www.fao.org.> (consulted on the 14/02//2022).

The protection of women inheritance Right in Cameroon. Available at https://www..research key.net (Consulted on the 02/12/2023).

The talented or gifted prevails; it should be complete cooperation among all so that there may be reasonable life for all. Available at https://en.m.wikipedia.org .(Consulted on the 20/05/2024)

The United Nations Fourth World Conference on Women, (1995). Platform for Action. Available at https://www.un.org (Consulted on 04/12/2023).

The World Bank (2016) Cameroon: creating opportunities for inclusive growth and poverty reduction. Available at https://www.worldbank.org. (Consulted on 10/02/2024).

The World Bank (2023). Indigenous people. Available at https://worldbank.org.

The World Bank: Small and Medium Enterprises (SMEs) Finances. Available at <https://www.worldbank.org.(consulted on the 18/03/2023 at 8:00pm)

Treece Dock (2023): Why Small Businesses are Good for local Communities. Available at https://www.businessnewsdaily.com

UN (2004). Inter-Agency Network on women and gender equality, Available at https://www.un.org. (Consulted on 14/08/2023).

UN (2017) Economic Commission for Africa Women's economic empowerment, Boosting Women's Entrepreneurship in Africa. Available at < www.uneca.org> (consulted on the 7/02/2020 at 8:05am).

UN (2017) UN Women Report, the sustainable development goals (SDGS) and Africa's Agenda 2063, Available at< www.uneca.org> (consulted on the 7/02/2020 at 8:05am)

UN Women (2016). Guidance on country portfolio evaluations in UN Women. Available at www.unwome.org (consulted on 11/02/2020 at 2:10pm).

UN WOMEN (2024). Facts and figures: Economic empowerment. Available at https//www.unwomen.org. (Consulted on 23/04/2024)

UN Women, (2019). The Journey along the gender road in Cameroon, Available at https://Africa .unwomen.org (consulted on the 12/02/2020 at 9:44am).

UN Women. Commission on the status of women. Available at <www.unwomen.org.> (consulted on the 10/02/2020 at 10:00am)

UN Women. World Conference on Women (1995). Available on https://www.unwomen .org. (consulted on 15/09/2023).

UN Women: Convention on the Elimination of ALL Forms of Discrimination against women. Available at https://www.Un.org.(Consulted on the 01/06/2023).

UNCDF (2014). Analysis: the National Economic and financial committee (CNEF) is an essential actor for financial inclusion in Cameroon. Available at https://eujournal.org.(consulted on 20/09/2023).

UNDP Cameroon (2024). Gender Equality and Women Empowerment. Available at https://www.undp.org.(Consulted on the 22/05/2024)

UNECE (2018). Road safety: Cameroon must redouble its efforts and strengthen coordination. Available at https://unece .org. (Consulted on the 30/09/2023).

United Nations (2023). The UN in General. Available at https://unis.unvienna.org. (Consulted on the 08/05/2024)

US Department of states archives. Cameroon. (2001).2007 investment climate statement-Cameroon openness to foreign investment. Available at http://2001-2009 state.gov

US Department of states archives. Cameroon. (2001).2007 investment climate statement-Cameroon openness to foreign investment. Available at http://2001-2009 state.gov.

Van O. T., (2012) World Bank Report on Gender Equality and Development Capacity, Available at <www.europa.eu> (consulted on the 10/02/2020 at 9:07am).

Vigiline Tise Esq. (2021). Privacy protection in electronic communications under Cameroon Law. Nico Halle & Co. Law Firm.Available at https://www.hallelaw.com (Consulted on 26/01/2024).

Wikipedia (2019): Global Entrepreneurship Monitor. Available at< https://en.wikipedia .org> (consulted on the 11/02/2020 at 11:01am).

Wikipedia (2022). Economic Crisis of Cameroon. Available https://en.wikipedia.org.(Consulted on 27/05/2024)

Wikipedia. Economic development. Available at https://en.m.wikipedia.org (Consulted on 01/05/2024).

Wirngo Alexanda Suiy Esq.(2016). Setting up a Non-Governmental Organisations in Cameroon. Available at https://www.linkedin.com. (Consulted on 8/10/2023)

World Bank, (2023), Women in the workforce statistics: Senior Roles, Maternity Leave, Pay Gap. Available at, https://teamstage.io> (consulted on the 26/11/2022)

World Bank, Cameroon: Rural population (% of total population) :(2022). Available at https://data worldbank.org. (Consulted on the 11/08/2023)

World Bank, Cameroon: Rural population (% of total population) :(2022). Available at https://data worldbank.org. (Consulted on the 11/08/20R23)

World Rainforest Movement. (2016). Women and Property in Cameroon. Laws and Reality. Available at https://www/wrm.org.(Consulted on the 17/05/2024).

Yitamben Gisele (2002). ASAFE (Association pour le Soutien et L'Appui a La Femme Entrepreneur) – Cameroon. Available at https://www.comminit.com.(Consulted on the 16/10/2023)

Zongabiro P. N. P., (2014). The Contribution of Village Palm Grove to the Cameroonian Rural Economic Development, Available at < https://www.researchgate.net> (consulted on the 14/02/2020).

www.ingramcontent.com/pod-product-compliance
Lightning Source LLC
Chambersburg PA
CBHW050426280326
41932CB00013BA/2003